AF556151

Hospitality Business and Enterprise

HOSPITALITY BUSINESS AND ENTERPRISE

Ravindra Verma

CENTRUM PRESS
NEW DELHI-110002 (INDIA)

CENTRUM PRESS
H.O.: 4360/4, Ansari Road, Daryaganj,
New Delhi-110002 (India)
Tel: 23278000, 23261597, 23255577, 23286875
B.O.: No. 1015, Ist Main Road, BSK IIIrd Stage,
IIIrd Phase, IIIrd Block, Bengaluru-560085 (INDIA)
Tel: 080-41723429
Email: centrumpress@gmail.com
Visit us at: www.centrumpress.com

Hospitality Business and Enterprise

First Edition, 2013

ISBN 978-93-81293-95-9

PRINTED IN INDIA

Printed at Balaji Offset, Delhi.

Contents

Preface

Hospitality exchange gives travellers the chance to experience what life is like for people living in other places. In addition, making interpersonal connections and fostering understanding of different cultures may in the long run also be important to international relations. During hospitality exchanges, hosts may show off their local knowledge and exciting places "off the tourist map". Not only may travellers get a distinct experience, but they will also get a feel for the everyday lives of local residents.

Hospitality management is part of the service industry—an industry that brings in more money and creates more jobs than any other. Business majors who have obtained a hospitality management degree, diploma, or certificate should have no problem securing a management position in this growing field. Business majors who study hospitality management usually focus on learning general management skills, as well as skills that are central to this industry. Examples include: purchasing, travel and tourism trends, and advertising. Educational requirements for aspiring hospitality managers vary depending upon the career goal. Someone wishing to work in casino management will need a different education than someone who wishes to work as an event planner. To get an idea of what might be expected of you in different hospitality management programs. There are thousands of schools that offer some type of hospitality management program. You can choose to earn anything from a certificate and a diploma to a full-fledged degree. Getting a formal education is often recommended in the field. Classroom time can supplement hands-on experience, and open up doors that may not have otherwise existed.

Depending on of the type of tourism business you start, you can often combine multiple services and components— such as accommodation, activities, attractions, meals and transportation — to create a variety of interesting and unique tourism packages. As few as two components can make up a package. The package can be of any duration from an hour to multiple days. As long as your foundation is solid, you can add or adjust components over time and modify the package to suit many different markets. It is important to price your product and services so you will be competitive and attract business, while also ensuring that your operations generate sufficient income. In order to establish a ballpark price, determine what it costs for you to deliver the experience you are selling, and then add on your desired profit. This is your net price. If you are selling your product directly to the public, your net price can also be your retail selling price. If you are marketing through trade travel partners, your price will also have to cover the commissions they charge to help sell your product. To market your tourism business outside the region, you will likely require the support of tour operators and/ or travel agents. To get their support, be prepared to pay them a commission on the retail price of your product. You must build in the commissions into the price of your package before establishing your retail selling price. Once you publish your retail price, this is the price that commissions must be based on. Further in this section you will be provided with information on the appropriate commissions for tour operators and travel agents. Working in partnership with marketing organizations or other tourism businesses can greatly increase the effectiveness of your marketing efforts. Destination Marketing Organizations, tour operators, travel agents, destination management companies, incentive planners and the travel media all have valuable experience and an established reputation in the tourism sector. Partnering with these organizations can benefit a new business by establishing your credibility, increasing your profile and broadening your marketing reach. In addition to Tour Operators, Travel Agents play an important role in selling a destination.

Travel agencies are the storefront where consumers can get information on travel products, obtain brochures, receive travel advice, and book their vacation or business trip. Many travel agencies are part of a chain such as American Express, Carlson Wagonlit, Cruise Ship Centres and Uniglobe, which undertake extensive marketing to promote products and destinations.

This book contains the fundamental and basic information of subject and the selection of contents makes it an appropriate textbook for the students.

—Author

1

The Economic Significance of Hospitality

Today, tourism is one of the largest and dynamically developing sectors of external economic activities.

Its high growth and development rates, considerable volumes of foreign currency inflows, infrastructure development, and introduction of new management and educational experience actively affect various sectors of economy, which positively contribute to the social and economic development of the country as a whole.

Most highly developed western countries, such as Switzerland, Austria, and France have accumulated a big deal of their social and economic welfare on profits from tourism.

According to recent statistics, tourism provides about 10% of the world's income and employs almost one tenth of the world's workforce. All considered, tourism's actual and potential economic impact is astounding.

Many people emphasize the positive aspects of tourism as a source of foreign exchange, a way to balance foreign trade, an "industry without chimney" – in short, manna from heaven. But there are also a number of other positive and negative sides of tourism's economic boom for local communities, which not always considered by advocates of tourism perspectives. Therefore in this chapter I will consider the main social and environment impacts of tourism at the country level.

The Positive and Negative Social and Environmental Impacts of Tourism

Socially tourism has a great influence on the host societies. Tourism can be both a source of international amity, peace and understanding and a destroyer and corrupter of indigenous cultures, a source of ecological destruction, an assault of people's privacy, dignity, and authenticity.

Here are possible positive effects of tourism:

- Developing positive attitudes towards each other
- Learning about each other's culture and customs
- Reducing negative perceptions and stereotypes
- Developing friendships
- Developing pride, appreciation, understanding, respect, and tolerance for each other's culture
- Increasing self-esteem of hosts and tourists
- Psychological satisfaction with interaction.

So, social contacts between tourists and local people may result in mutual appreciation, understanding, tolerance, awareness, learning, family bonding respect, and liking. Residents are educated about the outside world without leaving their homes, while their visitors significantly learn about a distinctive culture. Local communities are benefited through contribution by tourism to the improvement of the social infrastructure like schools, libraries, health care institutions, internet cafes, and so on. Besides, if local culture is the base for attracting tourists to the region, it helps to preserve the local traditions and handicrafts which maybe were on the link of the extinction.

For example in Uzbekistan, particularly in such famous regions as Samarqand, Buhara, and Horezm tourists contribute significantly to the preservation of traditional handcrafting wood carving, hammered copper work, handmade silk and carpets, and of course to preservation and maintenance of architectural and historical monuments.

Since Uzbekistan proclaimed its independence in 1991 many museums and monuments were renovated or opened to promote the national culture and traditions. Growing interest in this culture makes the local people proud of their way of life.

On the other side tourism can increase tension, hostility, and suspicion. Claims of tourism as a vital force for peace are exaggerated. Indeed there is little evidence that tourism is drawing the world together (Robinson 1999). In this context economic and social impacts on the local community depend on how much of the incomes generated by tourists go to the host communities. In most all-inclusive package tours more than 80% of travellers' fees go to the airlines, hotels and other international companies, not to local businessmen and workers. On the other hand large hotel chain restaurants often import food to satisfy foreign visitors and rarely employ local staff for senior management positions, preventing local farmers and workers from reaping the benefit of their presence. Tourism has the power to affect cultural change. Successful development of a resource can lead to numerous negative impacts. Among these are overdevelopment, assimilation, conflict, and artificial reconstruction. While presenting a culture to tourists may help preserve the culture, it can also dilute or even destroy it. The point is to promote tourism in the region so that it would both give incomes and create respect for the local tradition and culture.

There are also both negative and positive impacts of tourism on the local ecology. Tourism often grows into mass-tourism. It leads to the over consumption, pollution, and lack of resources.

However, from the ecological point of view tourism is often more acceptable and preferable than any other industrial production, as it is environmentally friendlier. The problem is that it is not easy to change the traditional way of life of the local communities. It often creates pseudo conflicts. Undoubtedly in some regions or countries the alternative industries are even more harmful to the environment than tourism.

Besides that in many countries of Asia and the Pacific, for example in Cook Islands, Samoa and others, tourism is the main source of income or the friendliest to the environment. It is at least better than chopping down the forests or destroying coral reefs.

Thus, the preceding paragraphs show that the impact of tourism on local communities can be both positive and negative, whether it comes to economic, social, or environmental effects. It depends to which extent tourism is developed in a particular region. Every region has its bearing capacity, that is to say the limit of the incoming influence that does not harm the host community.

The combined effects of major expenditures on investments in infrastructure and the associated influx of visitors mean that tourism can have significant impacts, both positive and negative, on an economy, on its culture, and on the environment (Brown, 1998). In practice, the dominant motive for the development of tourism is economic (improvements in employment, incomes and exports), but the very process of developing tourism will impose costs elsewhere. If governmental and non-governmental organisations are to make sensible and rational decisions with respect to the current and future development of tourism, they must have reliable information on its costs and benefits (Fletcher, 1989). Without such information, there is the risk that significant investment opportunities may be missed, that key infrastructure developments may be starved of funds, or that developments may take the wrong form or take place in the wrong location.

While recognising the variety of different impacts that tourism may have, this discussion will focus particular attention on the economic impact of tourism. Economic benefits are probably the main reason why so many countries are interested in the development of tourism and the contribution of tourism to the world economy is considerable.

The purpose of this discussion is to examine the main economic costs and benefits associated with tourism and to highlight the difficulties associated with their measurement. Having highlighted the potential economic contribution of tourism, we will then examine the role played by tourism satellite accounts in providing a consistent and reliable source of information on the economic dimensions of tourism. Finally, the use of economic impact modelling techniques will be introduced to present an integrated framework for the evaluation of the economic impact of tourism.

The Economic Benefits of Tourism

Before discussing the various economic benefits of tourism in detail, it is perhaps appropriate to clarify the current position of tourism in the world economy. Arguably, tourism is the second largest industry in the world; estimates from the World Travel and Tourism Council (WTTC) suggest that it generates around 200 million jobs world-wide and accounts for 10% of global GDP (WTTC, 2003). Although there may be debates about the precise scale of tourism's impact on the world economy, few would argue with the view that it does make a major contribution. The scale of that contribution will vary considerably across countries partly because the extent of domestic tourism will vary and partly because the numbers and spending of international visitors will also vary. Relatively speaking, the impact of international visitors is probably greater than the impact of domestic tourists, although the importance of the latter should not be underestimated and for many large countries (eg US, Brazil, India), domestic tourism is often of far greater economic significance than international tourism.

Businesses and public organizations are increasingly interested in the economic impacts of tourism at national, state, and local levels. One regularly hears claims that tourism supports X jobs in an area or that a festival or special event generated Y million dollars in sales or income in a community. "Multiplier effects" are often cited to capture secondary effects of tourism spending and show the wide range of sectors in a community that may benefit from tourism.

Tourism's economic benefits are touted by the industry for a variety of reasons. Claims of tourism's economic significance give the industry greater respect among the business community, public officials, and the public in general. This often translates into decisions or public policies that are favourable to tourism. Community support is important for tourism, as it is an activity that affects the entire community. Tourism businesses depend extensively on each other as well as on other businesses, government and residents of the local community. Economic benefits and costs of tourism reach virtually everyone in the region in one way or another. Economic impact analyses provide tangible estimates of these economic interdependencies and a better understanding of the role and importance of tourism in a region's economy.

Tourism activity also involves economic costs, including the direct costs incurred by tourism businesses, government costs for infrastructure to better serve tourists, as well as congestion and related costs borne by individuals in the community. Community decisions over tourism often involve debates between industry proponents touting tourism's economic impacts (benefits) and detractors emphasizing tourism's costs. Sound decisions rest on a balanced and objective assessment of both benefits and costs and an understanding of who benefits from tourism and who pays for it.

Tourism's economic impacts are therefore an important consideration in state, regional and community planning and economic development. Economic impacts are also important factors in marketing and management decisions. Communities therefore need to understand the relative importance of tourism to their region, including tourism's contribution to economic activity in the area. A variety of methods, ranging from pure guesswork to complex mathematical models, are used to estimate tourism's economic impacts. Studies vary extensively in quality and accuracy, as well as which aspects of tourism are included. Technical reports often are filled with economic terms and methods that non-economists do not understand. On the other hand, media coverage of these studies tend to oversimplify and frequently misinterpret the results, leaving decision makers and the general public with a sometimes distorted and incomplete understanding of tourism's economic effects.

How can the average person understand these studies sufficiently to separate good studies from bad ones and make informed choices? The purpose of this bulletin is to present a systematic introduction to economic impact concepts and methods. The presentation is written for tourism industry analysts and public officials, who would like to better understand, evaluate, or possibly conduct an economic impact assessment. The bulletin is organized around ten basic questions that either are asked or should be asked about the economic impacts of tourism.

Ten Questions about the Economic Impacts of Tourism;

1. What is an economic impact analysis?
2. What questions does an economic impact assessment answer?
3. What economic impacts does tourism have?
4. What are multiplier effects?
5. How are tourism's economic impacts measured?
6. What are the typical approaches for an economic impact assessment?
7. What are some examples of economic impact assessment approaches in tourism?
8. What are the steps for conducting a tourism economic impact study?
9. What are some questions to ask when evaluating or interpreting a tourism economic impact study?
10. What will an economic impact study cost?

What is an Economic Impact Analysis?

A variety of economic analyses are carried out to support tourism decisions. As these different kinds of economic analysis are frequently confused, let's begin by positioning economic impact studies within the broader set of economic problems and techniques relevant to tourism. These same techniques may be applied to any policy or action, but we will define them here in the context of tourism. Each type of analysis is identified by the basic question(s) it answers and the types of methods and models that are appropriate.

Types of Economic Analysis

Economic impact analysis — What is the contribution of tourism activity to the economy of the region?

An economic impact analysis traces the flows of spending associated with tourism activity in a region to identify changes in sales, tax revenues, income, and jobs due to tourism activity. The principal methods here are visitor spending surveys, analysis of secondary data from government economic statistics, economic base models, input-output models and multipliers. (Frechtling 1994a)

Fiscal impact analysis – Will government revenues from tourism activity from taxes, direct fees, and other sources cover the added costs for infrastructure and government services?

Fiscal impact analysis identifies changes in demands for government utilities and services resulting from some action and estimates the revenues and costs to local government to provide these services.

Financial analysis – Can we make a profit from this activity?

A financial analysis determines whether a business will generate sufficient revenues to cover its costs and make a reasonable profit. It generally includes a short-term analysis of the availability and costs of start-up capital as well as a longer-range analysis of debt service, operating costs and revenues. A financial analysis for a private business is analogous to a fiscal impact analysis for a local government unit.

Demand analysis – How will the number or types of tourists to the area change due to changes in prices, promotion, competition, quality and quantity of facilities, or other demand shifters?

A demand analysis estimates or predicts the number and/ or types of visitors to an area via a use estimation, forecasting or demand model. The number of visitors or sales is generally predicted based on judgement (Delphi method), historic trends (time series methods), or using a model that captures how visits or spending varies with key demand determinants (structural models) such as population size, distance to markets, income levels, and measures of quality & competition.

Benefit Cost analysis (B/C) – Which alternative policy will generate the highest net benefit to society over time?

A B/C analysis estimates the relative economic efficiency of alternative policies by comparing benefits and costs over time.

B/C analysis identifies the most efficient policies from the perspective of societal welfare, generally including both monetary and non-monetary values. B/C analysis makes use of a wide range of methods for estimating values of non-market goods and services, such as the travel cost method and contingent valuation method.

Feasibility study – Can/should this project or policy be undertaken?

A feasibility study determines the feasibility of undertaking a given action to include political, physical, social, and economic feasibility. The economic aspects of a feasibility study typically involve a financial analysis to determine financial feasibility and a market demand analysis to determine market feasibility. A feasibility study is the private sector analogue of benefit cost analysis. The feasibility study focuses largely on the benefits and costs to the individual business or organization, while B/C analysis looks at benefits and costs to society more generally (Warnell 1986).

Environmental Impact assessment – What are the impacts of an action on the surrounding environment? An environmental assessment determines the impacts of a proposed action on the environment, generally including changes in social, cultural, economic, biological, physical, and ecological systems. Economic impact assessment methods are often used along with corresponding measures and models for assessing social, cultural and environmental impacts. Methods range from simple checklists to elaborate simulation models.

Benefit cost analysis and economic impact analysis are frequently confused as both discuss economic "benefits". There are two clear distinctions between the two techniques. B/C analysis addresses the benefits from economic efficiency while economic impact analysis focuses on the regional distribution of economic activity. The income received from tourism by a destination region is largely offset by corresponding losses in the origin regions, yielding only modest contributions to net social welfare and efficiency. B/C analysis includes both market and non-market values (consumer surplus), while economic impact analysis is restricted to actual flows of money from market transactions. While each type of economic analysis is somewhat distinct, a given problem often calls for several different kinds of economic analysis. An economic impact study will frequently involve a demand analysis to project levels of tourism activity. In other cases demand is treated as exogenous and the analysis simply estimates impacts if a given number of visitors are attracted to the area. A comprehensive impact assessment will also examine fiscal impacts, as well as social and environmental impacts.

Be aware that an economic impact analysis, by itself, provides a rather narrow and often one-sided perspective on the impacts of tourism. Studies of the economic impacts of tourism tend to emphasize the positive benefits of tourism. On the other hand environmental, social, cultural and fiscal impact studies tend to focus more on negative impacts of tourism. This is in spite of the fact that there are negative economic impacts of tourism (e.g., seasonality and lower wage jobs) and in many cases positive environmental and social impacts (e.g., protection of natural & cultural resources in the area and education of both tourists and local residents).

An economic impact assessment (EIA) traces changes in economic activity resulting from some action.

An EIA will identify which economic sectors benefit from tourism and estimate resulting changes in income and employment in the region. Economic impact assessment procedures do not assess economic efficiency and also do not generally produce estimates of the fiscal costs of an action. For many problems economic impact analysis will be part of a broader analysis. Environmental, social, and fiscal impacts are often equally important concerns in a balanced assessment of impacts.

What Questions does a Tourism Economic Impact Study Answer?

An economic impact analysis will assess the contribution of tourism activity to a region's economy. The basic questions an economic impact study usually addresses are:

- How much do tourists spend in the area?

- What portion of sales by local businesses is due to tourism?
- How much income does tourism generate for households and businesses in the area?
- How many jobs in the area does tourism support?
- How much tax revenue is generated from tourism?

An economic impact analysis also reveals the interrelationships among economic sectors and provides estimates of the changes that take place in an economy due to some existing or proposed action. The most common applications of economic impact analysis to tourism are:

- To evaluate the economic impacts of changes in the supply of recreation and tourism opportunities. Supply changes may involve a change in quantity, such as the opening of new facilities, closing of existing ones, or expansions and contraction in capacity. Supply changes may also involve changes in quality, including changes in (a) the quality of the environment, (b) the local infrastructure and public services to support tourism, or (c) the nature of the tourism products and services that are provided in an area.
- To evaluate the economic impacts of changes in tourism demand. Population changes, changes in the competitive position of the region, marketing activity or changing consumer tastes and preferences can alter levels of tourism activity, spending, and associated economic activity. An economic impact study can estimate the magnitude and nature of these impacts.
- To evaluate the effects of policies and actions which affect tourism activity either directly or indirectly. Tourism depends on many factors at both origins and destinations that are frequently outside the direct control of the tourism industry itself. Economic impact studies provide information to help decision makers better understand the consequences of various actions on the tourism industry as well as on other sectors of the economy. For example, increased air pollution standards

have been opposed in some regions due to the predicted economic consequences of the closing of plants that cannot meet the new standards. Tourism interests counter these arguments with estimates of the potential gains in income and jobs in tourism industries that depend on good air quality and visibility.

- To understand the economic structure and interdependencies of different sectors of the economy. Economic studies help us better understand the size and structure of the tourism industry in a given region and its linkages to other sectors of the economy. Such understandings are helpful in identifying potential partners for the tourism industry as well as in targeting industries as part of regional economic development strategies. Issues such as economic growth, stability, and seasonality may be addressed as part of these studies.
- To argue for favourable treatment in allocation of resources or local tax, zoning or other policy decisions. By showing that tourism has significant economic impacts, tourism interests can often convince decision-makers to allocate more resources for tourism or to establish policies that encourage tourism. Tax abatements and other incentives frequently given to manufacturing firms have also been granted to hotels, marinas and other tourism businesses based on demonstrated economic impacts in the local area.
- To compare the economic impacts of alternative resource allocation, policy, management or development proposals. Economic impact analyses are commonly used to assess the relative merits of distinct alternatives. The economic contribution of expanded tourism offerings may be compared for example with alternatives such as resource extraction activities (mining, timber harvesting) or manufacturing. Impacts of alternative tourism development proposals may also be evaluated, e.g., tourism strategies that emphasize outdoor recreation, camping development, a convention facility, or a factory outlet mall.

What Economic Impacts does Tourism have?

Tourism has a variety of economic impacts. Tourists contribute to sales, profits, jobs, tax revenues, and income in an area. The most direct effects occur within the primary tourism sectors —lodging, restaurants, transportation, amusements, and retail trade. Through secondary effects, tourism affects most sectors of the economy. An economic impact analysis of tourism activity normally focuses on changes in sales, income, and employment in a region resulting from tourism activity.

A simple tourism impact scenario illustrates. Let's say a region attracts an additional 100 tourists, each spending $100 per day. That's $10,000 in new spending per day in the area. If sustained over a 100 day season, the region would accumulate a million dollars in new sales.

The million dollars in spending would be distributed to lodging, restaurant, amusement and retail trade sectors in proportion to how the visitor spends the $100. Perhaps 30% of the million dollars would leak out of the region immediately to cover the costs of goods purchased by tourists that are not made in the local area (only the retail margins for such items should normally be included as direct sales effects). The remaining $700,000 in direct sales might yield $350,000 in income within tourism industries and support 20 direct tourism jobs. Tourism industries are labour and income intensive, translating a high proportion of sales into income and corresponding jobs.

The tourism industry, in turn, buys goods and services from other businesses in the area, and pays out most of the $350,000 in income as wages and salaries to its employees. This creates secondary economic effects in the region. The study might use a sales multiplier of 2.0 to indicate that each dollar of direct sales generates another dollar in secondary sales in this region. Through multiplier effects, the $700,000 in direct sales produces $1.4 million in total sales.

These secondary sales create additional income and employment, resulting in a total impact on the region of $1.4 million in sales, $650,000 in income and 35 jobs. While hypothetical, the numbers used here are fairly typical of what one might find in a tourism economic impact study. A more complete study might identify which sectors receive the direct and secondary effects and possibly identify differences in spending and impacts of distinct subgroups of tourists (market segments). One can also estimate the tax effects of this spending by applying local tax rates to the appropriate changes in sales or income. Instead of focusing on visitor spending, one could also estimate impacts of construction or government activity associated with tourism.

There are several other categories of economic impacts that are not typically covered in economic impact assessments, at least not directly. For example:

- Changes in prices — tourism can sometimes inflate the cost of housing and retail prices in the area, frequently on a seasonal basis.
- Changes in the quality and quantity of goods and services – tourism may lead to a wider array of goods and services available in an area (of either higher or lower quality than without tourism).
- Changes in property and other taxes – taxes to cover the cost of local services may be higher or lower in the presence of tourism activity. In some cases, taxes coilected directly or indirectly from tourists may yield reduced local taxes for schools, roads, etc. In other cases, locals may be taxed more heavily to cover the added infrastructure and service costs. The impacts of tourism on local government costs and revenues are addressed more fully in a fiscal impact analysis.
- Economic dimensions of "social" and "environmental" impacts-There are also economic consequences of most social and environmental impacts that are not usually addressed in an economic impact analysis. These can be positive or negative. For example, traffic congestion will increase costs of moving around for both households and businesses. Improved amenities that attract tourists may also encourage retirees or other kinds of businesses to locate in the area.

Direct, Indirect and Induced Effects

A standard economic impact analysis traces flows of money from tourism spending, first to businesses and government agencies where tourists spend their money and then to :

- other businesses – supplying goods and services to tourist businesses,
- households – earning income by working in tourism or supporting industries, and
- government – through various taxes and charges on tourists, businesses and households.

Formally, regional economists distinguish direct, indirect, and induced economic effects. Indirect and induced effects are sometimes collectively called secondary effects. The total economic impact of tourism is the sum of direct, indirect, and induced effects within a region. Any of these impacts may be measured as gross output or sales, income, employment, or value added.

Direct effects are production changes associated with the immediate effects of changes in tourism expenditures. For example, an increase in the number of tourists staying overnight in hotels would directly yield increased sales in the hotel sector. The additional hotel sales and associated changes in hotel payments for wages and salaries, taxes, and supplies and services are direct effects of the tourist spending.

Indirect effects are the production changes resulting from various rounds of re-spending of the hotel industry's receipts in other backward-linked industries (i.e., industries supplying products and services to hotels).

Changes in sales, jobs, and income in the linen supply industry, for example, represent indirect effects of changes in hotel sales. Businesses supplying products and services to the linen supply industry represent another round of indirect effects, eventually linking hotels to varying degrees to many other economic sectors in the region.

Induced effects are the changes in economic activity resulting from household spending of income earned directly or indirectly as a result of tourism spending. For example, hotel and linen supply employees, supported directly or indirectly by tourism, spend their income in the local region for housing, food, transportation, and the usual array of household product and service needs. The sales, income, and jobs that result from household spending of added wage, salary, or proprietor's income are induced effects.

By means of indirect and induced effects, changes in tourist spending can impact virtually every sector of the economy in one way or another. The magnitude of secondary effects depends on the propensity of businesses and households in the region to purchase goods and services from local suppliers. Induced effects are particularly noticed when a large employer in a region closes a plant. Not only are supporting industries (indirect effects) hurt, but the entire local economy suffers due to the reduction in household income within the region. Retail stores close and leakages of money from the region increase as consumers go outside the region for more and more goods and services. Similar effects in the opposite direction are observed when there is a significant increase in jobs and household income. Final demand is the term used by economists for sales to the final consumers of goods and services. In almost all cases, the final consumers of tourism goods and services are households. Government spending is also considered as final demand. The same methods for estimating impacts of visitor spending can be applied to estimate the economic impacts of government spending, for example, to operate and maintain a park or visitor centre.

Regional Economic Models

An input-output model (I-O model) is a mathematical model that describes the flows of money between sectors within a region's economy. Flows are predicted by knowing what each industry must buy from every other industry to produce a dollar's worth of output. Using each industry's production function, I-O models also determine the proportions of sales that go to wage and salary income, proprietor's income, and taxes. Multipliers can be estimated from input-output models based on the estimated re-circulation of spending within the region.

Exports and imports are determined based upon estimates of the propensity of households and firms within the region to purchase goods and services from local sources (often called RPC's or regional purchase coefficients).

The more a region is self-sufficient and purchases goods and services from within the region, the higher the multipliers for the region.

Input-output models make a number of assumptions. The basic ones are that:

- All firms in a given industry employ the same production technology (usually assumed to be the national average for that industry), and produce identical products.
- There are no economies or diseconomies of scale in production or factor substitution. I-O models are essentially linear —double the level of tourism activity/ production and you double all of the inputs, the number of jobs, etc.
- The model doesn't explicitly keep track of time, but analysts generally report the impact estimates as if they represent activity within a single year.
- One must assume that the various model parameters are accurate and represent the current year.

I-O models are firmly grounded in the national system of accounts, which relies on a standard industrial classification system (SIC codes) and various federal government economic censuses, in which individual firms report sales, wage and salary payments and employment. I-O models will generally be at least a few

years out-of-date, although this isn't usually a major problem unless the region's economy has changed significantly. An I-O model represents the region's economy at a particular point in time. Tourist spending estimates are generally price adjusted to the year of the model.

Multiplier computations for induced effects generally assume that jobs created by additional spending are new jobs, involving new households in the area. Induced effects are computed assuming linear changes in household spending with changes in income. Estimates of induced effects may be inflated due to the

violation of these assumptions. Induced effects tend to account for the vast majority of the secondary effects of tourism, and therefore should be used with caution.

What are Multipliers and Multiplier Effects of Tourism?

Multipliers capture the secondary economic effects (indirect and induced) of tourism activity. Multipliers have been frequently misused and misinterpreted in tourism studies (Archer 1984) and are a considerable source of confusion among non-economists. Multipliers represent the economic interdependencies between sectors within a particular region's economy. They vary considerably from region to region and sector to sector. There are many different kinds of multipliers reflecting which secondary effects are included and which measure of economic activity is used.

For example;

The Type I sales multiplier = direct sales + indirect sales direct sales.

The Type II or III sales multiplier = direct sales + indirect sales + induced sales direct sales.

Multiplying a Type I sales multiplier times the direct sales gives direct plus indirect sales. Multiplying a Type II or III sales multiplier times the direct sales gives total sales impacts including direct, indirect and induced effects. The multipliers defined above are called ratio type multipliers as they measure the ratio of a total impact measure to the corresponding direct impact. Comparable income and employment ratio type multipliers may be defined by replacing sales with measures of income or employment in the above equations. Ratio multipliers should be used with caution.

A common error is to multiply a sales multiplier times tourist spending to get total sales effects. This will generate an inflated estimate of tourism impacts. The problem is that tourism spending or sales is not exactly the same as the "direct effects", appearing in the multiplier formula. Tourist purchases of goods (vs. services) are the primary source of the problem.

To properly apply tourist purchases of goods to an input-output model (or corresponding multipliers), various margins (retail, wholesale and transportation) must be deducted from the "purchaser price" of the good to separate out the "producer price". In an I-O model, retail margins accrue to the retail trade sector, wholesale margins to wholesale trade, transportation margins to transportation sectors (trucking, rail, air etc.) and the producer prices of goods are assigned to the sector that produces the good.

In most cases the factory that produces the good bought by a tourist lies outside of the local region, creating an immediate "leakage" in the first round of spending and therefore no local impact from production of the good. Before applying a multiplier to tourist spending, one must first deduct the producer prices of all imported goods that tourists buy (i.e. only include the local retail margins and possibly wholesale and transportation margins if these firms lie within the region). Generally, only 60 to 70% of tourist spending appears as final demand in a local region. While all tourist purchases of services will accrue to the local region as final demand, only the margins on goods purchased at retail stores should be counted as local final demand. The ratio of local final demand to tourist spending is called the capture rate.

Capture rate = local final demand / tourism spending in local area.

The distinction between Type II and Type III multipliers involves a technical difference in how the induced effects are computed. Type II approaches include households as a sector of the economy and invert the technical coefficient matrix including the household sector, while Type III approaches treat households as exogenous.

Capture rates, like multipliers, will vary with the size and nature of the region as well as the kind of tourist spending included. One must therefore be cautious in taking a multiplier or capture rate cited in one study and using it in another.

Another way of calculating a multiplier (generally the preferred approach among economists) is as a ratio of income or employment to sales. This kind of multiplier is sometimes called a Keynesian multiplier or response coefficient.

Type III Income multiplier = Total direct, indirect, and induced income direct sales Type III Employment multiplier = Total direct, indirect, and induced employment direct sales This income (employment) multiplier produces total income (employment) impacts when multiplied by the direct sales. One must still be careful in distinguishing between tourism spending/sales and direct sales effects. Some studies may embed the capture rate in the multiplier, expressing the ratio in terms of tourism spending rather than direct sales.

How are Tourism's Economic Impacts Measured?

The economic impacts of tourism are typically estimated by some variation of the following simple formula:

The formula suggests three distinct steps and corresponding measurements or models:

Estimate the change in the number and types of tourists to the region due to the proposed policy or action.

Estimates or projections of tourist activity generally come from a demand model or some system for measuring levels of tourism activity in an area. Economic impact estimates will rest heavily on good estimates of the numbers and types of visitors. These must come from carefully designed measurements of tourist activity, a good demand model, or good judgement. This step is usually the weakest link in most tourism impact studies, as few regions have accurate counts of tourists, let alone good models for predicting changes in tourism activity or separating local visitors from visitors from outside the region.

Estimate average levels of spending (often within specific market segments) of tourists in the local area.

Spending averages come from sample surveys or are sometimes borrowed or adapted from other studies. Spending estimates must be based on a representative sample of the population of tourists taking into account variations across seasons, types of tourists, and locations within the study area. As spending can vary widely across different kinds of tourists, we recommend estimating average spending for a set of key tourist segments based on samples of at least 50-100 visitors within each tourism segment. Segments should be defined to capture differences in spending between local residents vs. tourists, day users vs. overnight visitors, type of accommodation (motel, campground, seasonal home, with friends and relatives), and type of transportation (car, RV, air, rail, etc.). In broadly based tourism impact studies, it is useful to identify unique spending patterns of important activity segments such as downhill skiers, boaters, convention & business travellers.

Multiplying the number of tourists by the average spending per visitor (be careful the units are consistent) gives an estimate of total tourist spending in the area. Estimates of tourist spending will generally be more accurate if distinct spending profiies and use estimates are made for key tourism segments. The use and spending estimates are the two most important parts of an economic impact assessment. When combined, they capture the amount of money brought into the region by tourists. Multipliers are needed only if one is interested in the secondary effects of tourism spending.

Apply the change in spending to a regional economic model or set of multipliers to determine secondary effects.

Secondary effects of tourism are estimated using multipliers or a model of the region's economy.

Multipliers generally come from an economic base or input-output model of the region's economy. In many cases multipliers are borrowed (often improperly) or adjusted from published multipliers or other studies. One should not take a multiplier estimated for one region and apply it in a region with a quite different economic structure.

Generally, multipliers are higher for larger regions with more diversified economies and lower for smaller regions with more limited economic development. A common error is to apply a statewide multiplier (since these are more widely published) to a local region. This will yield inflated estimates of local multiplier effects. Multipliers can also be used to convert estimates of spending or sales to income and employment. Simple ratios can be used to capture how much income or jobs are generated per dollar of sales. These ratios will vary from region to region and across individual economic sectors due to the relative importance of labour inputs in each industry and different wage and salary rates in different regions of the country. Be aware that job estimates are generally not full time equivalents, making them difficult to compare across industries with different proportions of seasonal and part time jobs. Income or value added are generally the preferred measures of the contribution of tourism to a region's economy.

What are the Typical Approaches for an Economic Impact Assessment?

At the simple, "quick and dirty" end of the spectrum are highly aggregate approaches that rely mostly on judgement to determine tourism activity, spending and multipliers. Such estimates can be completed in a couple hours at little cost and rest largely on the expertise and judgement of the analyst. At the other extreme are studies that gather primary data from visitor spending studies and apply the spending estimates to formal regional economic models for the area in question. In between are a wide range of options that employ varying degrees of judgement, secondary data, primary data, and formal models. Different levels of detail and corresponding expense (time and money) and accuracy are possible for each of the three steps – estimating tourist volume, spending, and multiplier effects. Four typical approaches illustrate the levels of detail that are possible and the associated methods.

1. Subjective estimates that rely mostly on expert opinion
2. Secondary data in aggregate form, adapting existing estimates to suit the problem
3. Secondary data in disaggregate form, permitting finer adjustment of data to fit the situation
4. Primary data and/or formal models, usually involving visitor surveys and regional economic models.

Summary

The economic significance of tourism has been subject to considerable debate. Resolving this debate requires reliable and rigorous information on the precise nature of tourism spending and its impact on different sectors of the economy. One problem which has always faced those seeking to analyse the economic contribution of tourism is that tourism simply does not exist as a distinct sector in systems of national accounts. There are sectors which are characteristic of tourism, such as transport, hotels and accommodation, but tourists spend their money across a range of different sectors and national accounts do not track this spending. These difficulties can be resolved through the construction of Tourism Satellite Accounts which provide an internationally recognised and standardised method of assessing the scale and impact of tourism spending and its links across different sectors. Although costly, investment in the construction of satellite accounts provides policy makers with information on the economic contribution of tourism and the ability to analyses its effects economy wide. Such information is the prerequisite to efficient and effective policy decisions to guide the future development of tourism. Moreover, satellite accounts provide a foundation for more sophisticated analyses of the impact of tourism and the assessment of different policy regimes using techniques such as computable general equilibrium modelling. These general equilibrium techniques do require significant investment, but are increasingly being utilised because of the benefits they generate in terms of understanding the extent and diversity of tourism's impact on an economy.

One can employ different levels of aggregation in visitor segments, spending categories, multipliers, and economic sectors to finely tune the data and models to a particular application and also yield more detailed information about the economic impacts. For example, spending data from previous surveys may be adjusted over time using consumer price indices (CPI). If spending is itemized in several categories, distinct CPI's may be used for food away from home, lodging, or gasoline. If not, an aggregate CPI, which may not reflect the mix of goods that tourists purchase, must be used. Data for distinct tourism market segments is also valuable in tailoring secondary data to a particular application. For example, separate estimates of the average spending for day users and overnight visitors allows one to adjust the spending estimate to reflect a given mix of day users and overnight visitors.

Tourism Growth Factors

A number of factors are responsible for the rapid growth and development of the tourism industry in the Asia Pacific region. These include the strong economic growth, increase in income, breakdown of political barriers, easing of travel restrictions, liberalization of air transport, and focused marketing campaigns. These factors are expected to accelerate the growth of tourism over the next decade.

Economic Growth

The rapid growth of the tourism industry is a reflection of the region's booming and diversified economies. Economic growth has ranged between an average of 6% to 9% in the last decade, in contrast to 3% to 4% growth achieved by the rest of the world. Only the industrialized countries of Australia, Japan, and New Zealand show a lower rate of growth than the rest of the region. China, which has achieved double-digit growth over the last 5 years, is poised to become one of the world's largest economies and surpass Japan in the next decade. The region is expected to maintain its growth at a rate between 6% to 8% over the next decade (IMF 1996b).

Strong economic growth in Asia is attributed to a focus on market reforms, export oriented industries, stable currencies, diversification of the economy, and massive injection of foreign capital. Billions of dollars are being poured into the tourism infrastructure to accommodate a burgeoning Asian tourism industry. This has intensified trade, investment, and travel within the region and with the rest of the world. Asian governments have also sought to avoid extremes of inflation and unemployment, and are keeping budget deficits small or running surpluses. It is no wonde.

2

Hospitality Management

The Caribbean hotel industry is positioned to reinvent itself in a way that improves profitability, enhances guest relations, builds bridges into the local communities, and preserves the Caribbean's natural beauty.

Over the past 2 years, this trend has been translated into results in Jamaica in the form of the Environmental Audits for Sustainable Tourism (EAST) project, sponsored by the Jamaica Hotel and Tourist Association and funded by the United States Agency for International Development (USAID).

This paper presents a case study of the USAID/Jamaica EAST project demonstrating the power of becoming an environmentally friendly hotel through the adoption of an environmental management system (EMS), a comprehensive organizational approach designed to achieve environmental care in all aspects of operations.

Partnering environmental protection with cost-saving environmental improvements and best practices, the EAST project is a model for the hotels and tourism destinations in the Caribbean region and beyond for environmental assessments and actions, as well as voluntary environmental audits that can lead to the GREEN GLOBE International Certification.

Introduction

A "quiet revolution" is taking place in the Caribbean-one less visible than the construction of new hotels and the building of new cruise ships. Nevertheless, its advent is profoundly changing the nature and shape of the tourism and hospitality industry, in every hotel guestroom, housekeeping, laundry or maintenance facility, and in every tourism destination that elects voluntarily to join the environmental movement. This revolution is environmentally sustainable tourism. The Caribbean hotel industry, particularly, is positioned to reinvent itself in a way that improves profitability, enhances guest relations, builds bridges into the local communities, and preserves the Caribbean's natural beauty. Over the past 2 years, this trend has been translated into results in Jamaica in the form of the Environmental Audits for Sustainable Tourism (EAST) project, sponsored by the Jamaica Hotel and Tourist Association and funded by the United States Agency for International Development (USAID).

USAID/Jamaica EAST Project Description

In 1997, the Jamaica Hotel and Tourist Association, Government of Jamaica, Jamaica Manufacturers Association, and a number of tourism-related public and private-sector industry organizations committed to undertake the Environmental Audits for Sustainable Tourism (EAST) project. With funding from the U.S. Agency for International Development, Hagler Bailly implemented a program of environmental audits within a corporate environmental management system aimed at the tourism and hospitality industry in Negril, with a smaller component focused on manufacturing industries in Kingston and St. Andrews. The project is a model for environmental action and voluntary audits for the tourism sector, combining promotion and outreach, training, audits, and investment.

The objectives of the EAST program are:

- to develop greater awareness and understanding of the benefits of environmental systems and audits among hotel and restaurant owners and allied tourism businesses;
- to upgrade the technical skills of Jamaicans who are expected to conduct the audits and advise on environmental management systems;

- to assist a select, representative number of tourism-related establishments in carrying out environmental audits, and
- to help finance in the tourism industry, on a cost-sharing basis, selected audit recommendations in order to demonstrate the financial benefits of the systematic application of environmentally friendly practices and, thereby, encourage others in the tourism industry to do likewise.

The activities of the EAST project include:

- institutionalizing environmental management in the tourism industry;
- performance monitoring of EAST demonstration hotels;
- environmental assessments, audits, and certification; environmental awareness and training; regulatory assistance in environmental licensing;
- audits and technical assistance in the manufacturing industry;
- targeted environmental investment fund feasibility and financing; performance awards programs, and international human resources exchange programs.

An important next step for Jamaica is to sustain and expand this improved level of environmental management among government and private-sector organizations.

East Findings and Results

The following is a discussion of some of the EAST findings and results. When Hagler Bailly began in June of 1997, the awareness was quite high in Negril (the target area for the EAST project) due primarily to the influx of questionnaires and surveys sent by European tour operators such as Tui and British Airways Holidays. These inquiries were from European markets interested in buying the export products, e.g., traveling to destinations supporting environmental best policies and management practices. Hagler Bailly started with a survey of hotels in Negril to ask hoteliers why they choose to become "environmentally friendly." The results showed a genuine concern about the impact their operations have on the physical environment and an appreciation for how this can be translated into cost savings. Interestingly, the government's enforcement of environmental laws and standards ranked lowest. This told us that hoteliers were interested in measurable results and that they would respond better to incentives than to government intervention. Initially, however, when we asked individual hoteliers what they thought "going green" implied, the most common answer was to replace plastic straws with paper straws. The obvious next question, since none of the respondents had achieved the "environmentally friendly" status, was what are the perceived barriers to becoming a green hotel. The results pointed to the up-front cost of learning how to make the transition, and then to the financing to implement it.

Hotel Environmental Management System

One of the most critical elements of becoming an environmentally friendly hotel is the adoption of a new culture that extends throughout the hotel organization, and between the hotel and its guest, local community, and even its vendors. We call this an environmental management system (EMS).

An EMS is defined as a comprehensive organizational approach designed to achieve environmental care in all aspects of operations. The International Standards Organization (ISO) 14000 series is an international standard for EMS. The World Travel and Tourism Council's GREEN GLOBE international certification has developed an EMS standard specifically for the travel and tourism industry.

An effective EMS can help a hotel assure its guests of its commitment to environmental management as partners in programs such as recycling, linen and towel reuse, etc. It can set specific and realistic performance objectives and targets, and allow the hotel to monitor to see if the objectives and targets are being met. As mentioned earlier, it can enhance a hotel's image in the marketplace and help reach nearly 43 million Americans, as well as hundreds of thousands of environmentally aware tourists from Europe and elsewhere interested in visiting environmentally friendly destinations and staying in accommodations with environmental policies and programs in place.

Most importantly, an EMS can improve efficiency and reduce operating costs. In fact, the savings alone should be sufficient for any hotel to commit to implementing an EMS.

Few hotels today have what we would consider an EMS. This is not to say that there are no hotels implementing environmental programs such as water conservation and composting, but it is typically not done as part of a larger management system, nor is it integrated with other environmental programs. There is a growing demand to have an EMS that meets international standards such as ISO 14001 and GREEN GLOBE. An EMS evaluation, because of its broad-reaching implications, will begin to encompass other concerns such as health, safety, and security, emergency preparedness, compliance with discharge and emissions standards, and employee training.

What constitutes an EMS? The principal components of an EMS, as defined by GREEN GLOBE, include the following: an environmental policy that clearly communicates the organization's commitment to maintaining the social, cultural and physical environment; an action plan to guide the property's actions and expenditure of resources; the implementation or operations of the EMS that encompasses all of the property's actions relative to the environment, including awareness and training, staff procedures, incentive programs, and community outreach among other things; corrective action or monitoring to ensure that the EMS performs as expected, allowing for responsive actions to capture things such as leaking toilets and chemical spills and review, typically by senior management, to determined how to improve the EMS and the level of compliance with the hotel's environmental policy.

EMS and Environmental Programs

Many will say, we already have hotels in the Caribbean that are operating in an environmentally responsible manner. That is to say that the hotel is currently composting much of its organic solid wastes, or that guestrooms have low flow showerheads installed.

We call these environmental programs. An EMS is the integration of those programs under a comprehensive organizational system. An EMS takes the following approach to addressing its environmental issues (or aspects as they are referred to in the standards).

- First, an assessment is done to determine what improvements can be made, how much they cost, and what types of changes in consumption or waste generation can be expected. The assessment also allows you to establish a baseline against which change can be measured.
- Next, the hotel sets objectives such as to reduce water consumption for the entire property by 10%. Each objective is supported by a set of specific targets, such as introduce towel and linen reuse program by June 31st, or install low-flow showerheads in guest rooms and staff locker rooms by August 1st.
- The individuals, or departments, responsible for achieving the targets are identified in an action plan. It is important to remember that the greatest improvements are made through changes in staff procedures.
- Finally, the impact or results, in terms of changes from the baseline, must be measured and documented. This provides the necessary feedback to determine whether the EMS is working.

The EMS can be viewed as the integration of multiple environmental programs. Environmental programs are typically designed to address a specific environmental problem or issue such as recycling or composting solid waste; or are focused on a specific department such as a linen reuse program in housekeeping and laundry. In some instances, particularly for smaller hotels, environmental programs may involve multiple properties, such as sharing the cost of a bottle crusher for glass recycling

East Environmental Management Audit Findings

Hagler Bailly designed a specific audit protocol that combines the attributes of an energy audit, an environmental audit, and a management audit —the EAST Environmental Management Audit. We tested the audit protocol on the full range of hotel properties, from 15 rooms to over 200 rooms. The audits covered the following areas energy use, water use, wastewater generation and disposal, solid waste generation and disposal, use of chemicals, and management and staff practices. Summarized below are some of the general findings of the EAST audits.

Inefficient use of Water: Leaking toilets accounted for 40% of the daily water use in one 35-room hotel. The cost of the leaks was US$600 per month. In another property, a defective drain valve on a washing machine increased laundry water use by more than 1 million gallons per year equivalent to US$6,000 of wasted water.

Inefficient use of Energy: Loose louvers and doors and poor insulation force air conditioners to work continuously in order to keep guest rooms cool. This mode of operation increases energy consumption and shortens the air conditioner's service life.

Excessive and Unnecessary use of Chemicals: Instead of manually cleaning the kitchen grease trap, a property used 420 gallons/year of sulfuric acid (or Drano) to do the job. This cost of this dangerous habit exceeded US$6,000 per year.

Excessive Solid Waste Generation: A 25-room property spent US$1,700 per year to purchase large plastic trash bags. Many properties place all yard waste in plastic bags and pay to send this material to the dump. Organic wastes from kitchen and landscaping accounts for up to 50% of a property's solid waste and can be easily composted.

Staff not Participating in Environmental Programs: In 90% of cases, housekeepers automatically replace all used guest towels in properties that have towel reuse programs.

Poor (or no) Monitoring: Approximately 70% of audited properties had no effective utilities monitoring program. Water and electricity bills are simply received and paid. A 20,000-

gallon per day leak went undetected for more than a week because the property didn't check the water meter daily. There was considerable variation in water use among 14 properties we audited ranging from 15 to 70 rooms.

To provide a common base for comparison, we calculated each hotel's consumption in terms of Imperial gallons per guest night. The results are shown in table below. The most efficient of the hotels used just one-third the water per guest night of the least efficient.

Water Use in Properties Audited by EAST Imperial gallons/ Guest Night

Most Efficient Hotel	116
Average Efficient	216
Least Efficient	351

A similar comparison was also done among audited properties for electricity consumption. The results are shown in table below. Again, the most efficient hotel used only one-quarter of the electricity per guest night of that of the least efficient hotel.

Electricity Use in Properties Audited by EAST KWH/Guest Night

Most Efficient Hotel	8.7
Average Efficient	21.4
Least Efficient	32.9

Detailed Analysis of Efficiency Improvements in the EAST Demonstration Hotels

The water and energy use indices of a hotel are affected by occupancy rates as well as by its conservation efforts and investments in efficient technologies. As a general rule, water and energy indices rise during low occupancy months and drop during high occupancy months.

Given the influence of occupancy and conservation efforts on efficiency, the monitoring data collected from the properties should be analyzed in greater detail to ensure that efficiency gains result from improved environmental practices rather than better occupancy rates. This higher scrutiny is particularly important, for example, in the case of a hotel that reduced its water and electricity use indices by more than 25% while simultaneously increasing its occupancy by 16%.

Figures below present the result of a more rigorous data analysis, and show how the hotel's monthly water and electricity use indices varied with respect to occupancy before and after its involvement with the EAST project.

Since the water and electricity use indices are consistently lower "after" the EAST audit, regardless of the actual occupancy levels, these graphs prove that the property's water and electricity savings are due to improved conservation practices rather than higher occupancy rates. The vertical distance separating the "before EAST" and "after EAST" trend lines represents the actual water and electricity savings achieved through the property's conservation efforts at any given occupancy level.

Electricity Use Index Versus Occupancy for a Hotel Before and After EAST/
Note: 1,000 GN/month is approximately equivalent to 100% occupancy.

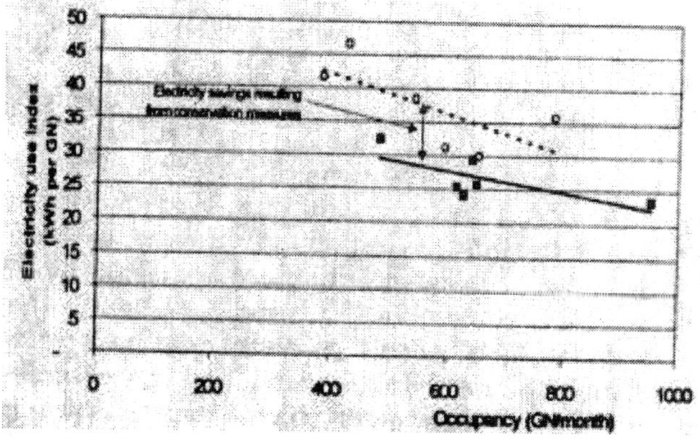

Source: Performance Monitoring Report on EAST Project Demonstration Hotels.

Water Use Index Versus Occupancy for a Hotel Before and after EAST

Note: 1,000 GN/month is approximately equivalent to 100% occupancy.

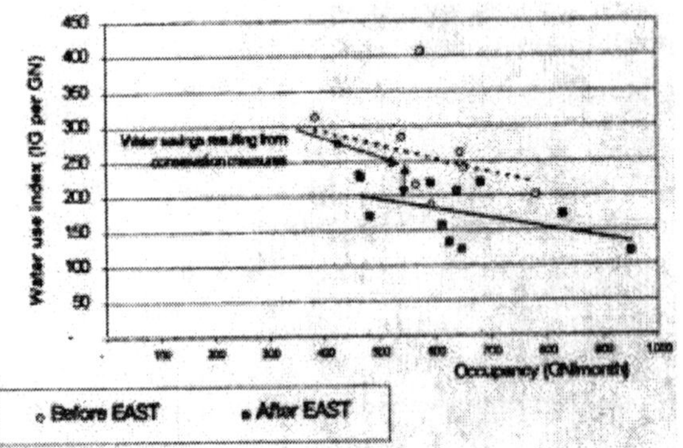

Source: Performance Monitoring Report on EAST Project Demonstration Hotels.

Recommendations for Improvement

So what did it take to improve performance in a typical Jamaican hotel?

Most of the recommendations made in the EAST Audit reports have the following characteristics. They have low implementation costs, rapid payback periods, and they are relatively simple and easy to implement.

The EAST auditors also found that the greatest environmental and financial benefits can be achieved by improving: frequent monitoring, particularly utility bills; management supervision, oversight to ensure that programs are operating effectively; staff practices, training, and providing incentives for staff to implement programs, and preventive and routine maintenance, particularly of energy-and water-using equipment. In the breakdown of EAST audit recommendations for a typical hotel, the following was evident. Over three-quarters of the recommendations cost less than US$10/guest room, 19% of the recommendations cost between US$10-50 per guest room and only 3% cost more than US$50 per guestroom.

Payback period is defined as the length of time required before the savings from a measure equal the cost to implement the measure. In terms of payback period for EAST audit recommendations: 62% of the recommendations had a payback of less than 2 months, another 36% had payback periods of between 2 months and 1 year, and only 2% had payback of greater than 1 year. Another way to break down the EAST audit recommendations is by area of activity (or department) in the hotel. Our auditors identified that the largest, by far, can be found in the maintenance and engineering department. We should note that more often than not, the problems lie in insufficient resources resulting in shortages of staff, parts, and supplies, and unwillingness to pay repair bills to fix a problem properly. Guest rooms (or housekeeping department) and restaurant and bar (or food and beverage department) accounted for 15 and 16 percent of the recommended actions, respectively. This is mainly due to the high degree of energy and water used in these areas.

Advantages of a "Green Hotel"

During our visits to Jamaica, we became aware of one small hotel in Port Antonio-Hotel Mocking Bird Hill-that has made considerable strides in improving environmental performance. For purposes of the following example, we will refer to Mocking Bird Hill's consumption levels as that of a "green hotel." Using the average from the 14 EAST hotels audited for both water and electricity; we show the difference relative to the "green hotel."

Looking now at an illustration of the cost advantages of a green hotel, let's assume a 50-room hotel, with 60% occupancy, and 2 guest per room. Over the course of a year, the water savings are over 3.6 million gallons, or savings of US$21,829 in water bills. The electricity savings are 186,000 kWh per year, or savings of US$23,886 in electricity bills. Total savings, for both water and electricity amounts to US$45,715 per year.

The savings can greatly improve a hotel's profitability. For example, if it takes US$10 of revenue to generate US$1 of profit, savings of US$45,715 in utility costs would have an impact equivalent to US$457,150 in additional revenue. Assuming average revenue of US$100 per guest night, the savings represent the equivalent to additional 4,571 guest nights worth of revenue.

Cash Flow Associated with "Going Green"

So how would the investment and savings look over an extended period of time? Most of the costs are incurred in the first 9 months. These include the cost of an external audit, energy and water savings equipment, and training of key staff. After the first year, the costs are only associated with preventative maintenance and preparing for the annual GREEN GLOBE certification. Over a 3-year period, the initial investment of US$40,000 will yield approximately US$112,000 in savings, or a net profit of about US$70,000.

Implications for the Jamaican Hotel Industry

Just to illustrate the point further, we asked the question: "What would becoming a green hotel mean for Jamaica as a whole?" Here we have used the Jamaican Tourist Product Development Company (TPDCo) hotel data for 1996, assumed 60% occupancy and 2 guests per room like the earlier example. Obviously, this over-simplifies the hotel industry, but the point is valid. For all of Jamaica, the difference between an industry comprised of green hotels and one comprised of average hotels is over 930 million gallons of water per year. The green hotel industry will use 77% less water than the average, and 86% less than the inefficient hotel industry. The reductions in water consumption also translate directly to the volume of wastewater coming from the hotel industry. We can do the same simulation for energy or specifically electricity consumption. For all of Jamaica, the difference between green hotels and the average hotel industry is over 47 million kilowatt-hours per year. The green hotel industry will use a third less electricity than the average, and two-thirds less electricity than the inefficient hotel industry.

So what does this all mean to the Caribbean hotel industry? First, it is a "win-win" proposition. You can improve your market share while reducing your operating costs. Second, it is neither rocket science nor is it untried or untested. The audit recommendations are relatively simple and proven to work right here in the Caribbean. Third, you have no choice.

Resorts throughout the Caribbean countries and hotels all over the world have recognized the advantages of going green. International certification programs like GREEN GLOBE are driving the industry toward improved performance. This means that instead of getting the marketing advantage of being a leader, those that fail to make the transition may soon be termed as "brown hotels." Know anyone who would prefer to stay in a brown hotel rather than in a green one?

We should also look at what it means to different stakeholders such as the government and local communities across the Caribbean. The reduced water, wastewater, and energy consumption levels of a green hotel industry translate directly to reduced shortages and lowered needs for infrastructure in water supply, wastewater treatment plants, and power plants. The same holds true for solid waste and the need for sanitary landfills.

So the more important question becomes, what are the hotels waiting for? Governments should begin laying out the necessary incentives and standards to move the industry in this direction. Banks should open special lines of credit to finance the improvements. And Caribbean Hotel Association, Caribbean Tourism Organization, and the tourist board of each island should find ways to link the marketing of Caribbean hotels directly to the computers of those millions of so-called "eco-tourists" in the U.S. and Europe who are beginning to plan their next family vacations.

Employee Recognition and Motivation

The foundation of recognition and motivation is that people need and want Acceptance, Approval and Appreciation. Almost all positive motivation is based on these needs. People want to know that what they do makes a difference. Just recognizing the staff is the most important step one can take. You may want to count the number of "we's that are said instead of "I's in order to assess the extent to which your staff feels part of the team and part of the business' future. One saying is, "Powerlessness corrupts, absolute powerlessness corrupts absolutely."

These nine actions will help immensely to give your staff what they need: Communicate, Communicate, Communicate, Recognize, Recognize, Recognize, Thank, Thank, and Thank!

From various sources, Vicki developed a list of ideas for ongoing weekly or monthly programs to keep employees connected to the hotel or restaurant emotionally, to create excitement and to make your business unique relative to your nearby competitors for employees.

Remember, the competition for staff may be from other industries such as retail, manufacturing, etc. Pick a few and try them for a while; but, you must give them a chance, one time will not do it. The staff will see right through you.

- Gift certificate for the most challenging question posed to the President
- Money or chocolates or lottery ticket to a spouse with a note thanking for his/her support during overtime
- Thumbs-up certificates redeemable for merchandise
- Soda, fruit, snacks to housekeeping staff all the time
- When anyone makes a negative comment, put $0.25 or $0.50 into a pot and use the money for a Fun Committee
- Bring Polaroid camera to work occasionally and take candids of staff and post pictures on a bulletin board for all to enjoy
- Selection of employee of the month/quarter/year by peers not just management
- When he/she is employee of the month, give him/her a special name tag highlighting that status
- Points given out at any time for anything, good attendance, helping out a guest, etc., and are redeemable for prizes
- When you reach a certain level in revenues, give all staff a reward, being sure to give them the goal in advance

- Spontaneous calls from corporate to line staff saying how they are appreciated
- Allow line workers to participate in all personnel function decisions, hiring, training, evaluating, firing, schedules
- Fine those who arrive late to a meeting and distribute the money to those who were there on time
- Create a symbol of the team, maybe just property logo but put it on T-shirts, mugs, caps
- Certificate of achievement, lunch, and mug for perfect attendance, gift certificate to the one with longest perfect attendance
- Allow those with perfect attendance record to enter a lottery to get a $100 or $200 gift certificate
- Quarterly teleconference with all employees and support staff, especially CEO
- Family orientation for new employees with slide show or video program with refreshments
- Several line staff call new hire to welcome him/her to the team the day before he/she starts
- Toll-free hot line to President where they can leave any question, suggestion, etc. and will get a response
- Hold a regular meeting to tell staff what is going on and how they are doing
- Always hang charts, graphs, etc. to depict regularly how the property is doing
- Full page ad in newspaper once a year thanking employees and name all individually
- Public praising of an individual at a department or hotel meeting
- Make sure all rewards, praise, bonuses, etc. are in public
- Have the General Manager spend at least an hour with every new employee
- Golden Broom Award to all (excluding housekeeping

staff) who are seen picking up trash-after two, they can redeem them for a gift

- Pick a trophy that is passed from rewardee to rewardee so it is much desired, it does not matter what it is and actually the odder the better so it is fun
- Pre-printed "you done good" or "a pat on the back" or "bravo" note cards to have management inscribe whenever appropriate spontaneously
- Praise immediately and tell them specifically what they did right and how it helps the company
- Always find ways to get staff's input into the operation-just simple suggestion box works great
- Work hard at finding a way to implement each suggestion and give a clear explanation why it cannot be used if that is the case
- Acknowledge all suggestions, even if not implemented, express appreciation perhaps also a small reward If you implement an idea, give a reward, and widely publicize it
- Pins for uniforms that say "The guest comes first" or "I will do my best" or "We're glad you're here" or something similar
- Periodically hold contests like a TV game show where employees answer questions about the property hotel, perhaps in teams
- Use an 800# service which employees call periodically to be given randomly selected test questions and win a prize if they get them all correct
- Give a small gift on the date of their anniversary
- Hold an annual banquet for those with more than a certain number of years of service
- Give every employee printed business cards
- At Ritz Carlton, all employees throughout the hotel are authorized to spend up to $2,000 each incident to resolve a guest's complaint, but few spend anywhere near that amount

- Ask employees regularly what else we can do for them to enable them to do a good job
- Tell employees regularly what else they can do for management to enable you to do a good job
- Hold weekly meetings with small groups of employees to discuss anything, serve food
- Hold a weekly 20 minute meeting with one employee to discuss anything
- Make it personal, people naturally commit themselves to other people, not to organizations
- Hold monthly employee meetings at which the financial performance of the previous month and other goals are discussed in specific
- Distribute daily reports of revenue performance last night and month-to-date
- Send employees and family to a competitive property and have them write a report
- Send employees and family to your property and have them write a report
- Imprint the hotel's four key business goals on T-shirts
- Include career development discussion in all performance reviews
- Send line staff to schools to do recruiting and interviewing
- Tell staff that if they achieve x,y,z, etc., you will call their mothers and tell them how great their child is and actually do it
- Always make sure their work environment is positive, attractive, and reflective of your goals and values
- Ideas for back-of-the-house areas: plants, framed art (let them choose), clean unworn carpets, adequate ventilation, natural light, meeting space, adequate work-space, well-functioning equipment, attractive break facilities
- Form a recreation committee to plan monthly activities
- Regular employee newsletter

- Ask for input on cost-cutting programs during times of low demand
- Implement management reviews where line staff assess management's performance

These are only a few of the infinite number of ideas to keep good staff members and motivate them to work hard toward common goals. Whatever you choose to do, keep doing it consistently and make sure that you are sincere. Good luck on making your hotel or restaurant a unique and rewarding place to work.

The Organisation and Operation

Meetings are a crucial part of an organization's overall strategy, and planning them requires special skills and tools. This article describes how to get the job done and where to turn for help.

Introduction

So you've been handed the responsibility of organizing an off-premises meeting. Welcome to a task that isn't as easy as it seems. Before long, you'll be making decisions and following up on all manner of details. You may find yourself searching madly for reference materials or interviewing professionals to help you organize. Don't worry, there's no shortage of either.

Measuring Value

The best meetings support an organization's business objectives and help convey its overall message to those attending. The best meeting planners actively participate in honing the content to ensure that the meeting furthers the goals of the organization and is consistent with its mission. To measure the meeting's effectiveness, they are prepared to demonstrate its return on investment (ROI) to management. Through ROI, organizations justify the dollars spent on meetings by measuring desired criteria, i.e., the knowledge gained by attendees or the increase in sales directly attributable to their participation. Determining ROI is accomplished through a variety of means, such as feedback from management, post-meeting evaluations, and surveys.

Questions to Ask

When handed the task of planning a meeting, first ask yourself whether there are alternatives to having a meeting at all. Is there a less costly way to communicate with this group, say, with videoconferencing or computer conferencing?

Chances are your organization will decide there is no substitute for a face-to-face gathering, so two other questions are in order:

- What is the objective of this meeting?
- Who will attend?

The answers to these questions will form the basis of all logistical decisions to come, such as where the meeting is to be held, the size of the budget, what type of hotel or other facility you will use, the content of the agenda, what type of recreation will be called for, and even how the chairs in the meeting room will be set up. The importance of these early steps cannot be overemphasized, in particular the question: "Why are we having this meeting?"

An incentive meeting held as a reward for salespeople, for example, will likely be held in an upscale resort hotel with recreation as part of the program. On the other hand, a short, hastily called brainstorming meeting is best staged at a business hotel, perhaps one located near an airport so that attendees can get in and out quickly. Obviously, fancy meals and recreation will not be necessary. And a meeting called to teach salespeople a new skill will best fit in a conference center that specializes in training and team-building programs. There, some form of recreation may provide a welcome break.

Venue Selection

Only after you are sure of the nature of the meeting and what type of hotel or facility you will use, can you go about selecting a venue. For openers:

- Contact the convention and visitors bureau in the destination you are considering. The bureau will send you literature that describes local hotels.
- Consult a hotel directory, such as SourceBook, a special

issue of Successful Meetings magazine, Gavel, a special issue of Meetings & Conventions magazine, or the Official Meetings & Facilities Guide, a web-based facility guide. (For details, see Publications.)

- Contact the sales offices of major hotel chains for directories of their properties.

After compiling a list of possible venues, send the sales department of each a request for proposal (RFP) outlining the requirements of your meeting. (If you're contacting several hotels in a destination, the convention and visitors bureau may serve as a middleman). The RFP should include such information as the preferred dates for your meeting, the number and type of sleeping rooms you require, the range of acceptable room rates, food and beverage requirements, a tentative agenda, and the amount and type of meeting space needed. This information will help the hotel decide whether it is able to host the meeting according to your specifications.

Based on the hotels' responses to your RFP, narrow down the field and arrange to inspect the hotel or hotels you're considering. Things to consider during a site inspection: overall appearance of the hotel and its guest rooms, lobby, and meeting space; proximity to the airport and availability of shuttle services; attitude of the service staff; whether meeting rooms have obstructions, such as pillars or overhangs, that interfere with audiovisual presentations; accessibility for people with disabilities.

If you cannot inspect the site in person, a detailed questionnaire will suffice. Also, many hotels have Web sites that include layouts of their meeting space.

Negotiating a Contract

By now, you should be ready to accept a letter of agreement from one property. This outlines the space reserved for your group. You can begin to negotiate with the salesperson from the property on the terms of the contract that will eventually be signed. If you've held a similar meeting before, you may strengthen your bargaining position by mentioning how much was spent on basic items.

Nearly everything is negotiable: the sleeping room rate; the meeting room rental, which may be waived if the group generates sufficient guest-room and food and beverage revenue; upgrades to suite accommodations; meeting room equipment; and the complimentary room ratio (typically, hotels "comp" one room for every 50 booked).

Negotiating with a conference center is simpler, because such properties offer a complete meeting package (CMP). This provides a per-person cost for everything from sleeping rooms and meals to conference space and audiovisual needs.

Regardless of the venue, make sure you have a written contract that outlines the guest room commitment, room rate, complimentary accommodations, reservation and deposit procedures, method of payment, meeting space, banquet space, and cancellation policy.

Before the contract is signed, however, you might want to include special provisions that could be difficult to add later on. For instance, you could insert a clause stipulating that certain organizations, such as a competing company, may not meet in the hotel at the same time. Or you could provide for financial relief in the event that the hotel is double-booked and can't honour its commitments.

Keep in mind that you have the option of outsourcing your meeting to meeting specialists who will undertake all logistics (or only those elements you wish to outsource) from site selection to on-site management of the meeting. This company need not be based in the city where you hold the meeting.

Details

After the contract is signed, your meeting file will be turned over to the property's convention services manager. Think of this person as your in-house meeting planner, the person who, from now until your meeting ends, will coordinate all your needs and serve as a liaison between you and other departments within the property. Leading up to the meeting, you will be confronted with countless details (meeting publications often publish diagrams showing what must be done and when). Among the critical details:

- *Transportation:* Will flights be booked by your organization's in-house travel department or an outside agency? Airlines have special departments that handle groups. They offer discounted fares and cargo rates, complimentary tickets (depending on the number of seats booked), and special ticketing and billing. How will attendees get from the airport to the meeting property? Taxi? Hotel shuttle? If you're expecting high-level executives or other VIPs, you'll have to arrange limousine transfers.
- *Check-in:* To expedite check-in, the property will need to be briefed on the arrival pattern of attendees.
- *Agenda:* As the meeting nears, a schedule of meeting-related activities and food-and-beverage functions should be drafted and shared with the convention services manager.
- Meeting-room setup depends on the nature of the sessions. Use an auditorium-style setup when a speaker is addressing the group. Arrange tables in a U for sessions where attendees will be interacting.
- *Audiovisual:* Well before the meeting, talk to the convention services manager about your requirements and how the equipment should be set up. Bear in mind that some rooms have structural elements that are not conducive to audiovisual presentations.
- *Food and Beverage:* Menus should be discussed and confirmed with the convention services manager and with the catering department.
- Recreation and special events. The convention services manager can assist in setting up recreational programs on the property, such as a golf tournament. Off-site events, such as dinners and outings, are best arranged through a destination management company (DMC), a type of tour operator that focuses on groups. Production companies can assist you with organizing themed banquets, Broadway-style shows, or multimedia presentations. Ask the local convention and visitors bureau for a list of such companies.

Making the Meeting Interactive

Interactive technology provides ways to improve understanding and learning at your meeting, then measure the progress. It gives planners a more precise and immediate system for evaluating the results of a meeting. A key interactive element is the audience response system, which enables a presenter to ask questions and have the answers displayed instantly on a large screen in front of the audience. (Questions and answers can also be printed out and distributed after the meeting.)

Attendees are each given a wireless keypad with which they answer questions. They can pick Yes or No or punch in a number that corresponds to a multiple-choice answer. Answers are tabulated by an on-site computer, then displayed on the screen in various formats, such as bar graphs or pie charts. Besides getting people involved in the learning process, the system makes it possible to obtain immediate feedback. That makes it especially useful for business meetings, media testing, and focus groups. Often, the audience is divided into teams that compete for the best score. Audience response systems can be used at virtually any meeting facility, whether in-house, off-site, or at several remote sites linked by videoconferencing.

Setup time is nominal. A 500-pad meeting can be set up in an hour and a half. The price varies, depending on the size and duration of the meeting and the amount of customization required.

On Site/Aftermath

Ideally, the meeting planner should arrive at least a day before the attendees. At that time, the meeting planner, the convention services manager, and the appropriate department heads can discuss last-minute needs.

Some form of post-meeting evaluation is necessary to determine the meeting's ROI. Example: a questionnaire distributed to attendees plus follow-up interviews with attendees and managers.

3

Managing the Hospitality Organization

Introduction

A hotel is an establishment that provides paid lodging, usually on a short-term basis. Hotels often provide a number of additional guest services such as a restaurant, a swimming pool or childcare. Some hotels have conference services and meeting rooms and encourage groups to hold conventions and meetings at their location. Hotels differ from motels in that most motels have drive-up, exterior entrances to the rooms, while hotels tend to have interior entrances to the rooms, which may increase guests' safety and present a more upmarket image.

In Australia, a hotel may also be an establishment that serves alcoholic drinks, and usually meals in a casual setting but which does not necessarily provide accommodation. This type of establishment would more usually be called a pub or bar in other countries. In general use in Australia the terms '"hotel" and *pub* are usually taken to be synonymous. In India, the word may also refer to a restaurant since the best restaurants were always situated next to a good hotel.

Origins of the Term

The word *hotel* derives from the French *hotel,* which referred to a French version of a townhouse, not a place offering accommodation (in contemporary usage, *hotel* has the meaning of "hotel", and *hotel particulier* is used for the old meaning). The

French spelling (with the circumflex) was once also used in English, but is now rare. The circumflex replaces the 's' once preceding the 't' in the earlier *hostel* spelling, which over time received a new, but closely related meaning.

Services and Facilities

Basic accommodation of a room with only a bed, a cupboard, a small table and a washstand has largely been replaced by rooms with en-suite bathrooms and, more commonly in the United States than elsewhere, climate control. Other features found may be a telephone, an alarm clock, a TV, and broadband Internet connectivity. Food and drink may be supplied by a mini-bar (which often includes a small refrigerator) containing snacks and drinks (to be paid for on departure), and tea and coffee making facilities (cups, spoons, an electric kettle and sachets containing instant coffee, tea bags, sugar, and creamer or milk).

In the United Kingdom a hotel is required by law to serve food and drinks to all comers within certain stated hours; to avoid this requirement it is not uncommon to come across "private hotels" which are not subject to this requirement.

However, in Japan the capsule hotel supplies minimal facilities and room space.

Classification

The cost and quality of hotels are usually indicative of the range and type of services available. Due to the enormous increase in tourism worldwide during the last decades of the 20th century, standards, especially those of smaller establishments, have improved considerably. For the sake of greater comparability, rating systems have been introduced, with the one to five stars classification being most common.

Boutique Hotels

"Boutique Hotel" is a term originating in North America to describe intimate, usually luxurious or quirky hotel environments. Boutique hotels differentiate themselves from larger chain or branded hotels by providing an exceptional and personalized level of accommodation, services and facilities. Boutique hotels are furnished in a themed, stylish and/or aspirational manner. Although usually considerably smaller than a mainstream hotel (ranging from 3 to 100 guest rooms) boutique hotels are generally fitted with telephone and wi-fi Internet connections, honesty bars and often cable/pay TV. Guest services are attended to by 24 hour hotel staff. Many boutique hotels have on site dining facilities, and the majority offer bars and lounges which may also be open to the general public.

Of the total travel market a small percentage are discerning travellers, who place a high importance on privacy, luxury and service delivery. As this market is typically corporate travellers, the market segment is non-seasonal, high-yielding and repeat, and therefore one which boutique hotel operators target as their primary source of income.

Famous Hotels

Some hotels have gained their renown through tradition, by hosting significant events or persons, such as Schloss Cecilienhof in Potsdam, Germany, which derives its fame from the so-called Potsdam Conference of the World War II allies Winston Churchill, Harry Truman and Joseph Stalin in 1945. Other establishments have given name to a particular meal or beverage, as is the case with the Waldorf Astoria in New York City, USA, known for its *Waldorf Salad* or the Raffles Hotel in Singapore, where the drink *Singapore Sling* was invented. Another example is the Hotel Sacher in Vienna Austria, home of the *Sachertorte*.

There are also hotels which became much more popular through films like the Grand Hotel Europe in Saint Petersburg, Russia when James Bond stayed there in the Blockbuster, Goldeneye. Cannes hotels such as the Carlton or the Martinez become the center of the world during Cannes Film Festival (France).

A number of hotels have entered the public consciousness through popular culture, such as the Ritz Hotel in London, UK ('Putting on The Ritz') and Hotel Chelsea in New York City, subject of a number of songs and also the scene of the alleged stabbing of Nancy Spungen by her boyfriend Sid Vicious. Hotels that enter folklore like these two are also often frequented by celebrities, as is the case both with the Ritz and the Chelsea.

Other famous hotels include the Beverly Hills Hotel, the Hotel Bel-Air and the Chateau Marmont, in California, Watergate complex in Washington DC, the Hotel Astoria in Saint Petersburg, Russia, the Hotel George V and Hotel Ritz in Paris, Palazzo Versace hotel on the Gold Coast, Queensland, Australia, Hotel Hermitage and Hotel de Paris in Monaco (in the French Riviera), Peninsula Hotel in Hong Kong and Hotel Leningradskaya in Moscow.

Unusual Hotels

Many hotels can be considered destinations in themselves, by dint of unusual features of the lodging and/or its immediate environment:

Treehouse Hotels

Some hotels, such as the Costa Rica Tree House in the Gandoca-Manzanillo Wildlife Refuge, Costa Rica, or Treetops Hotel in Aberdare National Park, Kenya, are built with living trees as structural elements, making them treehouses.

The Ariau Towers near Manaus, Brazil is in the middle of the Amazon, on the Rio Negro. Bill Gates even invested and had a suite built there with satellite internet/phone.

Another hotel with treehouse units is Bayram's Tree Houses in Olympos, Turkey.

Cave Hotels

Desert Cave Hotel in Coober Pedy, South Australia and the Cuevas Pedro Antonio de Alarcon (named after the author) in Guadix, Spain, as well as several hotels in Cappadocia, Turkey, are notable for being built into natural cave formations, some with rooms underground.

Capsule Hotels

Capsule hotels are a type of economical hotels that are quite common in Japan.

Ice Hotels

Ice hotels, such as the Ice Hotel in Jukkasjarvi, Sweden, melt every spring and are rebuilt out of ice and snow each winter.

Snow Hotels

The Mammut Snow Hotel in Finland is located within the walls of the Kemi snow castle, which is the biggest in the world. It includes The Mammut Snow Hotel, The Castle Courtyard, The Snow Restaurant and a chapel for weddings, etc. Its furnishings and its decorations, such as sculptures, are made of snow and ice.

There is snow accommodation also in Lainio Snow Hotel in Lapland (near Yllas), Finland.

Garden Hotels

Garden hotels, famous for their gardens before they became hotels, includes Gravetye Manor, the home of William Robinson and Cliveden, designed by Charles Barry with a rose garden by Geoffrey Jellicoe.

Underwater Hotels

As of 2005, the only hotel with an underwater room that can be reached without Scuba diving is Utter Inn in Lake Malaren, Sweden. It only has one room, however, and Jules' Undersea Lodge in Key Largo, Florida, which requires scuba diving, is not much bigger.

Hydropolis is an ambitious project to build a luxury hotel in Dubai, UAE, with 220 suites, all on the bottom of the Persian Gulf, 20 meters (66 feet) below the surface. Its architecture will feature two domes that break the surface and an underwater train tunnel, all made of transparent materials such as glass and acrylic.

Other unusual Hotels

The Library Hotel in New York City is unique in that its ten floors are arranged according to the Dewey Decimal System. The Rogers Centre, formerly SkyDome, in Toronto, Canada is the only stadium to have a hotel connected to it, with 70 rooms overlooking the field. The Burj al-Arab hotel in Dubai, United Arab Emirates, built on an artificial island, is structured in the shape of a sail of a boat.

The RMS Queen Mary in Long Beach, California is the only 1930s ocean liner still in existence. Its elegant first-class staterooms are now used as a hotel. The Oriental Pearl Tower in Shanghai houses an extremely expensive hotel with only 20 rooms.

World-record Setting Hotels

Tallest

The tallest hotel in the world is the Burj al-Arab in Dubai, United Arab Emirates, at 321 metres, which however will soon be surpassed by the nearby Rose Rotana Suites at 333 meters (1,091 feet). The Ryugyong Hotel in Pyongyang was intended to reach 330 meters (1,083 feet), but is unlikely to be completed; it has been under construction since 1987 and was abandoned in 1992.

The highest hotel rooms are in the *Grand Hyatt* in the Jin Mao Building in Shanghai, the highest floor being at around 350 m.

Largest

The largest hotel in the world is the MGM Grand Las Vegas in Las Vegas, Nevada, USA with a total of 6,276 rooms as of December 20, 2006. On December 18, 2006 Guinness World Records listed the First World Hotel in Genting Highlands, Malaysia as the worlds largest hotel. It has a total of 6,118 rooms and is part of the Genting Highlands Resort and Casino. The First World Plaza which is joined to the two hotel towers boasts 500,000 square feet of indoor theme park, shopping centres, casino gaming areas, and eateries. Previously, Guinness had listed the MGM Grand Las Vegas in Las Vegas, Nevada, USA with 5,005 rooms as the largest hotel in the world.

Oldest

According to the Guinness Book of World Records, the oldest hotel still in operation is the Hoshi Ryokan, in Awazu, Japan. It opened in 717, and features hot springs.

Hotel Occupations

The owner, chairman, or CEO of a hotel or hotel group is known as a *hotelier*.

Living in Hotels

The American billionaire Howard Hughes lived much of his life in hotels. He moved with his entourage from hotel to hotel and from Beverly Hills to Boston before deciding to move to Las Vegas and become a casino baron. Less than a month after his November 27, 1966 arrival, Hughes made a public offer to buy the Desert Inn.

The hotel's 8th floor became the nerve center of his empire and the 9th floor penthouse became Hughes's personal residence. Hughes moved to the Bahamas, Vancouver, London and several other locations — always taking up residence in the top floor penthouse of the hotel. Between 1966 and 1968, he also purchased several other hotel-casinos from the Mafia: Castaways, New Frontier, The Landmark Hotel and Casino, Sands and Silver Slipper.

Coco Chanel made the Hotel Ritz in Paris her home for more than thirty years, until the day of her death, at 87, in a suite now named "Coco Chanel Suite".

King Peter II of Yugoslavia spent much of the Second World War at Claridge's, a hotel in London. His son, Aleksandar Karadordevis, was born in the hotel.

Prince Felix Yusupov lived in the Hotel Vendome in Paris.

Alois Brunner, Austrian Nazi war criminal, is believed to have lived in the Meridian Hotel in Damascus, Syria, under the name Georg Fischer.

Sultan Said Bin Taimur of Muscat lived at Dorchester Hotel in London after he was deposed by Qaboos of Oman in 1970, He died in the hotel in 1972.

Eleftherios Venizelos, Greek statesman and diplomat, lived in the Hotel Ritz Paris while he was in exile in France from 1935-1936.

Hotels in Fiction

Hotels have been chosen by authors as settings for crime fiction, farce and mystery works. A hotel is perfect as a mysterious, anonymous setting where various characters may gather. Hotels also feature in films, television series, songs and even theme park rides.

Taj Hotels

Taj Hotels Resorts and Palaces is the largest Indian luxury hotel chain. A wholly owned subsidiary of the Tata Group, Taj Hotels Resort and Palaces comprises 57 hotels in 39 locations across India with an additional 18 international hotels in the Maldives, Mauritius, Malaysia, Seychelles, United Kingdom, United States of America, Bhutan, Sri Lanka, Africa, the Middle East and Australia.

Their first and most well known property is the Taj Mahal Palace & Tower in Colaba, Mumbai. The Taj Mahal Palace & Tower, Mumbai was opened on December 16, 1903, by the founder of the Tata Group, Jamshetji Nusserwanji Tata. Taj President-a business hotel and Taj Land's End-an ultimate luxury boarding are also located in Mumbai.

It operates TajAir, a luxury private jet operation with state-of-the-art Falcon 2000 aircraft designed by Dassault Aviation, France; and Taj Yachts, two 3-bedroom luxury yachts which can be used by guests in Mumbai and Kochi.

Falaknuma Palace

Falaknuma Palace is situated on a hill 650 meters in height, in the Old City of Hyderabad, India. It was built by Nawab Vikar-ul-Umra. It was purchased by the then Nizam VI during 1897 for use as a royal guest house. The palace provides a good view of Hyderabad.

The palace is spread out in a scorpion shape with two pincers spread out as wings on the north. The middle part occupies the main building. The Harem quarters and the kitchen stretch towards the south. The palace was designed by an Italian architect. The palace boasts of lavishly decorated interiors made of the Italian marble, and follows a western architectural style. It took almost nine years to complete. This famous palace houses a large collection of rare treasures, paintings, statues, furniture, manuscripts and books collected by the Nizam. The jade collection displayed here is considered to be unique in the world. Some old models of artillery are also exhibited in the front. The Palace is being converted into a heritage hotel by the Taj Hotels group.

Operations of the Hotels

No hotel company operating today can be unaware of the swift pace of global change and its impact on every facet of the hospitality industry. With just five years left in this century, we can expect change to be the only constant. New business practices are evolving virtually as fast as our technologies, while resistance to change has become one of the primary causes of business failure.

The specter of constant change raises fundamental questions as to the creation of shareholder wealth in a capital-constrained, highly competitive environment. How will hotel organizations build shareholder wealth, and what key drivers will result in success? What future products and services will be essential in a technology-driven, global environment marked by rising customer expectations? Moreover, what alternative approaches and skills must organizations develop to ensure market success? The future success of hotel organizations will be driven in large part by the ability to foresee--and capitalize--on change. Beyond this truism, however, there is an urgent need to identify what will be required in the competitive environment of the future with its intense focus on serving customer needs.

The hospitality industry--as is the case with business generally--is subject to deep currents of change set in motion as economic and social systems shaped in the industrial era evolve to a knowledge-based era driven by technology advances.

In this period of global transition, it behooves hotel organizations to examine the key factors that will not only define success, but the ability to survive in coming years. Many of these issues were spotlighted in a global study undertaken by the Economist Intelligence Unit and co-sponsored by Arthur Andersen. The Successful Corporation of the Year 2000 surveyed more than 600 senior executives around the world. Its mission was to identify the characteristics needed to lead successful businesses in the next century. These executives offer a number of compelling messages regarding the key success factors of the future.

Customers will have the strongest influence on the corporation in the year 2000. Indeed, these executives believe that the customer will be "king" in the new century. Exceptional leadership was by far the attribute most frequently cited by CEOs and senior executives; the consensus appears to be that successful companies in the year 2000 will be led by corporate visionaries.

A strategic planning focus is not only essential, but must embody a concept of planning for the future that anticipates change, rather than being based exclusively on historical models. In structuring organizations for the future, companies must build management capabilities to deal with one of the most critical challenges--diversity in the marketplace. Employing information technology to drive business success in this information-driven era is not only the path of least resistance, but vital to virtually every aspect of operations.

The study's top-line results create an excellent backdrop to address key issues confronting the hotel industry, and what factors will lead to membership--rather than rejection--in the elite club of the world's corporate success stories in the year 2000.

From an Asset to Customer Focus

Recognizing that the hotel industry has a somewhat split personality reflecting the inherent conflicts between its real estate and operational aspects, it is important to understand the industry's real estate origins and how they are shaping the challenges ahead. The origins of the industry's real estate persona are embodied in the classic theory of location-"if we build it, they will come." As a result of this "building" complex, the industry has tended to have a real estate and asset orientation, rather than a customer focus. From the hotel company perspective--especially that of the brand-oriented "chain"--the varied interests of a diffused property ownership group can be quite different than the singular interest of the chain that operates and markets the properties.

Even when the ownership of geographically dispersed hotel properties is controlled by a single hotel organization, the financial structuring tends to be property-specific. Corporate financial strategies are frequently subjugated to the needs of the last property deal brought into the company's fold.

Each property in a so-called "chain," is frequently the subject of a unique and distinctive ownership and financial structure. This phenomenon--quite common in the real estate sector, but unusual for business enterprises generally--makes for elusive economies of scale in the structuring and financing of property-driven expansion.

Collectively, these factors have produced low comparative returns in real estate, although criticism leveled at commercial real estate returns is somewhat less germane to the hotel industry, where management and franchise fees can produce high returns for those companies where property ownership is held by third parties. Nevertheless, average returns in the real estate industry in the United States, for example, are just over 10 percent, compared to small company stock returns at almost 20 percent and large company stocks at an average of about 15 percent.

While hotel chains have adopted traditional corporate frameworks, there are a number of predominantly real estate-driven, family-owned businesses in the hotel sector that continue to operate as relatively unstructured organizations. In meeting the future, these businesses will need plans, people and processes in order to establish viable corporate forms that can compete in tomorrow's marketplace and capitalize upon its opportunities.

In today's changed environment, the hotel organization must deal with a number of new realities. Investors in our industry are no longer satisfied with long-term capital appreciation and psychic income that heretofore were often the justification for otherwise seemingly uneconomic investments in hotel property or, indeed, hotel chains.

The first reality is that there is a very specific and identifiable relationship between bottom line performance and value. Improvements in business operations raises values. It is not surprising, therefore, that the new owners attracted to this industry in recent years have new sets of demands. This transformation from an old-guard group of investors and owners to income and return-driven newcomers has meant that the once "quiet enjoyment" of operators in their management of hotels for third parties is being disturbed, interrupted and overturned.

These challenges all take place in an environment where capital has become extremely selective in markets that have little stability. A global shortage of capital will not remain a short-term problem, and future hotel organizations must have a stronger alignment to capital providers--a critical "customer" group. Hotel companies will need to compete by offering better returns and performance than in the past. Hotel chains have found their development timetables quashed in recent years, making it difficult to achieve goals of critical mass often required to improve performance. These factors are driving consolidation in the brand "sweepstakes." Capital markets, therefore, continue to favour well-established companies, a reality that must drive entrepreneurial organizations to meet the future now by planning for an evolving corporate context in which to operate.

Key Success Factors

Within this broad context, hotel developers, owners and management companies will all need to develop new strategies, skills and processes that look forward to the competitive demands of the future. These ultimately must address issues related to vision and planning, as well as organizational skill sets and processes to attract and retain customers. To stake a claim in the future, current business practices should be examined in light of what can be expected to be the key success factors in the year 2000.

Embrace a global change orientation. As the information age produces greater worldwide integration of business activities, a global knowledge base will become invaluable. Success in local and regional hotel markets will be shaped decisively by a global business environment that defines capital movement, customer expectations and applications of new technologies.

Focus on the Customer. If the customer is "king" in the 21st century, hotel organizations will be best served by focusing less on their hotel assets as measures of success, and more on their customers.

This involves a fundamental shift in viewing the real estate asset as the wealth creator--to the customer as the key to building shareholder wealth. A customer focus must imbue business decisions at all levels of developing and operating a hotel organization. Pursuing such a course will inevitably impact shareholder wealth. To accomplish this, however, customers need to participate in the product development process.

Fully realizing a customer focus in the industry poses a significant challenge. The hotel industry must confront problems due to conflicts between operational needs and real estate goals. Quite simply, an operator must remain customer-focused, but the short-term strategies to meet these needs may be inconsistent with the long-term objectives of property owners. Balancing those goals will be essential. A customer focus implies a significant shift in what drives hotel development--placing primary emphasis on the customer with the locations to follow. Nevertheless, a hotel organization with its large investment in fixed assets--the real estate--can never be as nimble as a consumer products company in adjusting products and services to match rapid shifts in the marketplace.

The Japanese taught us that the concept of "zero defects" in products and services can yield tremendous benefits. But today an even more rigorous standard dominates--quality that surprises. In practical terms, the hotel industry finds it extremely difficult to meet the standard of zero defects in service. Hotel services are based primarily on people, not computers or other equipment. Quality that surprises takes the concept of zero defects a step further. Yesterday's surprising product or service is today's status quo.

Twenty years ago, a business executive did not expect a consistent and predictable level of service wherever he or she travelled in the world. Today that is a standard--not the exception--as is the expectation for sophisticated technology in hotel rooms to support business needs. With customer discrimination so acute, it is not surprising that brand loyalty is a diminishing "commodity" in the hotel industry.

Find the ingredients for visionary leadership. Today's hotel organizations need to recognize the need for visionary leadership. The ability to forecast the future--to anticipate change rather than react to it--will be one of the single greatest determinants of market dominance in the years ahead. The old "command and control" model of leadership is giving way to a focus on leadership in ideas, information, inspiration, vision and teamwork. Warren Bennis, an authority on leadership in the U.S., puts it this way--"For the most part, failing organizations tend to be over-managed and under-led. The leader sets the tone for the moral character, the vision, the corporate culture and the fiber of the institution."

While visionary leadership is essential, it must be linked to business operations and foster a risk bias, rather than a procedural bias. This will allow the organization to stretch and, in turn, change. And it must be shared by empowered professionals and staff throughout the organization, including those who meet the customer. Overcoming the resistance to change can be a daunting task, particularly in large hotel organizations in which diversions from the status quo may threaten established management lines. It suggests that a culture based on conformance may need to be replaced by an emphasis on flexibility, learning and cooperation. Management competencies will need to be aligned in order to achieve the desired result. For many organizations, this may mean a shift from traditional hierarchies typical of companies in an industrial era to a flatter organization with a more transparent interface between leadership, organizational functions and employees.

Create a defensible position through corporate strategy. For many of the industry's leaders, vision is driven by the strategic planning process, a function which has become critical for success.

Strategic planning, however, has at times been a step-child in the hotel industry, and it is often the first to be cut when organizations are downsized. It is clearly in transition. There also has been a tendency to decentralize and simplify this function--both actions of potential benefit. Strategic planning must be led by the top people in the organization--the CEO and COO. On the other hand, it should be close enough to the customer to ensure that planners can "listen" to and be influenced by customer needs.

Empower Management: Beyond the ability to envision the future, core management capabilities will make the difference--they are essential. A clear vision without the management skills to support it cannot be a recipe for success. First and foremost, hotel management must have strategic development skills and the ability to integrate complex factors affecting success. Market volatility has become the norm, in part caused by the rapidly changing tastes of customers. Customers are increasingly approaching the hotel industry with widely different social, economic and political backgrounds, to say nothing of employees. Being able to deal with these diversities in a positive and constructive fashion that capitalizes on the differences, rather than working to find ways to mitigate them, is the clear path for successful management in the future.

The organization will also need to be imbued with a sense of entrepreneurship that reacts proactively to the market's diversity. Traditional organizations that follow well-documented rules must give way to leaders who can balance a sense of discipline with that of flexibility. Talent and resources must be marshalled and leveraged. In an industry with high fixed costs and labour intensity, the concept of leverage in the hotel business is an all-important one. Improving labour productivity through technology must be a goal for today's forward-looking hotel organization.

Management must also be able to narrow the gap between the employer and the employee, forcing a flatter organization in the process. This will put management closer to the customer and speed the two-way communication process up and down the organization.

Be in the Information Fast Lane: The traditional role of information technology (IT) as a back office support for accounting and bookkeeping has clearly moved front and center stage.

IT today influences all aspects of business from corporate strategies to organizational structure--and from the very business processes it is designed to support to performance measurement. In a world where the customer is "king," IT must also deliver in two critical areas: sales and marketing and customer service.

Technology was once viewed as a way to reduce costs by replacing people. That attitude has been firmly supplanted by one that seeks IT support for the creative work that all organizations must pursue. IT must allow organizations to react more speedily to market needs and, of course, produce the fulfilment of customer demands both quickly and accurately. To do this IT must operate on a decentralized basis. IT delivers, but it has to be the right information to the right people, and it needs to be done on a timely basis.

Improving Management (GEF) Project

Improving Management of NGO and Privately Owned Nature Reserves and High Biodiversity Islands in Seychelles Project funded by the Global Environment Facility through the World Bank

The Seychelles is known world wide as a storehouse of rare biodiversity. Historically, most of the islands and ecosystems have been severely impacted by human activities. Nevertheless, a few examples of whole island ecosystems have been protected and restored. These islands are Cousin, Cousine, Aride, Fregate and Aldabra, all managed, surprisingly, by civil society organisations. Nevertheless, there are significant barriers to sustainability of conservation efforts by these organisations.

The focus of the project is two islands, Cousin and Cousine, which are host to numerous rare and endemic species, and immense biodiversity. These include shared resources such as 10 species of breeding seabirds, 5 species of endemic land birds, rare floral species, 8 species of reptiles and hundreds species of invertebrates, the most important population of hawksbill turtles in the Western Indian Ocean and the highest biomass of reef fish in the granitic islands of Seychelles.

The project is to ensure the islands' function as a reserve for the preservation of globally important biodiversity through understanding processes and changes in sites, species and habitats in the islands for better management and decision-making on activities to preserve this globally important biodiversity.

Cousin and Cousine are adjacent to Praslin-the second most populous island of the Seychelles. Cousin was purchased in the 1960's through a world wide appeal at a time when unique biodiversity in Seychelles was in jeopardy. An international NGO held the title to the island because land tenureship was the only method of securing the island for perpetuity and thereby restoring the ecosystems. This NGOs also assisted the previous owners of Cousine in the early years to conserve its biodiversity. This proved to be a very wise move because the islands are remarkable in that unlike other granitic islands of Seychelles, endemic and globally important fauna and flora have been saved.

They have been protected by NGO/private resources and management, and at least for Cousin, through national legislation and policy.

The ownership and management regimes by civil society organisations and the relative remoteness, which are the main reasons why biodiversity has been saved, are now proving to be constraints for not only continuing with established activities but also for initiating new programs; the civil society organisations cannot source adequate resources from the local private sector, governmental or international sources. In addition, anthropogenic impacts and lack of knowledge of ecosystem-level changes, all mean that science and conservation action on each of them cannot move beyond present capacity and limits. The project assumption is that conservation of island biodiversity can be sustained and at the same time greatly improved through an inter-island integrated and collaborative approach geared to clear management outcomes and also to the development of public education and community buy-in. The project recognises the importance of developing financial sustainability to maintain these conservation programs. The project intends to build long-term capacity for sustainable conservation and use of island biodiversity through program and capacity building, infrastructure acquisition and installation, co-management, and education and advocacy.

The two islands are small, close to each other, and share similar and sensitive ecosystems, associated conservation activities and problems. They are both focused on biodiversity conservation, chiefly concerning globally threatened endemic land birds and internationally important colonies of breeding seabirds. Each island also hosts similar important reptile, botanical and invertebrate species. Both islands have a distinguished conservation history and offer a slightly different model and philosophy for biodiversity conservation. Cousin Island is owned by an international NGO but managed by an independent, locally registered, not-for-profit Association. Cousine Island is owned and managed by a private limited company registered in Seychelles. Management of the islands are supposed to be undertaken with in-country resources.

Project Vision

The project will remove barriers that currently prevent civil society organisations from augmenting and enhancing their capacity to conserve and restore species, sites and habitats.

The project will aims to create partnerships between neighbouring islands which have shared globally important biodiversity and similar environmental issues. This will be done through a substantial number of new and improved linked programs, the creation of a common resource and management center, institutional strengthening and capacity building, and public education and advocacy.

The ultimate aim of this model partnership is to catalyze further collaboration and public buy-in, to remove other barriers and to mitigate negative ecosystem changes. The process set in motion by the project will improve the management of high biodiversity islands as well as increase the number of managed conservation sites in Seychelles. This project will thus have global biodiversity benefits, lead to greater sustainability of biodiversity and permit the sharing of these benefits to be directed principally at local levels. The vision mirrors the three principal objectives of the 1992 Convention of Biological Diversity.

Overall Goal of the Project

The Goal of the project is to improve management of biodiversity-rich islands by installing a shared multi-pronged programme framework and infrastructure for enhanced and sustainable conservation, financing and use of biodiversity. The project vision and overall goal will be delivered through two principal components namely Small Island Ecosystem Management, and Public Education and Advocacy.:.

Component 1: Small Island Ecosystem Management

A. Improved management of terrestrial and marine habitats and important species.

B. Establish collaborative management and resource center on Praslin

C. Institutional strengthening

D. Capacity building and training

Component 2: Public Education and Advocacy

A. Develop biodiversity awareness and advocacy programs

B. Establish community outreach, partnerships and stakeholder participation programs

Project Partners

Nature Seychelles, formerly known as Bird Life Seychelles, is a local not-for-profit association registered in Seychelles. It is currently the largest independent environment organisation in Seychelles. The association is involved in a suite of activities including species and habit conservation, monitoring, research, island restoration, eco-tourism, education and awareness and advocacy.

Nature Seychelles manages Cousin Island Special Reserve and has a presence on several other islands. It has a multi-stakeholder and result-oriented approach through its programs such as the Seychelles Magpie-robin Recovery Team (SMART) and the Seychelles Seabird Group (SSG) as well with other organisations such as the Wild Life Clubs of Seychelles, Ministry of Environment and Ministry of Education.

Its donors and partners include the World Bank/GEF and the Royal Society for Protection of Birds. It is a member of the Bird Life International network, WIOMSA, the African Bird Club and IUCN, works in close collaboration with WWF, the Mauritian WildLife Foundation and many others.

Cousine Island LTD (Owner and Manger of Cousine Island): is a private limited company registered in the Seychelles. The company has built a very small and ecologically friendly luxury hotel. The island is not legally protected and the owner is not obliged to conserve its biodiversity. The company has voluntarily put in a system for biodiversity conservation using its own resources. It delegates management responsibility for the island to a Conservation Warden.

The Warden works in close collaboration with the hotel manager. The purpose of setting up the small hotel is to bring in sufficient revenues to maintain the conservation and research programs on the island and to maintain it as a high biodiversity area. The company supports other conservation programs in Seychelles, for example the Magpie Robin Recovery Program and the Seychelles Rare Birds Committee.

Landmarks Achievements

Hotel Association of India, established on 24th October 1996, within a short span of less than a decade of its inception, has successfully provided an integrated hospitality platform produced ground breaking results and recorded several notable 'firsts' for the hospitality industry described in the ensuing pages:

Export House Status for Tourism and Hospitality Industry

Among the path breaking industry 'first' initiatives of Hotel Association of India is the unique recognition secured for tourism and hospitality sectors in India as 'export industries'. This was an unparelled achievement of the Association which undertook the entire groundwork and created consensus in support of according export status for hospitality industries.

HAI organized series of inter-active meetings with the concerned Ministries of the Government of India, culminating in a high level Conclave presided over by Shri Ramakrishna Hegde, then Hon'ble Minister of Commerce, Government of India, on 16th July 1998 at the Oberoi Hotel, New Delhi which cleared the decks for the action plan blue-printed by HAI receiving the official seal of approval of the Government of India manifested in the a Gazette Notification of November 26th, 1998 declaring Hotels and Tourism Units eligible for the benefits of Service Export House/International Service Export House/International Star Service Export House/International Super Star Service Export House categories on the basis of their quantum of foreign exchange earnings.

This extraordinary recognition placed hotels and tourism units on par with industries engaged in export of products for imports of projects and products against their foreign exchange entitlements and facilitated hotels in acquiring competitive edge vis-a-vis hotels overseas in providing world class facilities.

Tourism Export Promotion Council

Another notable first for hospitality and tourism industries, synchronizing with the grant of Export House Status, was notched by the Hotel Association of India by formulating the Constitution of the Tourism Export Promotion Council (TEPC) on 20th November 1998. The approval of the Company Law Board was also secured for the new body under Section 25 of the Companies Act 1956. TEPC represented an unique experiment in bringing together for the first time all constituents of the tourism sector-hotels, travel agents, tour operators, transporters, airlines, tourism finance companies-under a single umbrella on a common platform.

Establishment of SAARC Hotel Association

HAI reached beyond the national boundaries to provide regional co-operation aiming hotels in South Asia and became the prime mover in the formation of the SAARC Hotel Association. This was achieved by developing close synergy between the hospitality industry organizations of Bangladesh, Bhutan, India, Maldives, Nepal, Pakistan and Sri Lanka. The SAARC Hotel Association was formally launched at Mumbai on 7th April 1999 with Nepal being assigned the responsibility of hosting the SAARC body for its initial two years and later by rotation by other member countries.

International Code of Conduct to Govern Relations Between Hoteliers, Travel Agents and Tour Operators

For the first time in the history of travel trade in India on 28.4.2000, HAI successfully evolved consensus among the Travel Agents Association of India (TAAI) and the Indian Association of Tour Operators (IATO) and the Hotel Association of India (HAl) resulting in the signing of the International Code of Practice governing the relations between Hoteliers, Travel Agents and Tour Operators.

The code represents a watershed for the tourism and travel industry in India, as protracted negotiations for adopting a code of practice for over three decades had not yielded any results till HAl took the lead and crafted consensus in favour of adopting the global practice. It's signing by the three national bodies signalled to the international travel fraternity and business travellers that India had opted for internationally approved policies of hotel bookings, cancellations, refunds, claims etc.

Legal 'First' for Hotel Industry

The Hotel Association of India took the lead in invoking the intervention of the High Court of Delhi in protecting the interests of hospitality industry in India on a matter of vital importance to the hotels as well as to the foreign and domestic tourist staying in hotels. Hotel Association of India filed a writ in the High Court Delhi against an arbitrary and ad hoc administrative directive requiring the hotels in approved categories, classified by the Ministry of Tourism, to follow a Single Tariff system. The directive would have proved detrimental and counter productive to national tourism interests. The industry perspective presented by HAI was accepted by the High Court of Delhi which granted a Stay in favour of hotel industry, signifying an unique legal validation of hospitality industry system of operation across the country.

Seeking Repeal of Anti-women Legislation

The Punjab Excise Act enacted during the British rule in India in 1914 contains an archaic and anti-women provision prohibiting the employment of women in licenced premises, i.e., bars and restaurants in hotels. The Hotel Association of India challenged the validity of this ancient legislation before the Hon'ble High Court to protect the interest of women. The HAI's Writ against the constitutional validity of the provisions of the Punjab Excise Act, 1914

Media Centric Initiatives

The large number of foreign correspondents stationed in India, representing powerful and popular foreign publications, newspapers, journals, T. V. Channels, Broadcasters play a major role in making or marring the image of India as a peaceful tourists destination country through their news reports and dispatches. HAI took the lead in organizing the first ever hospitality industry meeting with the foreign correspondent stationed in New Delhi.

The event was organized with the objective to discuss adverse the impact of Travel Advisories issued by foreign Governments on the State of Indian hospitality and tourism industry and correct their perspective to restore consumer confidence in travel, tourism and hospitality sectors adversely affected by global events of preceding years. Because of the unique nature of the special event and its potential for future tourists arrivals in India, the Ministry of Tourism fully associated with HAI.

Survey on the Impact of Travel Advisories in Hospitality Industry

Foreign Embassies and Missions are often instrumental in advising their respective countries to issue "Travel Advisories" to caution their citizens from undertaking visits to specific countries owing to adverse conditions of safety and security. Travel Advisories against visiting India were issued by several countries following global events like the terrorist attacks on 9/11 in USA and 13/12 in New Delhi, War in Afghanistan and tension on Indo-Pak borders etc. The adverse travel advisories affected tourists arrivals to India over a prolonged period.

The Hotel Association of India stepped in by organizing an innovative Survey among foreign tourists staying in hotels to obtain their reactions to such advisories issued by the foreign governments.

The HAI Survey brought out that a preponderant majority of tourists declared India as a safe and peaceful destination and foreign travellers viewed the travel advisories and warnings as "coloured by political considerations" and based on "inadequate knowledge of ground realities". Some of them opined that they found New Delhi "safer than Manhattan". HAI Survey facilitated the Governments of the respective countries in reviewing and withdrawing the adverse travel advisories and re-assured tourists of their safety and security in India.

Setting Up of Confederation of Indian Travel and Tourism Industry

Another first initiative mooted by the Association related to the need for creating a Confederation of Indian Travel and Tourism Industry (CITTI) as an umbrella organization to represent all components of the Travel & Travel industry in India. Unlike other industries, there has never been an umbrella organization in the tourism industry. To fill this gap, HAI proposed the setting up of CITTI which would address the policy issues and concerns of the industry. The Constitution of the proposed new body has been drawn up and made available to all sectoral associations to facilitate its establishment in the future.

Study of Tariff System in Hotels

The first ever 'While Paper' on Tariff Systems in Hotels in India, produced by a Central Government Autonomous Organisation the National Institute of Public Finance and Policy (NIPFP), was undertaken at the behest of the Hotel Association of India. The NIPFP headed by eminent economists of the standing of Dr. Raja J Chelliah, former Chief Economic Advisor of the Government of India and Dr. C. Rangarajan, former Governor of the Reserve Bank of India, provided the Indian hospitality industry with its most appropriate perspective and authentic study of tariff systems.

First Afro-Asian Infotech Hotels Expo

HAI-led initiative resulted in Afro-Asian Region's first Conference-cum-Exposition on Information Technology being institutionalized as 'an annual event in New Delhi for countries in the South Asian Region.

The first Conference-cum-Expo organized by HAl on April 10-11, 2000 at the ITC Maurya Sheraton Hotel, New Delhi received support from the United Nations Economic and Social Commission for Asia and the Pacific, and the SAARC Tourism Council. The Ministries of Tourism and Information Technology, Government of India, extended official support to HAl as Co-sponsors of the event.

Second Afro-Asian Infotech-hotels Expo

The Second Conference-cum-Exposition on Information Technology in Hotels was organized on March 15-16, 2001 at the Taj Palace Hotel, New Delhi. This Afro-Asian conference was supported by United Nation Economic and Social Commission for Asia and like the front conference the Pacific (UN-ESCAP); Ministry of Tourism, Ministry of Information Technology, Government of India, SAARC Tourism Council and SAARC Hotel Association, Pacific Asia Travel Association (PATA) and International Hotel & Restaurant Association (IH&RA).

Creating a National Network of HAI Chapters

The Hotel Association of India, established in April 1997, enlisted co-operation on a voluntary basis of professional hoteliers in twenty five State and fifty three cities to monitor hospitality related developments to enable the Association to address the concerns of the hospitality industry at the grass-roots level.

Going Global with Knowledge Exchange Partners

Knowledge Exchange partnerships were formed with international organization such as the World Travel and Tourism Council (WTTC); the Pacific Asia Travel Association (PATA); World Tourism Organisation (WTO); the International Hotel and Restaurant Association (IH&RA); the United Nation Economic and Social Commission for Asia and the Pacific (UN-ESCAP); the South Asia Association of Regional Countries (SAARC), the World Health Organisation (WHO) and the European Union's South Asia Integrated Tourism Human Resource Development Programme (EU-SAITHRDP).

Inter-sectoral Linkages With Apex National Fora

At the National level working partnerships were established with apex industry for a like the Federation of Indian Chamber of Commerce and Industry (FICCI); Associated Chamber of Commerce and Industry of India (ASSOCHAM); Confederation of Indian Industry (CII); to provide hospitality industry perspective in the formation of national industrial policies and development.

Affiliation with World Health Organisation (WHO)

HAI's pioneered the concept of 'Healthy Hotels' in line with WHO's 'Healthy Cities' campaign by initiating programmes for the hospitality industry on 'Hygiene Management in Hotels' at Agra in 1997. The WHO representative in India delivered the keynote address at the First Hygiene Management Seminar.

Innovative-"India Quiz Contest" at ITB Berlin 2002

A new promotional first was scored by the HAI at ITB Berlin, held from 16th to 20th March 2002. This was the first time 25 leading Indian hotels were brought together by HAI on the industry net to sponsor prizes of FAM Holiday Tours to Travel Trade visitors at the ITB.

The India Quiz Contest brochure of HAI provided a high visibility to the Indian hospitality industry products among visitor to the ITB, Berlin. The participating hotels received excellent marketing exposure of their properties in the Quiz brochure. This also offered unique opportunities for prospective agents and operator for the familiarization and experience of the hotels.

Guidelines for Provision of Disabled Friendly Facilities in Hotels

The Association undertook a pioneering role in formulating a comprehensive set of Guidelines for provision of Disabled Friendly facilities in Hotels, especially in parking and Approach Areas, Lobbies, Public Areas, Lifts, Rooms, Bathrooms and to install special Fire Prevention measures for the disabled.

Promoting Public-Private Partnership

The Association in a step towards promoting the public-private partnership called upon its members to extend their full corporation to the Archeological Survey of India in the maintenance of the National monuments, which has translated into following public-private sector partnership:-

(i) Illumination of Humayun's Tomb at Delhi by the Oberoi Group of Hotels.

(ii) Development of facilities for visitors at the Agra Fort by the ITC Hotels Ltd.

(iii) Main entrance of the Jantar Mantar observatory at New Delhi by the Apeejay Surrendra Park Hotels Pvt. Ltd.

(iv) Illumination of the Safdarjung Tomb, New Delhi by the Grand Group of

62 Special Promotional Packages in Hotels

A major initiative undertaken by HAI galvanized the entire Indian hospitality industry to come together under the Association's banner to offer for the first time in the history of the industry as many as 62 special promotional packages in hotels for marketing averages in association with Air India.

Memorandum of Undertakings Signed with the Hotel Association of Nepal and the Uganda Investment Authority

The Hotel Association of India signed two Memorandum of Understanding which aimed at fostering and promoting tourism in their respective countries by inter alia agreeing to exchange information in respect to development and trend in the fields of tourism, hospitality and hotel sectors and encourage interaction between their respective hotels and Hospitality Association of India for Tourism Promotion and exploring investment opportunities in these sectors.

India Quiz Contest Brochure at 51st PATA Annual Conference

Encouraged by the overwhelming response received from the ITB Berlin, HAI launched its exclusive India Quiz Contest at the 51st PATA Annual Conference held in New Delhi from 14.04.2002 to 18.04.2002 offering opportunities of FAM Holiday in 14 leading Hotels.

Study Project on Management of Cross-cultural Tourists Movements in Hospitality Sector

HAI initiated a study project on Management of cross-cultural tourism movements in hospitality sector to assess and promote awareness among staff in smaller hotel and upgrade their knowledge and skills for handling of foreign tourists.

Grant of Fiscal Benefits to the Hospitality Industry

For the first time the tourism industry's aspirations elaborated in the Hotel Association of India's various memoranda to the Central Government were translated into "tourism-friendly", measures in the Union Budget of 2003-04.

These measures were aimed at making India more affordable destination, fuelling growth of hospitality infrastructure, facilitating business re-organisation, re-structuring hospitality industry and motivating State Governments to rationalize tourism tax regime. The major incentives extended to hospitality industries included and exemption of Service tax in hotels relating to Conference and Banquet business, which have been excluded from the service tax net.

Encouraging Investments

Hotel Association of India orchestrated the strategy leading to announcement in the Union Budget 2003 of benefits under Section 10(23) (g) on loans to hotels (3 star and above categories) for increasing the availability of funds for the hotel industry.

This provision has allowed lending institutions to make available funds to hotel projects at reduced rates of interest. The financial institutions will get a tax break on the interest income they earn on loans extended to such borrowers.

Inclusion of finance to the hotel projects of three star category and above for the first time under Section 10 (23)(g) of the Income Tax Act "signals" the positioning of hotels on the threshold of securing full infrastructure status as granted to other industries. HAI is now carrying this agenda forward to securing the wider benefits of infrastructure under Section 84 I/A of Income Tax Act.

Restructuring Hospitality Business

Amalgamation and Merger

It is at the behest of HAI that the Finance Ministry constituted a Working group under Chief Commissioner of Income Tax Mumbai which recommended the grant of benefits under Section 72 A of the Income Tax Act (which relates to the set-off of accumulated losses and depreciation on amalgamation), for the hotel industry to help loss-making hotel companies in re-organising their business. The facility of mergers and acquisitions was hitherto available only to industrial undertakings and manufacturing units. With its extension to hotel companies, it has facilitated moves towards consolidation with the hospitality industry and releasing of resources blocked in non-performing assets. This measure has now enabled smaller hotel units to enter into franchisee arrangements with established hotel groups/ chains which in turn has led to improvements in occupancy levels and service standards.

Zero Duty Facility for Imports by Hotels

HAI pursued with the Ministry of Commerce, Government of India for grant of the zero duty import facility to hotels and standalone restaurants. The Industry has now been granted under the "Served from India Scheme", the zero duty facility to all hotels including one star, two star hotels for import of food items and alcoholic beverages sell which would make India an affordable destination.

HAI Directory of Hotels Going Global

The exclusive HAI Directory of Hotels is an annual publication promoted with a singular aim of fulfilling the promotional need for tourists and visitor coming to India for an authentic compendium of leading Indian hotels recognized by the Ministry of Tourism. For the first time in 2005 the Directory was utilized by the Ministry of Tourism for distribution among foreign travel agents and tour operators in 12 countries through the Government of India's Tourist Offices abroad.

World Tourism Day Celebration

A new promotional first was scored by HAI for creating awareness about the World Tourism Day on 27th Sept. 2005 amongst not only the member-hotels but also the school children. To encourage and facilitate the member-hotels in celebrating the World Tourism Day on 27th September 2005, HAI outlined a bouquet of activities to be organized by the member-hotels. The member-hotels came forward in large numbers and organized the activities with enthusiasm and excitement. In New Delhi, HAI collaborated with the Sanskriti School to launch a Quiz Contest on Tourism for school children on the World Tourism Day.

Members Services

Variety of professional member-services are provided by HAI to its members these include:-

(i) INFORMATION BULLETINS sent out regularly with updates on latest developments concerning hotel industries, policy changes and pronouncements by

Ministry of Tourism, Ministry of Finance, Ministry of Commerce, CBEC, CBDT, State Governments and affiliate international organizations such as WTTC, IH&RA, WTO etc.;

(ii) HAI TODAY-the first hospitality industry magazine of its kind in India;

(iii) HAI DIRECTORY OF HOTELS-an exclusive high quality reference manual of recognized hotels in India;

(iv) HAI PRIVILEGE CARDS which are offered to members in the Gold and Silver Categories entitling them to discounts on hotel room tariffs and restaurants outlets in all member hotels on reciprocal basis;

(v) HAI LEGAL SERVICES which enables members to avail benefits of highest calibre legal advice on issues of concern them and interventions on their behalf in courts.

HAI Green Weeks

HAI has successfully institutionalized the concept of celebrating annual green weeks in hotels to exhibit its commitment to conservation of environment through use of bio-degradable and environment-friendly products by efficient management of waste generated and by adopting measures for efficient utilization of day light to conserve upon electricity etc. HAI has this year celebrated its ninth annual green week, reaching out to large number of tourists, employees, their families, school children and society with its environment message.

Fundamentals of Revenue Management will be Revealed in a Special Report Commissioned by HSMAI Special Interest Group

MCLEAN, VA The Hospitality Sales & Marketing Association International (HSMAI) Revenue Management Special Interest Group has taken on an ambitious project to produce the first-ever comprehensive "Fundamentals of Revenue Management" special report.

The report will be a practitioner-friendly publication that addresses the fundamentals of revenue management for a broad audience of hospitality professionals. With comprehensive content that is both readable and actionable, it will deliver tools and information for revenue management education, incorporating expert advice from interviews with industry executives and educators, case studies, and practical checklists for implementing successful revenue management strategies at the property level.

"Creating relevance for members and the industry at large through groundbreaking initiatives such as this Revenue Management Special Report is in keeping with HSMAI's mission to be the leading source for sales and marketing information, knowledge and business development for professionals in tourism, travel, and hospitality," states Robert A. Gilbert, CHME, CHA, president and CEO of HSMAI.

"We are very excited about this debut project, and expect it will be a springboard for other initiatives including certification and revenue management research," notes Tim Wiersma, vice president of revenue management for Host Marriott and chair of HSMAI's Revenue Management Tangible Resources Committee.

The publication will be produced in a manner similar to the recent special report produced by HSMAI and TIG Global entitled DeMystifying Distribution, widely praised by the industry for its insight, accuracy and comprehensive coverage of the topic.

The commissioned report, which will be released at the third annual HSMAI Revenue Management Strategy Conference on June 19, 2005 in Minneapolis, will be co-authored by Caryl Helsel and Kathleen Cullen of the Solutionz Group, a business development and strategic consulting group based in Florida. Helsel heads the hospitality practice and previously held executive positions with Kimpton Hotels, Pegasus Solutions and Mandarin Oriental Hotel Group, and is the former president of the Hotel Electronic Distribution Network Association (HEDNA).

Cullen is a lead consultant on the hospitality team and is a hospitality revenue management and distribution veteran, holding executive positions with Swissotel and Raffles Hotels, as well as past vice president of HEDNA. Delving deep into the fundamentals, nuances and specifics of revenue management, the special report will address the following:

- Ideas and initiatives to maximize revenue opportunities, optimize profits by managing revenues and develop an infrastructure (strategies, policies, procedures, reports, etc.) to make informed decisions about accepting or rejecting business.
- An overview of the external market such as segmentation, demand forecasting, revenue strategy, operational forecast, interdepartmental integration, strategic pricing, inventory control strategies and internal performance analysis.
- Tactics including rate-level maintenance, inventory management and rate offer assessment (for group and negotiated rates).
- The optimal environment, characteristics and descriptors.

The Revenue Management Special Interest Group is made up of a group of HSMAI members who advance the revenue management discipline through education, certification, participation, resources and guidance, enabling leaders to optimize revenue and performance within their own organizations.

4

Process of Hospitality Organizing

A key issue in accomplishing the goals identified in the planning process is structuring the work of the organization. Organizations are groups of people, with ideas and resources, working toward common goals. The purpose of the organizing function is to make the best use of the organization's resources to achieve organizational goals. Organizational structure is the formal decision-making framework by which job tasks are divided, grouped, and coordinated. Formalization is an important aspect of structure. It is the extent to which the units of the organization are explicitly defined and its policies, procedures, and goals are clearly stated. It is the official organizational structure conceived and built by top management. The formal organization can be seen and represented in chart form. An organization chart displays the organizational structure and shows job titles, lines of authority, and relationships between departments.

The informal organization is the network, unrelated to the firm's formal authority structure, of social interactions among its employees. It is the personal and social relationships that arise spontaneously as people associate with one another in the work environment. The supervisor must realize that the informal organization affects the formal organization. The informal organization can pressure group members to conform to the expectations of the informal group that conflict with those of the formal organization. This can result in the generation of false information or rumors and resistance to change desired by management. The supervisor should recognize the existence of information groups, identify the roles member play within these groups, and use knowledge of the groups to work effectively with them. The informal organization can make the formal organization more effective by providing support to management, stability to the environment, and useful communication channels.

Organizational Structure

Even though the differences among organizations are enormous, there are many similarities that enable them to be classified. One widely used classification is the twofold system (mechanistic versus organic forms of organizational structure) developed by Tom Burns and G. M. Stalker in their study of electronics firms in the United Kingdom. (See Burns, Tom and G. M. Stalker, Management of Innovation, London: Tavistock Publications, 1961, p. 19.)

The mechanistic structure is the traditional or classical design, common in many medium-and large-size organizations. Mechanistic organizations are somewhat rigid in that they consist of very clearly delineated jobs, have a well-defined hierarchical structure, and rely heavily on the formal chain of command for control.

Bureaucratic organizations, with their emphasis on formalization, are the primary form of mechanistic structures. According to Max Weber, bureaucracy is a form of organization characterized by a rational, goal-directed hierarchy, impersonal decision making, formal controls, and subdivision into managerial positions and specialization of labour. Bureaucratic organizations are tall consisting of hierarchies with many levels of management.

In a tall structure, people become relatively confined to their own area of specialization. Bureaucracies are driven by a top-down or command and control approach in which managers provide considerable direction and have considerable control over others. Other features of the bureaucratic organization include functional division of labour and work specialization.

On the other hand, the organic structure is more flexible, more adaptable to a participative form of management, and less concerned with a clearly defined structure. The organic organization is open to the environment in order to capitalize upon new opportunities.

Organic organizations have a flat structure with only one or two levels of management. Flat organizations emphasize a decentralized approach to management that encourage high employee involvement in decisions. The purpose of this structure is to create independent small businesses or enterprises that can rapidly respond to customers' needs or changes in the business environment. The supervisor tends to have a more personal relationship with his or her employees.

Rensis Likert has conducted extensive research on a non-bureaucratic organization design referred to as System 4 (participative-democratic). Management and employees interact in a friendly environment characterized by mutual confidence and trust.

Contingency organization means that the most appropriate organization structure for each situation depends upon technology, organizational size, goals and strategy, environmental stability, and characteristics of the employees. Mechanistic organizations are best suited to repetitive operations and stable environments, while organic organizations are best suited to an uncertain task and a changing environment.

Organization Design

Designing an organization involves choosing an organizational structure that will enable the company to most effectively achieve its goals. Organization design is the creation of an organization's structure, traditionally functional, divisional, and/or matrix.

Functions or divisions arrange traditional organizations. In a functional organization, authority is determined by the relationships between group functions and activities. Functional structures group similar or related occupational specialties or processes together under the familiar headings of finance, manufacturing, marketing, accounts receivable, research, surgery, and photo finishing. Economy is achieved through specialization. However, the organization risks losing sight of its overall interests as different departments pursue their own goals.

In a divisional organization, corporate divisions operate as relatively autonomous businesses under the larger corporate umbrella. In a conglomerate organization, divisions may be unrelated. Divisional structures are made up of self-contained strategic business units that each produces a single product. For example, General Motors' divisions include Chevrolet, Oldsmobile, Pontiac, and Cadillac. A central headquarters, focusing or results, coordinates and controls the activities, and provides support services between divisions. Functional departments accomplish division goals. A weakness however, is the tendency to duplicate activities among divisions.

In a matrix organization, teams are formed and team members report to two or more managers. Matrix structures utilize functional and divisional chains of command simultaneously in the same part of the organization, commonly for one-of-a-kind projects. It is used to develop a new product, to ensure the continuing success of a product to which several departments directly contribute, and to solve a difficult problem. By superimposing a project structure upon the functional structure, a matrix organization is formed that allows the organization to take advantage of new opportunities. This structure assigns specialists from different functional departments to work on one or more projects being led by project managers. The matrix concept facilitates working on concurrent projects by creating a dual chain of command, the project (program, systems, or product) manager and the functional manager. Project managers have authority over activities geared toward achieving organizational goals while functional managers have authority over promotion decisions and performance reviews. An example is an aerospace firm with a contract from NASA.

Matrix organizations are particularly appealing to firms that want to speed up the decision-making process. However, the matrix organization may not allow long-term working relationships to develop. Furthermore, using multiple managers for one employee may result in confusion as to manager evaluation and accountability. Thus, the matrix system may elevate the conflict between product and functional interests.

Boundaryless organizations are not defined or limited by horizontal, vertical, or external boundaries imposed by a predetermined structure. They share many of the characteristics of flat organizations, with a strong emphasis on teams. Cross-functional teams dissolve horizontal barriers and enable the organization to respond quickly to environmental changes and to spearhead innovation. Boundaryless organizations can form relationships (joint ventures, intellectual property, distribution channels, or financial resources) with customers, suppliers, and/or competitors. Telecommuting, strategic alliances and customer-organization linkages break down external barriers, streamlining work activities. Jack Welch, former CEO of General Electric, to facilitate interactions with customers and suppliers, first used this un-structure.

A boundaryless environment is required by learning organizations to facilitate team collaboration and the sharing of information. When an organization develops the continuous capacity to adapt and survive in an increasingly competitive environment because all members take an active role in identifying and resolving work-related issues, it has developed a learning culture. A learning organization is one that is able to adapt and respond to change. This design empowers employees because they acquire and share knowledge and apply this learning to decision-making. They are pooling collective intelligence and stimulating creative thought to improve performance. Supervisors facilitate learning by sharing and aligning the organization's vision for the future and sustaining a sense of community and strong culture.

Organizing Function

The organizing function deals with all those activities that result in the formal assignment of tasks and authority and a coordination of effort. The supervisor staffs the work unit, trains employees, secures resources, and empowers the work group into a productive team. The steps in the organizing process include (1) review plans, (2) list all tasks to be accomplished, (3) divide tasks into groups one person can accomplish-a job, (4) group related jobs together in a logical and efficient manner, (5) assign work to individuals, (6) delegate authority to establish relationships between jobs and groups of jobs.

The nature and scope of the work needed to accomplish the organization's objectives is needed to determine work classification and work unit design. Division of labour, or work specialization, is the degree to which tasks in an organization are divided into separate jobs. Work process requirements and employee skill level determine the degree of specialization. Placing capable people in each job ties directly with productivity improvement. In order to maximize productivity, supervisors match employee skill level with task requirements.

Supervisors should perform workflow analysis to examine how work creates or adds value to the ongoing processes in an organization. Workflow analysis looks at how work moves from the customer or the demand source through the organization to the point at which the work leaves the organization as a product or service to meet customer demand.

Thus, workflow analysis can be used to tighten the connection between employees' work and customers' needs. Also, it can help to make major performance breakthroughs throughout business process reengineering (BPR), a fundamental rethinking and radical redesign of business processes to achieve dramatic improvements in costs, quality, service, and speed. BPR uses workflow analysis to identify jobs that can be eliminated or recombined to improve company performance.

Departmentalization

After reviewing the plans, usually the first step in the organizing process is departmentalization. Once jobs have been classified through work specialization, they are grouped so those common tasks can be coordinated. Departmentalization is the basis on which work or individuals are grouped into manageable units. There are five traditional methods for grouping work activities.

- Departmentalization by function organizes by the functions to be performed. The functions reflect the nature of the business. The advantage of this type of grouping is obtaining efficiencies from consolidating similar specialties and people with common skills, knowledge and orientations together in common units.
- Departmentalization by product assembles all functions needed to make and market a particular product are placed under one executive. For instance, major department stores are structured around product groups such as home accessories, appliances, women's clothing, men's clothing, and children's clothing.
- Departmentalization by geographical regions groups jobs on the basis of territory or geography. For example, Merck, a major pharmaceutical company, has its domestic sales departmentalized by regions such as Northeast, Southeast, Midwest, Southwest, and Northwest.
- Departmentalization by process groups jobs on the basis of product or customer flow. Each process requires particular skills and offers a basis for homogeneous categorizing of work activities. A patient preparing for an operation would first engage in preliminary diagnostic tests, then go through the admitting process, undergo a procedure in surgery, receive post operative care, be discharged and perhaps receive out-patient attention. These services are each administered by different departments.
- Departmentalization by customer groups jobs on the basis of a common set of needs or problems of specific customers. For instance, a plumbing firm may group its work according to whether it is serving private sector, public sector, government, or not-for-profit organizations. A current departmentalization trend is to structure work according to customer, using cross-functional teams. This group is chosen from different functions to work together across various departments to interdependently create new products or services.

For example, a cross-functional team consisting of managers from accounting, finance, and marketing is created to prepare a technology plan.

Power and Authority

Organizational structure is a means of facilitating the achievement of organizational objectives. Such structures are not static, but dynamic. They reorganize in response to changing conditions that occur in the environment, new technology, or organizational growth. Organization structures are dependent upon the employees whose activities they guide. Supervisors rely upon power and authority to ensure that employees get things done.

Authority

The organizational structure provides the framework for the formal distribution of authority. Formalization is the degree to which tasks are standardized and rules and regulations govern employee behaviour. It influences the amount of discretion an employee has over his or her job. In an organization with high degrees of formalization, job descriptions and policies provide clear direction.

Where formalization is low, employees have a great deal of freedom in deciding how thy conduct their work. Within the same organization, different departments may have different degrees of formalization. For example, in a hospital, doctors have freedom in selecting treatments, drugs, and methods for treating patients. However, the hospital physical plant staff has a strict schedule for cleaning buildings, mowing lawns, and maintaining the facilities. Authority is the legitimate power of a supervisor to direct subordinates to take action within the scope of the supervisor's position. Formal authority in the organization can be traced all the way back to the U.S. constitutional right to own property. The owner of the organization has the authority to make decisions. For example, entrepreneurial firms have an informal arrangement of employees and centralization of decision-making authority, the owner.

Forms of Authority

Three forms of authority are line authority, staff authority, and team authority.

Line authority is direct supervisory authority from superior to subordinate. Authority flows in a direct chain of command from the top of the company to the bottom. Chain of command is an unbroken line of reporting relationships that extends through the entire organization that defines the formal decision-making structure. It helps employees know to whom they are accountable, and whom to go to with a problem. Line departments are directly linked to the production and sales of specific products. Supervisors--in line departments, such as marketing and production--give direct orders, evaluate performance, and reward or punish those employees who work for them. Unity of command within the chain states that each person in an organization should take orders from and reports to only one person. This helps prevent conflicting demands being placed on employees by more than one boss. However, the trend toward employee empowerment, fuelled by advances in technology and changes in design from downsizing and reengineering have tempered the importance of being accountable to only one superior. Span of control refers to the number of employees that should be placed under the direction of one manager. Spans within effective organizations vary greatly. The actual number depends on the amount of complexity and the level of specialization. In general, a wide span of control is possible with better-trained, more experienced, and committed employees.

Staff authority is more limited authority to advise. It is authority that is based on expertise and which usually involves advising line managers. Staff members are advisers and counsellors who aid line departments in making decisions but do not have the authority to make final decisions. Staff supervisors help line departments decide what to do and how to do it. They coordinate and provide technical assistance or advice to all advisors, such as accounting, human resources, information technology, research, advertising, public relations, and legal services.

Team authority is granted to committees or work teams involved in an organization's daily operations. Work teams are groups of operating employees empowered to plan and organize their own work and to perform that work with a minimum of supervision. Team-Based structures organize separate functions into a group based on one overall objective. Empowered employees create their own schedules, design their own processes, and are held responsible for outcomes. This facilitates efficiencies in work process, and the ability to detect and react to changes in the environment. Employees with the skills and knowledge to manage more than one specialized task are able to promptly provide customers with quality products and services. Cross-functionally training team members allows any member to perform a variety of problem-solving tasks.

Teamwork is an imperative in a flat, boundaryless organizational structure. A team is a small number of people with complementary skills who work toward common goals for which they hold themselves mutually accountable. Self-managed teams are responsible for producing an entire product, a component, or an ongoing service. In most cases, members are cross-trained on the different tasks assigned to the team. Often, these teams are trained in technical, administrative, and interpersonal skills. Problem-solving teams do not affect an organization's structure because they exist for only a limited period. They are often used when organizations decide to make improvements in the quality of a product or service. Special-purpose teams consist of members who span functional or organizational boundaries and whose purpose is to examine complex issues such as introducing new technology, improving the quality of work process, or encouraging cooperation between labour and management in a unionized setting.

Power

In addition to authority, supervisors have more personal sources of power to draw upon for getting things done. Everyone has power in one form or another and it is by exercising this power that organizations get things accomplished. Supervisors who are capable of achieving their objectives independently of others are said to possess strength. When these "strong" supervisors involve and incorporate others into their plans and activities they are making use of power, and in fact increasing the total amount of power available to incorporate into a particular situation or problem. Involving employees in setting objectives and making decisions as it relates to their jobs empowers everyone, and results in greater job satisfaction and commitment, as well as increased productivity. Empowering employees provides them with greater autonomy.

Power is the ability to exert influence in the organization beyond authority, which is derived from position. The supervisor's personal power could include job knowledge, personal influence, interpersonal skills, and ability to get results, empathetic ability, persuasive ability, and physical strength. J.P. French and B. Raven ("The Bases of Social Power" in Studies in Social Power, edited by D. Cartwright, Institute for Social Research, 1959, pp. 150-167) identify six sources of power: legitimate, coercive, reward, expert, referent, and information. Legitimate power is a result of the position a person holds in the organization hierarchy. This position power is broader than the ability to reward and punish, as members need to accept the authority of the position. Coercive power is the threat of sanctions. It is dependent on fear and includes, but is not limited to the ability to dismiss, assign undesirable work, or restriction of movement. Reward power results in people doing what is asked because they desire positive benefits or rewards. Rewards can be anything a person values (praise, raises, and promotions). Expert power comes from expertise, skill, or knowledge. Referent power refers to a person who has desirable resources or personal traits. It results in admiration and the desire to emulate. Information power is based upon the persuasiveness or content of a communication and is independent of the influencing individual.

In most instances, supervisors do not need to offer incentives or threaten retribution to get employees to do what they request. They influence employees because the employees want to follow. This power to influence comes from the employee granting authority to the supervisor.

Centralization versus Decentralization

Centralization is the degree to which decision-making is concentrated in top management's hands. Decentralization is the extent to which decision-making authority is pushed down the organization structure and shared with many lower-level employees. Centralized organizations have more levels of management with narrow spans of control. Employees are not free to make decisions. Decentralized organizations have fewer levels of management with wide spans of control giving employees more freedom of action. All other things being equal, a wide span of control is more efficient because it requires fewer managers. However, it is important to recognize that, at some point, effectiveness will decline.

The current trend is toward broadening decentralization. As competition intensifies, the need for organizations to be responsive increases. This has made employees, usually those at the lower levels, who are closest to customers extremely important. They are an excellent source of knowledge and implement changes that directly impact performance. Giving this group more input into certain decision-making activities can result in increased firm performance.

Teamwork is an imperative in a flat, boundaryless organizational structure. A team is a small number of people with complementary skills who work toward common goals for which they hold themselves mutually accountable. Self-managed teams are responsible for producing an entire product, a component, or an ongoing service. In most cases, members are cross-trained on the different tasks assigned to the team.

Often, these teams are trained in technical, administrative, and interpersonal skills. Problem-solving teams do not affect an organization's structure because they exist for only a limited period.

They are often used when organizations decide to make improvements in the quality of a product or service. Special-purpose teams consist of members who span functional or organizational boundaries and whose purpose is to examine complex issues such as introducing new technology, improving the quality of work process, or encouraging cooperation between labour and management in a unionized setting.

Power

In addition to authority, supervisors have more personal sources of power to draw upon for getting things done. Everyone has power in one form or another and it is by exercising this power that organizations get things accomplished. Supervisors who are capable of achieving their objectives independently of others are said to possess strength. When these "strong" supervisors involve and incorporate others into their plans and activities they are making use of power, and in fact increasing the total amount of power available to incorporate into a particular situation or problem. Involving employees in setting objectives and making decisions as it relates to their jobs empowers everyone, and results in greater job satisfaction and commitment, as well as increased productivity. Empowering employees provides them with greater autonomy.

Power is the ability to exert influence in the organization beyond authority, which is derived from position. The supervisor's personal power could include job knowledge, personal influence, interpersonal skills, and ability to get results, empathetic ability, persuasive ability, and physical strength. J.P. French and B. Raven ("The Bases of Social Power" in Studies in Social Power, edited by D. Cartwright, Institute for Social Research, 1959, pp. 150-167) identify six sources of power: legitimate, coercive, reward, expert, referent, and information.

Legitimate power is a result of the position a person holds in the organization hierarchy. This position power is broader than the ability to reward and punish, as members need to accept the authority of the position. Coercive power is the threat of sanctions. It is dependent on fear and includes, but is not limited to the ability to dismiss, assign undesirable work, or restriction of movement. Reward power results in people doing what is asked because they desire positive benefits or rewards. Rewards can be anything a person values (praise, raises, and promotions). Expert power comes from expertise, skill, or knowledge. Referent power refers to a person who has desirable resources or personal traits. It results in admiration and the desire to emulate. Information power is based upon the persuasiveness or content of a communication and is independent of the influencing individual.

In most instances, supervisors do not need to offer incentives or threaten retribution to get employees to do what they request. They influence employees because the employees want to follow. This power to influence comes from the employee granting authority to the supervisor.

Centralization versus Decentralization

Centralization is the degree to which decision-making is concentrated in top management's hands. Decentralization is the extent to which decision-making authority is pushed down the organization structure and shared with many lower-level employees. Centralized organizations have more levels of management with narrow spans of control. Employees are not free to make decisions. Decentralized organizations have fewer levels of management with wide spans of control giving employees more freedom of action. All other things being equal, a wide span of control is more efficient because it requires fewer managers. However, it is important to recognize that, at some point, effectiveness will decline.

The current trend is toward broadening decentralization. As competition intensifies, the need for organizations to be responsive increases. This has made employees, usually those at the lower levels, who are closest to customers extremely important. They are an excellent source of knowledge and implement changes that directly impact performance. Giving this group more input into certain decision-making activities can result in increased firm performance.

It is impractical for the supervisor to handle all of the work of the department directly. In order to meet the organization's goals, focus on objectives, and ensure that all work is accomplished, supervisors must delegate authority. Authority is the legitimate power of a supervisor to direct subordinates to take action within the scope of the supervisor's position. By extension, this power, or a part thereof, is delegated and used in the name of a supervisor. Delegation is the downward transfer of formal authority from superior to subordinate. The employee is empowered to act for the supervisor, while the supervisor remains accountable for the outcome. Delegation of authority is a person-to-person relationship requiring trust, commitment, and contracting between the supervisor and the employee.

The supervisor assists in developing employees in order to strengthen the organization. He or she gives up the authority to make decisions that are best made by subordinates. This means that the supervisor allows subordinates the freedom to make mistakes and learn from them. He or she does not supervise subordinates' decision-making, but allows them the opportunity to develop their own skills. The supervisor lets subordinates know that he or she is willing to help, but not willing to do their jobs for them. The supervisor is not convinced that the best way for employees to learn is by telling them how to solve a problem. This results in those subordinates becoming dependent on the supervisor. The supervisor allows employees the opportunity to achieve and be credited for it.

An organization's most valuable resource is its people. By empowering employees who perform delegated jobs with the authority to manage those jobs, supervisors free themselves to manage more effectively. Successfully training future supervisors means delegating authority. This gives employees the concrete skills, experience, and the resulting confidence to develop themselves for higher positions. Delegation provides better managers and a higher degree of efficiency. Thus, collective effort, resulting in the organization's growth, is dependent on delegation of authority.

Responsibility and Accountability

Equally important to authority is the idea that when an employee is given responsibility for a job, he or she must also be given the degree of authority necessary to carry it out. Thus, for effective delegation, the authority granted to an employee must equal the assigned responsibility. Upon accepting the delegated task, the employee has incurred an obligation to perform the assigned work and to properly utilize the granted authority. Responsibility is the obligation to do assigned tasks. The individual employee is responsible for being proficient at his or her job. The supervisor is responsible for what employees do or fail to do, as well as for the resources under their control. Thus, responsibility is an integral part of a supervisor's authority.

Responsibilities fall into two categories: individual and organizational. Employees have individual responsibilities to be proficient in their job. They are responsible for their actions. Nobody gives or delegates individual responsibilities. Employees assume them when they accept a position in the organization. Organizational responsibilities refer to collective organizational accountability and include how well departments perform their work.

For example, the supervisor is responsible for all the tasks assigned to his or her department, as directed by the manager. When someone is responsible for something, he or she is liable, or accountable to a superior, for the outcome. Thus, accountability flows upward in the organization. All are held accountable for their personal, individual conduct. Accountability is answering for the result of one's actions or omissions. It is the reckoning, wherein one answers for his or her actions and accepts the consequences, good or bad. Accountability establishes reasons, motives and importance for actions in the eyes of managers and employees alike. Accountability is the final act in the establishment of one's credibility. It is important to remember that accountability results in rewards for good performance, as well as discipline for poor performance.

The Delegation Process

The delegation process has five phases: (1) preparing, (2) planning, (3) discussing, (4) auditing, and (5) appreciating. The first step in delegating is to identify what should and should not be delegated. The supervisor should delegate any task that a subordinate performs better. Tasks least critical to the performance of the supervisor's job can be delegated. Any task that provides valuable experience for subordinates should be delegated. Also, the supervisor can delegate the tasks that he or she dislikes the most. But, the supervisor should not delegate any task that would violate a confidence.

- Preparing includes establishing the objectives of the delegation, specifying the task that needs to be accomplished, and deciding who should accomplish it.
- Planning is meeting with the chosen subordinate to describe the task and to ask the subordinate to devise a plan of action. As Andrew Carnegie once said, "The secret of success is not in doing your own work but in recognizing the right man to do it." Trust between the supervisor and employee-that both will fulfill the commitment-is most important.
- Discussing includes reviewing the objectives of the task as well as the subordinate's plan of action, any potential obstacles, and ways to avoid or deal with these obstacles. The supervisor should clarify and solicit feedback as to the employee's understanding. Clarifications needed for delegation include the desired results (what not how), guidelines, resources available, and consequences (good and bad). Delegation is similar to contracting between the supervisor and employee regarding how and when the work will be completed. The standards and time frames are discussed and agreed upon. The employee should know exactly what is expected and how the task will be evaluated.
- Auditing is monitoring the progress of the delegation and making adjustments in response to unforeseen problems.
- Appreciating is accepting the completed task and acknowledging the subordinate's efforts.

Since motivation influences productivity, supervisors need to understand what motivates employees to reach peak performance. It is not an easy task to increase employee motivation because employees respond in different ways to their jobs and their organization's practices. Motivation is the set of processes that moves a person toward a goal. Thus, motivated behaviours are voluntary choices controlled by the individual employee. The supervisor (motivator) wants to influence the factors that motivate employees to higher levels of productivity.

Factors that affect work motivation include individual differences, job characteristics, and organizational practices. Individual differences are the personal needs, values, and attitudes, interests and abilities that people bring to their jobs. Job characteristics are the aspects of the position that determine its limitations and challenges. Organizational practices are the rules, human resources policies, managerial practices, and rewards systems of an organization. Supervisors must consider how these factors interact to affect employee job performance.

Simple Model of Motivation

The purpose of behaviour is to satisfy needs. A need is anything that is required, desired, or useful. A want is a conscious recognition of a need. A need arises when there is a difference in self-concept (the way I see myself) and perception (the way I see the world around me). The presence of an active need is expressed as an inner state of tension from which the individual seeks relief.

Theories of Motivation

Many methods of employee motivation have been developed. The study of work motivation has focused on the motivator (supervisor) as well as the motivatee (employee). Motivation theories are important to supervisors attempting to be effective leaders. Two primary approaches to motivation are content and process.

The content approach to motivation focuses on the assumption that individuals are motivated by the desire to fulfill inner needs. Content theories focus on the needs that motivate people.

Maslow's Hierarchy of Needs identifies five levels of needs, which are best seen as a hierarchy with the most basic need emerging first and the most sophisticated need last. People move up the hierarchy one level at a time. Gratified needs lose their strength and the next level of needs is activated. As basic or lower-level needs are satisfied, higher-level needs become operative. A satisfied need is not a motivator. The most powerful employee need is the one that has not been satisfied. Abraham Maslow first presented the five-tier hierarchy in 1942 to a psychoanalytic society and published it in 1954 in Motivation and Personality (New York: Harper and Row).

Level I-Physiological needs are the most basic human needs. They include food, water, and comfort. The organization helps to satisfy employees' physiological needs by a paycheck.

Level II-Safety needs are the desires for security and stability, to feel safe from harm. The organization helps to satisfy employees' safety needs by benefits.

Level III-Social needs are the desires for affiliation. They include friendship and belonging. The organization helps to satisfy employees' social needs through sports teams, parties, and celebrations. The supervisor can help fulfill social needs by showing direct care and concern for employees.

Level IV-Esteem needs are the desires for self-respect and respect or recognition from others. The organization helps to satisfy employees' esteem needs by matching the skills and abilities of the employee to the job. The supervisor can help fulfill esteem needs by showing workers that their work is appreciated.

Level V-Self-actualization needs are the desires for self-fulfilment and the realization of the individual's full potential. The supervisor can help fulfill self-actualization needs by assigning tasks that challenge employees' minds while drawing on their aptitude and training.

Alderfer's ERG identified three categories of needs. The most important contribution of the ERG model is the addition of the frustration-regression hypothesis, which holds that when individuals are frustrated in meeting higher level needs, the next lower level needs reemerge.

Existence needs are the desires for material and physical well being. These needs are satisfied with food, water, air, shelter, working conditions, pay, and fringe benefits. Relatedness needs are the desires to establish and maintain interpersonal relationships. These needs are satisfied with relationships with family, friends, supervisors, subordinates, and co-workers.

Growth needs are the desires to be creative, to make useful and productive contributions and to have opportunities for personal development.

McClelland's Learned Needs divides motivation into needs for power, affiliation, and achievement.

Achievement motivated people thrive on pursuing and attaining goals. They like to be able to control the situations in which they are involved. They take moderate risks. They like to get immediate feedback on how they have done. They tend to be preoccupied with a task-orientation towards the job to be done.

Power motivated individuals see almost every situation as an opportunity to seize control or dominate others. They love to influence others. They like to change situations whether or not it is needed. They are willing to assert themselves when a decision needs to be made.

Affiliation motivated people are usually friendly and like to socialize with others. This may distract them from their performance requirements. They will usually respond to an appeal for cooperation.

Herzberg's Two-Factor Theory describes needs in terms of satisfaction and dissatisfaction. Frederick Herzberg examined motivation in the light of job content and contest. Motivating employees is a two-step process. First provide hygienes and then motivators. One continuum ranges from no satisfaction to satisfaction. The other continuum ranges from dissatisfaction to no dissatisfaction. Satisfaction comes from motivators that are intrinsic or job content, such as achievement, recognition, advancement, responsibility, the work itself, and growth possibilities. Herzberg uses the term motivators for job satisfiers since they involve job content and the satisfaction that results from them. Motivators are considered job turn-ons. They are necessary for substantial improvements in work performance and move the employee beyond satisfaction to superior performance. Motivators correspond to Maslow's higher-level needs of esteem and self-actualization.

Dissatisfaction occurs when the following hygiene factors, extrinsic or job context, are not present on the job: pay, status, job security, working conditions, company policy, peer relations, and supervision. Herzberg uses the term hygiene for these factors because they are preventive in nature.

They will not produce motivation, but they can prevent motivation from occurring. Hygiene factors can be considered job stay-ons because they encourage an employee to stay on a job. Once these factors are provided, they do not necessarily promote motivation; but their absence can create employee dissatisfaction. Hygiene factors correspond to Maslow's physiological, safety, and social needs in that they are extrinsic, or peripheral, to the job. They are present in the work environment of job context.

Motivation comes from the employee's feelings of accomplishment or job content rather than from the environmental factors or job context. Motivators encourage an employee to strive to do his or her best. Job enrichment can be used to meet higher-level needs. To enrich a job, a supervisor can introduce new or more difficult tasks, assign individuals specialized tasks that enable them to become experts, or grant additional authority to employees.

The process approach emphasizes how and why people choose certain behaviours in order to meet their personal goals. Process theories focus on external influences or behaviours that people choose to meet their needs. External influences are often readily accessible to supervisors.

Vroom's Expectancy Model suggests that people choose among alternative behaviours because they anticipate that particular behaviours will lead to one or more desired outcomes and that other behaviours will lead to undesirable outcomes. Expectancy is the belief that effort will lead to first-order outcomes, any work-related behaviour that is the direct result of the effort an employee expends on a job.

Equity is the perception of fairness involved in rewards given. A fair or equitable situation is one in which people with similar inputs experience similar outcomes. Employees will compare their rewards with the rewards received by others for their efforts. If employees perceive that an inequity exists, they are likely to withhold some of their contributions, either consciously or unconsciously, to bring a situation into better balance. For example, if someone thinks he or she is not getting enough pay (output) for his or her work (input), he or she will try to get that pay increased or reduce the amount of work he or she is doing. On the other hand, when a worker thinks he or she is being paid too much for the work he or she is doing, he or she tends to increase the amount of work. Not only do workers compare their own inputs and outputs; they compare their input/output ratio with the input/output ratio of other workers. If one work team believes they are doing more work than a similar team for the same pay, their sense of fairness will be violated and they will tend to reduce the amount of work they are doing. It is a normal human inclination to want things to be fair.

Bowditch and Buono note (see Bowditch, James L. and Anthony F. Buono, A Primer on Organizational Behaviour, 4th, John Wiley & Sons, 1997) that while equity theory was originally concerned with differences in pay, it may be applied to other forms of tangible and intangible rewards in the workplace. That is, if any input is not balanced with some fair output, the motivation process will be difficult. Supervisors must manage the perception of fairness in the mind of each employee. If subordinates think they are not being treated fairly, it is difficult to motivate them.

Reinforcement involves four types of consequence. Positive reinforcement creates a pleasant consequence by using rewards to increase the likelihood that a behaviour will be repeated. Negative reinforcement occurs when a person engages in behaviour to avoid unpleasant consequences or to escape from existing unpleasant consequences. Punishment is an attempt to discourage a target behaviour by the application of negative outcomes whenever it is possible. Extinction is the absence of any reinforcement, either positive or negative, following the occurrence of a target behaviour. Employees have questions about their jobs. Can I do what management is asking me to do? If I do the job, will I be rewarded? Will the reward I receive be satisfactory to me?

Reinforcement is based primarily on the work of B.F. Skinner, a psychologist, who experimented with the theories of operant conditioning. Skinner's work shows that many behaviours can be controlled through the use of rewards. In fact, a person might be influenced to change his or her behaviour by giving him or her rewards.

Employees who do an exceptionally good job on a particular project should be rewarded for that performance. It will motivate them to try to do an exceptional job on their next project. Employees must associate the reward with the behaviour. In other words, the employee must know for what specifically he or she is being rewarded! The reward should come as quickly as possible after the behaviour. The reward can be almost anything, but it must be something desired by the employee. Some of the most powerful rewards are symbolic; things that cost very little but mean a lot to the people who get them. Examples of symbolic rewards are things like plaques or certificates.

New Organising Techniques

To meet the many demands of performing their functions, managers assume multiple roles. A role is an organized set of behaviours. Henry Mintzberg has identified ten roles common to the work of all managers. The ten roles are divided into three groups: interpersonal, informational, and decisional. The informational roles link all managerial work together. The interpersonal roles ensure that information is provided. The decisional roles make significant use of the information. The performance of managerial roles and the requirements of these roles can be played at different times by the same manager and to different degrees depending on the level and function of management. The ten roles are described individually, but they form an integrated whole.

The three interpersonal roles are primarily concerned with interpersonal relationships. In the figurehead role, the manager represents the organization in all matters of formality. The top level manager represents the company legally and socially to those outside of the organization. The supervisor represents the work group to higher management and higher management to the work group. In the liaison role, the manger interacts with peers and people outside the organization. The top level manager uses the liaison role to gain favours and information, while the supervisor uses it to maintain the routine flow of work. The leader role defines the relationships between the manger and employees.

The direct relationships with people in the interpersonal roles place the manager in a unique position to get information. Thus, the three informational roles are primarily concerned with the information aspects of managerial work. In the monitor role, the manager receives and collects information. In the role of disseminator, the manager transmits special information into the organization. The top level manager receives and transmits more information from people outside the organization than the supervisor. In the role of spokesperson, the manager disseminates the organization's information into its environment. Thus, the top level manager is seen as an industry expert, while the supervisor is seen as a unit or departmental expert.

The unique access to information places the manager at the center of organizational decision making. There are four decisional roles. In the entrepreneur role, the manager initiates change. In the disturbance handler role, the manger deals with threats to the organization. In the resource allocator role, the manager chooses where the organization will expend its efforts. In the negotiator role, the manager negotiates on behalf of the organization. The top level manager makes the decisions about the organization as a whole, while the supervisor makes decisions about his or her particular work unit. The supervisor performs these managerial roles but with different emphasis than higher managers. Supervisory management is more focused and short-term in outlook. Thus, the figurehead role becomes less significant and the disturbance handler and negotiator roles increase in importance for the supervisor. Since leadership permeates all activities, the leader role is among the most important of all roles at all levels of management

In order to perform the functions of management and to assume multiple roles, managers must be skilled. Robert Katz identified three managerial skills that are essential to successful management: technical, human, and conceptual. Technical skill involves process or technique knowledge and proficiency. Managers use the processes, techniques and tools of a specific area. Human skill involves the ability to interact effectively with people. Managers interact and cooperate with employees. Conceptual skill involves the formulation of ideas. Managers understand abstract relationships, develop ideas, and solve problems creatively. Thus, technical skill deals with things, human skill concerns people, and conceptual skill has to do with ideas. A manager's level in the organization determines the relative importance of possessing technical, human, and conceptual skills. Top level managers need conceptual skills in order to view the organization as a whole. Conceptual skills are used in planning and dealing with ideas and abstractions. Supervisors need technical skills to manage their area of specialty. All levels of management need human skills in order to interact and communicate with other people successfully.

As the pace of change accelerates and diverse technologies converge, new global industries are being created (for example, telecommunications). Technological change alters the fundamental structure of firms and calls for new organizational approaches and management skills.

Successful organizations continually innovate and change based upon customer needs and feedback. Values, mission, and vision form the foundation for the execution of the functions of management. They are an organization's guidelines that affect how it will operate. They work only if visible and used in everyday activities and decisions. An organization's values are its beliefs or those qualities that have intrinsic worth and will not be compromised. Its mission is its purpose for existing. The vision is the image of itself in the future.

Values

Each supervisor's approach to management will reflect his or her values, as well as those of the organization. Building trust starts with creating culture based on shared values. Values are traits or qualities having intrinsic worth, such as courage, respect, responsibility, caring, truthfulness, self-discipline, and fairness. Values serve as a baseline for actions and decision-making and guide employees in the organization's intentions and interests.

The values driving behaviour define the organizational culture. A strong value system or clearly defined culture turns beliefs into standards such as best quality, best performance, most reliable, most durable, safest, fastest, best value for the money, least expensive, most prestigious, best designed or styled, easiest to use. If asked, "What do we believe in?" or "List our organization's values" all employees in the organization should write down the same values. For example, McDonald's values were captured in its motto of "Q.S.C. & V." which stands for quality, service, cleanliness, and value.

Supervisors need to appreciate the significance of values and value systems. Values affect how a supervisor views other people and groups, thus influencing interpersonal relationships. Values affect how a supervisor perceives situations and solves problems. Values affect how a supervisor determines what is and is not ethical behaviour. Values affect how a supervisor leads and controls employees. Since employees often base behaviour on perceived values it is critical to ensure their perceptions reflect organizational values. Supervisors must communicate, encourage and reinforce the desired values and related behaviours to integrate them into the organizational culture.

Geert Hofstede identified a work-related value framework that has four dimensions: power distance, uncertainty avoidance, individualism, and polarization. Power distance is the attitude to human inequality and relationships to superiors and inferiors in any hierarchy. Uncertainty avoidance is the tolerance for uncertainty that determines choices and rituals to cope with it in social structures and belief systems. Individualism is the relationship between the individual and the collectivity, especially in the way individuals choose to live and work together. Polarization is the extent to which differences such as masculinity or femininity have implications for social organization and the organizations of beliefs. Every person has a different mental program, based on patterns of thinking, feeling, and acting, which are learned throughout a lifetime. The effects of these differences have many practical implications for those who work or are managers in multinational business and for those involved in international negotiations.

Mission

A mission is a broad definition of a business that differentiates it from all other organizations. It is the justification for the organization's existence. The mission statement is the "touchstone" by which all offerings are judged. In addition to the organization's purpose other key elements of the mission statement should include whom it serves, how, and why. The most effective mission statements are easily recalled and provide direction and motivation for the organization.

Since an organization exists to accomplish something in the larger environment, its specific mission or purpose provides employees with a shared sense of opportunity, direction, significance, and achievement. An explicit mission guides employees to work independently and yet collectively toward the realization of the organization's potential.

Thus, a good mission statement gets the emotional bonding and commitment needed. It allows the individual employee to say; "I know how I should do my job differently." For example, many people might think that The Walt Disney Company's mission is to run theme parks. But, Disney's mission is always moving toward an expanded view. Disney provides entertainment. "Disney's overriding objective is to create shareholder value by continuing to be the world's premier entertainment company from a creative, strategic, and financial standpoint."

Also, many people might think that Revlon's mission is to make cosmetics. Yet, Revlon provides glamour, excitement and innovation. Charles Revson, Revlon's founder understood the importance of mission. He said "In the factory, we make cosmetics; in the store, we sell hope."

Vision

Erich Fromm pointed out; "The best way to predict your future is to create it." A vision might be a picture, image, or description of the preferred future. A visionary has the ability to foresee something and sees the need for change first. He or she challenges the status quo and forces honest assessments of where the industry is headed and how the company can best get there. A visionary is ready with solutions before the problems arise.

A study over the period from 1926 to 1990 found visionary companies that set a purpose beyond making money outperformed other companies in the stock market by more than six to one. (See Gilbert Fuchsberg, "Visioning' Mission Becomes Its Own Mission," The Wall Street Journal, January 7, 1994, B1, 3.) Managers require more vision than ever because change is coming faster than ever. Leaders have the ability to make their vision real by engaging the minds, as well as the hearts of others.

Microsoft's early vision statement was "A Computer on Every Desk and In Every Home." (At approximately the same time, President John Akers said IBM's goal was to become a $100 billion company by then end of the century. At that time IBM sales were $50 billion.) Microsoft's vision has evolved [1998 the "Connected PC and the Connected TV"-the idea of integrating the intelligence and interactivity of PCs with the video and sound of TV] to 2002 "to enable people and businesses throughout the world to realize their full potential."

Life consists in what a man is thinking of all day.--Ralph Waldo Emerson.

A goal is an end that the organization strives to attain. However, the supervisor cannot "do" a goal. Supervisors break down processes, analyze them, set objectives and then drive hard to achieve them. Doing the same thing and expecting different results doesn't work. The supervisor must write an objective for what he or she is trying to accomplish. Thus, an objective is the object or aim of an action. It implies an explicit direction for the action to take and a specific quality of work to be accomplished within a given period of time. Objectives reflect the desired outcomes for individuals, groups and organizations. They provide direction for decision-making and a criterion against which outcomes are measured. Thus, objectives are the foundation of planning.

Management by Objectives

An effective planning tool to help the supervisor set objectives is Management by Objectives (MBO). MBO gained recognition in 1954 with the publication of Peter Drucker's book The Practice of Management. MBO is a collaborative process whereby the manager and each subordinate jointly determine objectives for that subordinate. To be successful MBO programs should include commitment and participation in the MBO process at all levels, from top management to the lowest position in the organization. MBO begins when the supervisor explains the goals for the department in a meeting. The subordinate takes the goals and proposes objectives for his or her particular job. The supervisor meets with the subordinate to approve and, if necessary, modify the individual objectives. Modification of the individual's objectives is accomplished through negotiation since the supervisor has resources to help the subordinate commit to the achievement of the objective. Thus, a set of verifiable objectives for each individual are jointly determined, prioritized, and formalized. The supervisor and the subordinate meet periodically to review the latter's progress. Communication is the key factor in determining MBO's success or failure. The supervisor gives feedback and may authorize modifications to the objectives or their timetables as circumstances dictate. Finally, the employee's performance is measured against his or her objectives, and he or she is rewarded accordingly.

Steps in MBO Process

Research has demonstrated that when top management is committed and personally involved in implementing MBO programs, they significantly improve performance. This finding is not surprising when one considers that during the MBO process employees determine what they will accomplish. After all, who knows what a person is capable of doing better than the person does him or herself?

Objectives are the driver of planning processes. It is imperative that top managers safeguard the intention of their goals to facilitate middle .and lower management's effective translation and implementation of them. Objectives guide managerial activities such as budgeting, the development of action plans, staffing, and the purchasing of equipment. The organization's success ultimately depends on the combined outcomes of its objectives.

Objectives

Most supervisors set objectives, but not with equal skill. Few, who do not correctly write objectives, will reap MBO's full benefits. An objective is simply a statement of what is to done and should be stated in terms of results. A mnemonic aid to write objectives is SMART (Specific, Measurable, Attainable, Result-oriented, Time-limited).

Specific

An objective must be specific with a single key result. If more than one result is to be accomplished, more than one objective should be written. Just knowing what is to be accomplished is a big step toward achieving it. What is important to you? Once you clarify what you want to achieve, your attention will be focused on the objective that you deliberately set. You will be doing something important to you.

Measurable

An objective must be measurable. Only an objective that affects behaviour in a measurable way can be optimally effective. If possible, state the objective as a quantity. Some objectives are more difficult to measure than others are. However, difficulty does not mean that they cannot be measured. Treatment of salespeople might be measured by looking at the absenteeism and turnover rates among the sales force. Also, salespeople could be asked to fill out a behavioural questionnaire anonymously giving their observations of the supervision they receive.

Customer service could be measured by such indices as the number of complaints received, by the number of customers lost, and by customer interviews or responses to questionnaires. Development of subordinates could be measured by determining the number of tasks the subordinate has mastered. Cooperation with other functions could be measured by length of delay in providing requested information, or by peer ratings of degree of cooperation.

Avoid statements of objectives in generalities. Infinitives to avoid include to know, to understand, to enjoy, and to believe. Action verbs are observable and better communicate the intent of what is to be attempted. They include to write, to apply, to recite, to revise, to contrast, to install, to select, to assemble, to compare, to investigate, and to develop.

Scaling the Progress

Attainable

An objective must be attainable with the resources that are available. It must be realistic. Many objectives are realistic. Yet, the time it takes to achieve them may be unrealistic. For example, it is realistic to want to lose ten pounds. However, it is unrealistic to want to lose ten pounds in one week.

What barriers stand between you and your objective? How will each barrier be overcome and within what time frame?

Result-oriented

The objective should be central to the goals of the organization. The successful completion of the objective should make a difference.

How will this objective help the organization move ahead? Is the objective aligned with the mission of the organization?

Time-limited

The objective should be traceable. Specific objectives enable time priorities to be set and time to be used on objectives that really matter. Are the time lines you have established realistic? Will other competing demands cause delay? Will you be able to overcome those demands to accomplish the objective you've set in the time frame you've established?

Write Meaningful Objectives

Although the rules are difficult to establish, the following may be useful when writing an objective.

1. Start with an action or accomplishment verb. (Use the infinitive form of the verb. This means to start the with "to.")
2. Identify a single key result for each objective.
3. Give the date of the estimated completion.
4. Be sure the objective is one you can control.
5. To test for validity of SMART objectives, ask yourself the following questions.

   * S = Exactly what is my objective?
   * M = What would a good job look like?
   * A = Is my objective feasible?
   * R = Is my objective meaningful?
   * T = Is my objective traceable?

The following fill-in-the-blank equation may be useful when writing an objective.

Objective: To (+ action verb + single key result + target date)

Organizing Process

In cases of management transfer, the estalishment process focuses on a level of user organization where no organization presently exists, that is, at a level of the irrigation network previously managed by the government irrigation agency. Typically this entails organizing federations of user groups at the tertiary level under a secondary-canal association. The challenge of creating a new organization of users is perhaps the most central feature of the management transfer process. The act of management transfer from the agency to the users depends upon a user organization that is capable of assuming those management responsibilities.

Before any organizing of the users is carried out, there needs to be a package of incentives in place for both the users and the agency staff whose jobs would be affected by the transfer program. Such incentives are needed both to make the program work, and to maintain credibility with farmers whose long-term support will be required. If organizing is attempted before an adequate incentive structure is established, the transfer program could well collapse, thus setting the entire program back by several years, as well as causing short-term hardships to those concerned. Thus, if the incentives are not clear and attractive to farmers, the organizing process should be delayed until the incentives are clarified.

First determine:

Who Will do the Organizing?

The first step is to decide on the type of organizers who will work directly with farmers in helping establish the organization. [We use the term "water user association" (WUA) to refer to this new organization, although the term, "WUA" can also refer to organizations at the tertiary level of the system which have always been outside the management control of the government irrigation agency.] In the Philippines, a special cadre of social organizers was recruited and trained by the National Irrigation Administration in the late1970s and early 80s. These organizers were mostly social workers or social scientists selected for their ability to work easily with farmers in village conditions. They were trained in irrigation management so they could better understand the technical problems of the farmers they were trying to organize.

The work of the Philippines social organizers was effective, yet this approach has not been widely replicated by irrigation agencies in other countries. The investment and bureaucratic difficulties involved in recruiting new temporary staff from a different discipline has led many irrigation agencies to try other approaches. In Mexico's transfer program, the National Water Commission's own staff were used along with staff from a sister agency, the Institute for Water Technology (IMTA).

In addition, a few consultants were brought in on a case by case basis. In India, some state irrigation departments have relied on extensionists from the Agriculture Department under the Command Area Development Program. Also in India, several NGOs have been involved in organizing, at the request of the irrigation departments. But the organizers of choice, for most irrigation agencies, will be their own field staff. These staff are already within the bureaucratic structure of the agency, so the lines of authority are clear, there is little additional expense involved, and these staff are already familiar with the physical systems and with the local farmers.

The problems with using irrigation agency field staff for organizing work, however, are considerable. These staff are not necessarily interested in organizing farmers, They have not received any prior training in social work (in most cases), and their superiors have also no training (nor interest) in these tasks. These would-be organizers must be re-trained for their organizing tasks, and just as importantly, their job assignments need to be re-defined to reflect their new role. In addition, their superiors need to be trained and re-oreinted so they understand and appreciate the new role to be played by their field staff.

What Training do the Organizers Need?

Assuming that agency staff will be used for the organizing, and assuming that their professional training has been in irrigation engineering, they would need to be re-tooled as organizers.

First of all they would need a thorough understanding of the rationale for PIM, so that they can present a clear message both to the farmers and to their own colleagues within the irrigation agency.

Secondly, they will need training in communcation skills (including listening skills) for effective interaction with the users.

Thirdly, they will need training in social analysis, including an understanding of social stratification (by caste, ethnicity, or class), kinship, patron-client relations, labour relations, religious factors, political affiliation, land tenure (tenants, share-croppers, owners), etc. And fourthly, they would need training in methods for gathering information from farmers (e.g., participatory rural appraisal) and in methods for organizing farmers.

Who will Provide the Training?

Irrigation management training institutes?

Universities?

Administrative staff colleges?

NGOs?

What capacity building do these organizations need?

skills training: TOT course on PIM?

structural change in the organization itself? (IMTI case)

financing?

new or clarified mandate?

Building support for capacity building may require training and consensus building at political levels, just to provide an enabling environment for the PIM program to get started.

Then,

Organizing Steps

Note: This assumes there are reasonable incentives for farmers to take over system, and for the government irrigation agency to hand over the system; if not, go back and work on the incentives!

- Organize the organizers: Arrange for supervision/ support for the organizers, and clear lines of communication with Departmental staff responsible for the overall project (Ensure that PIM component of program is well integrated with rest of project).
- Meet the farmers and other irrigation stakeholders/ Discuss plans formulated during participatory design phase:
  - village head
  - local administrative officials
  - local political leaders (MLAs/MPs)
  - leaders of other farmer organizations (producer cooperatives)

- Identify key power relations among farmers; develop strategy for organizing
- Establish provisional boundaries of the system (through consultation with key power brokers among the farmers); conduct inventory of potential members; draw map showing command area and irrigation system.
- Arrange series of meetings between farmers and Departmental field staff to discuss improvements that need to be made prior to handover.
  - arrange canal walk-through to discuss specifics of design/infrastructure improvements
  - discuss general terms of WUA contracts
- Arrange farmer visits to other associations to discuss with those farmers (and invite those farmers to visit new association).
- Organizational Assistance:
  - Help prospective WUA leaders arrange farmer meetings to discuss plans
  - Help formulate/revise by-laws
  - Advise on elections/selections
  - Assist with legal registration
  - Arrange management training for WUA leaders
- Arrange meetings between WUA leaders and Department staff to discuss details of WUA contract and terms of transition phase leading to hand-over;
- Advise on staff recruitment(?)
- Assist with formal hand-over
- Visit periodically to monitor WUA's performance

Organizing Systems

One of the main problems that each enterprise faces is to organize the efforts of the people working on common goals. Most of the solutions to this problem originate from the time before computers became available for practically any company.

However, it's a general practice even now, that the developers follow the old management scheme when the company is being computerized, whereas modern computers offer unique opportunities for implementing new, far more effective approaches to management. We discovered the limitations of existing management schemes while computerizing a small trading company. Our objective was to develop a system able to assist the office workers in all aspects of their routine work. One of our tasks was a conventional one-to support such activities as taking orders, delivering goods, making a phone call, etc. The other one was more ambitious-to register all completed activities and to help plan new activities based on the completed ones.

We realized very soon that our second objective could not be achieved within the functional management scheme adopted in the company. To cope with our task we started to consider the company's activity as a number of processes (such as "processing an order", "closing a deal") without regard to the way these processes were being managed. As a result a new approach to management was developed which we call a process-oriented management. This approach can be described as a project management without project managers, a project manager's functions, e.g., planning, controlling the execution of activities, etc., being distributed among the workers involved in a particular process.

The main point with the process-oriented management is that it permits a company to gain full control over all the processes within the frame of the existing, often functionally-oriented, organizational structure. This type of management facilitates also the communication between the workers involved in the same process, and it provides them with actual information on the state of the process, as well as on all activities performed and planned.

Below, we present the main ideas of the process-oriented management, and the requirements for a computer system needed to support it. We tried our best to do that in a very informal way to make it easily understood by all concerned. It should also be mentioned that the author is not a specialist in the field of management, but he worked with experts on management throughout the project. The paper reflects a fresh view of an application developer not spoiled by the experience of the pre-computer management era.

The rest of this paper is organized as follows. In section 2, we outline our view on the management of routine work. In section 3, we present the main principles of the process-oriented management. We look at existing approaches to management of the routine work-the function-oriented management and project-oriented management, and then move on to describing the ways of transforming the project-oriented management into the process-oriented one. We discuss the process-oriented management without regards to computer systems, however, this type of management can't be implemented without computers. Requirements for a computer system designed to support the process-oriented management are discussed in section 4. In section 5, we discuss the major issues of the development and implementation of such systems. In section 6, we present a short summary of our practical and research work that lead to the development of a process-oriented approach to management.

Management of Routine Work

It's generally recognized that the main objective of management is to ensure a successful achievement of a company's goals at minimal costs. A company has several different types of goals to achieve at any given moment-long-term, short-term, etc.

As we are concerned with the management of routine work, it's the "conventional" everyday goals that are of primary interest to us; we call them "operational" goals. A typical operational goal for a trading company is, for example, to "drive" an incoming order through a delivery to receiving payment within certain time limits. A typical operational goal for a hospital is to administer the appropriate treatment to a patient that would lead to his discharging from the hospital. A typical operational goal for a software development company is to build a software system according to the specifications. But for the section of technical support of such company, a typical operational goal is to process a bug report so that the bug is fixed or/and a work-around solution is found.

Though operational goals may be quite unsophisticated, they, nevertheless, constitute the backbone of any business, as they have to be achieved on a day-to-day basis to ensure the proper functioning of the company. The character of operational goals depends on the type of business, but they have a number of common features:

- operational goals pop up more or less regularly;
- there is, usually, a standard procedure for achieving the operational goals of a given kind, which doesn't mean, of course, that a particular goal can't be approached in a different way if needed;
- there is often a set time limit for achieving an operational goal. If the goal is impossible to achieve within the time limit, it is discarded in a standard way.

To achieve an operational goal, a series of activities should be completed. For example, a series of activities aimed at getting payment for an incoming order includes delivery of goods and sending an invoice to the customer. This series may include more items in certain circumstances, for example, if the ordered goods are out of stock, they should be produced or ordered from the suppliers.

The activities aimed at achieving an operational goal are not, usually, executed immediately one after another, e.g., if the ordered goods are out of stock, it takes some time to get them from the suppliers. The execution of these activities is a process that continues over some period of time. The main objective for management of operational goals is to ensure that this process results in achieving the goal.

Different activities concerning the same goal can be completed by different workers from different divisions. Another objective of management is, therefore, to coordinate the work of all workers participating in the process of achieving an operational goal.

A Race Towards a Process-Oriented Management

Approaches to management of operational goals may be divided in two types-function-oriented and project-oriented. The function-oriented management (Fn-management) is usually used in the environments where a lot of relatively simple operational goals pop up very frequently. The Fn-management implies that operational goals are handled in a routine manner by the staff where each member has his own function in achieving operational goals. A manager does not coordinate the execution of activities for each goal, workers just react on the incoming documents, phone calls, etc., by completing activities they are assigned, and forwarding the received or newly composed documents further to their colleagues.

The project-oriented management (Pj-management) is usually used with more sophisticated goals such as construction or software projects. The Pj-management implies that a process for a new goal is planned in detail before the work on it starts, and there is someone (e.g., a project manager) who supervises all the work being done.

Fn-management is most cost-effective, but it works poorly when a process of achieving an operational goal deviates from a standard pattern, as it lacks control over individual processes. Pj-management gives full control over an individual process, but it's inefficient when a lot of coexisting processes are involved. There are working environments where one or the other type of management fits well. But in most environments a combination of these two approaches would be the way to obtain both full control over all processes and efficiency.

Below, we discuss our proposals for integration of the Fn- and Pj-managements. The result is a new type of management which we call the process-oriented management, or Pc-management, for short. This name highlights the main objective of the Pc-management-to control the processes, in contrast to Fn-management that places the emphasis on the execution of activities, and the Pj-management that emphasizes plans. We describe the Pc-management here in the following way. We consider an environment typical for the function-oriented management-a trading company, and try to introduce the project-oriented management in it. The process-oriented management is presented thus as a result of tailoring the project-oriented approach to fit a different kind of environment. We find this way most convenient for discussing our ideas, but it's not, naturally, the only possible one.

The Pc-management is based on the notions of "orgobject", "history" and "dynamic and distributed planning", which we can now turn our attention to.

Orgobjects

The Pj-management involves developing a detailed plan for achieving a project's goal before the work on the project can start. This plan is premised on certain assumptions that may turn out wrong after the project is under way. The plan should then be adapted to the changed conditions. For this purpose, a clear picture of the current state of the project is required to figure out what should be done to complete the project.

A project often involves developing some product that is a physical object, e.g. a software system, a building, etc. This product comes into existence in some form already at the earlier stages of the project, e.g. a half-ready software system or a building under construction. This half-ready product serves as a good representation of the current state of the project. As the half-ready product can be studied without regards to how it has been produced, the plan can be revised without going into details of the project's history.

In cases where the Fn-management is involved, there is no half-ready product to represent the current state of achieving an operational goal. A kind of an abstract object that contains all information on the current state of the process would be helpful here. As it would serve as an organizing device for achieving the goal, we call it an "orgobject".

For example, an orgobject representing a process of "Get payment for an incoming order" may be a record that contains information on: the name and address of the buyer, a description of each kind of goods ordered, the quantity and price per unit of each kind, the quantities of goods already delivered; the amount of money invoiced; the amount of money received. Having this orgobject, the conditions for the successful achievement of the "get payment" goal could be formulated as follows:

- have the numbers representing the quantities of 'goods ordered' and 'goods delivered' equal for each goods kind,
- have 'money invoiced' equal to the sum of 'ordered' multiplied by 'price per unit' for all goods kinds, and
- have 'money received' equal to 'money invoiced'.

As the process develops, the corresponding orgobject should change so that it reflects all the time the current state of the process. As soon as some activity is completed, the orgobject representing the process is to be modified. Thus, in the above example, after the delivery (full or partial), the quantities of the goods delivered are modified; if the customer has changed the order, the types and quantities of the goods ordered are modified, etc. To ensure that the orgobjects are always up-to-date, the routines for every type of activity should list not only the operations required for completing the activity (e.g., packing and shipping for delivery), but also instructions for the appropriate modifications of the relevant orgobjects.

Thus, the current state of an orgobject reflects the overall result of all activities completed earlier, and shows what actions should be taken to achieve the goal. To return to our example, if the quantity of the goods ordered is greater than the quantity of the goods delivered, the missing goods are to be delivered. If, on the other hand, the quantity of the goods ordered is less than the quantity of the goods delivered, then the customer should be asked to return some of the goods. Other examples: if the amount of money invoiced exceeds the payment received, then the customer should pay the difference. If the amount of the money received exceeds that of invoiced, then a credit note should be issued.

History

The current state of an orgobject contains only the result of the completed activities, but not a list of them, e.g.: the quantity of the goods delivered, but not the number of separate deliveries; the amount of money invoiced, but not the number of separate invoices, etc. This is OK if all goes as it should. But if something goes wrong, e.g., some goods sent off did not arrive, then the information on all activities performed is vital when figuring out what actions should be taken. This information can be collected through logging all the activities completed in the frame of the given process. Let's consider the following logging scheme. Every time a worker executes an activity, he/she doesn't physically change the previous state of the relevant orgobject. He/she makes a new record instead which contain the new state of the orgobject and leaves the former one unchanged. For example, after a delivery, a new record is made containing the same information as the previous one except the information on the quantities of the goods delivered. The latter is updated according to the packing list.

The record on the previous state of an orgobject is placed in a special file containing the history of the given orgobject. The worker who completes an activity composes also a report where he/she records: the kind of activity completed, the name of a person who completed it, the date, time, comments, etc. This report is saved together with the previous state of the orgobject in the history file. Given two consequent states of an orgobject and an activity report, we can reconstruct exactly what happened during the activity execution. For example, in case of delivery, we know exactly by whom and when the goods were delivered, and in what quantities. Thus, our log provides an easy access to the information on both the activity performed, and the state of events before and after it was performed.

Dynamic and Distributed Planning

As it was mentioned above, the Pj-management involves designing a detailed plan for each new process. If we try to apply the same to a Fn-management environment, two problems would arise:

- as Fn-processes are often trivial, their plans would be trivial too, e.g.: 'delivering goods'-'invoicing the buyer'-'getting payment'. It would be meaningless to record such plan for every process (and there are many in this kind of environments),

- unpredictable external events that often occur in Fn-management environments would demand revising the whole plan, e.g.: a customer has changed his order-additional delivery can be required, an invoice is to be sent later than it was initially planned, etc.

Dynamic planning is our answer to these problems. Dynamic planning involves planning only the first few activities at the first stage. As soon as one or several of these are completed, new activities are planned with regard to the emerging state of the relevant orgobject (and standard routines adopted in the company). For example, after a delivery, another delivery is planned if not all ordered goods have been delivered, or invoicing is planned if all goods have been delivered. The use of dynamic planning is fully beneficial in case of processes that follow a standard pattern. Otherwise, the usual planning is preferable. In case the character of the process (standard/deviating) is difficult to foresee, dynamic planning can be used at first, followed by conventional planning if necessary.

Another poser when trying to introduce the Pj-management in an Fn-environment is how to supervise a process. In cases where the Pj-management is involved, there is usually a project manager who supervises the execution of planned activities, and corrects the plan if needed. In an environment typical for the Fn-management, a project manager supervising each process would result in significant overheads.

A solution to this can be described as "distributed planning". Distributed planning implies that the worker who has completed a planned activity himself plans the subsequent activities. Moreover, he/she can assign these new activities not only to himself, but to other people too. For example, a worker who completes a delivery himself plans invoicing to be completed by another worker.

Distributed planning doesn't exclude the possibility of a centralized supervision of a process. In fact, a supervisor may intervene at any time and correct the plan if needed. Moreover, any member of staff can consult the supervisor in case he/she has some problems with his/her work on a particular process. He/she can do it by planning a special activity, e.g., "asking for help", and assigning his/her supervisor to complete it.

Let's have a look at the issue of implementing dynamic and distributed planning. Above, we considered orgobjects and plans as separate entities. Now, we put a plan inside the orgobject representing the corresponding process. As a result an orgobject besides the information on the current state of the process (e.g., on the customer, goods, delivery and payment) will also include a list of planned activities (e.g., delivery, invoicing, etc.), each of them containing information on what should be done, who's to do that and when.

Thus, a plan becomes part of an orgobject. Consequently, we can treat correction of the plan as one of the operations of changing the orgobject in the course of completing an activity. In section 3.1, we've already mentioned that instructions for modifying orgobjects should be included in the working procedures for each type of activities. To ensure proper dynamic planning, these instructions should embrace modification of the process's plan. In a simple case, a worker who has completed an activity modifies the relevant orgobject by removing this activity from the list of planned activities. In more complex cases, he/she adds new activities to the list, and/or removes some other activities from it.

Being an integral part of the orgobject representing a process, a plan is subjected to the logging we described above. As a result, all acts of replanning are registered in the same way as other modifications of orgobjects. Thus, for example, the name of a person who modified the plan is recorded, which may prove to be useful in case of conflicts.

Advantages

The main advantage of the Pc-management is its flexibility. The Pc-management permits to choose the optimum approach to coping with each process, and within the same management scheme. Thus, simple processes that follow a standard pattern are dealt with in a completely decentralized manner, whereas some more sophisticated case will be dealt with by centralized individual planning and supervising. Moreover, the same process may be treated differently at different stages. For example, it may be started as a standard one, but later it can be planned and supervised individually. As a result, full control over all kinds of processes is gained and efficiency is not sacrificed.

Another important thing is that the Pc-management is not bound to any particular type of organizational structure. It can be used both in case the same member of staff completes all the activities required for achieving an operational goal, and in case each activity type is assigned to a particular worker. This permits to preserve the same management scheme when the organizational structure is changed, e.g., in case of a company's expansion.

Some other advantages are as follows:

1. Orgobjects provide a perfect insight into the company's state of affairs. The information stored in the orgobjects is of great help to the management staff as it permit to quickly evaluate the state of a process (without going into its history). It also helps to give prompt answers to customers' questions. This kind of information is not easily obtainable when traditional managements schemes are used. Thus, when the Fn-management is used, only the information on the executed activities of a given type is easily accessible, and when the Pj-management is used, only the information on the state of the plans execution is easily accessible.
2. Histories of orgobjects permit to easily trace all the activities completed on a given process, which helps to devise plans for complicated cases. They are also a very important source of data for all kinds of statistical analysis, and other types of information processing required for decision-making.
3. The company's staff becomes goal-and process-conscious, as it is easy for any person to overview all the activities (one's own and those of others) completed in a process he/she is involved in. The history of old

orgobjects is useful for "learning by example", which may help a worker to find solutions in difficult cases. The goal-and process-consciousness isn't easy to acquire with a traditional management scheme. Under the Fn-management, a worker doesn't see how a process he/she's in is accomplished. His/her personal goal becomes to complete as efficient as possible the activities he/she is responsible for. That may result in, e.g., a seller concentrating on making telephone calls most of which don't get him to closing a deal.

4. The Pj-management emphasizes following the schedule, which becomes the main goal of the workers engaged in a project. There is a danger that the workers do not keep their eyes open for changes in the surrounding world, which is, e.g., the main reason why large software projects often produce out-of-day systems.
5. As all the information on the past is being stored, the management staff is in a better position concerning various kinds of conflicts, internal conflicts among workers engaged in the same process, and external ones, e.g., with customers or suppliers.
6. Distributed planning is a very powerful tool for coordinating the work which makes unnecessary the intensive communication (exchanges of documents, phone calls, etc.) among the workers engaged in the same processes. They get the required information from the current states of orgobjects and their histories.

An Orgsystem Wanted

Let's imagine you are fascinated by the Pc-management and decide to implement it in your company. A lot of orgobjects start circulating around, each accompanied by a huge history file. You don't find the one you need, you never know which of the orgobjects contains the planned activities assigned to you, and when these activities should be completed. You strove for a better order and got yourself into a mess. And, as if that were not enough, you have a lot of extra work to do. You should construct a new state of an orgobject for each completed activity, and remember to put the new activities on the list and assign them to yourself and others. You wanted to improve the efficiency, but it sinks instead.

There is no need to worry, there is a means to restore the order and efficiency, and that's, naturally a computer system. It's primary aim is to make you happy with the Pc-management doing away with the chaos, that's why we call it an "organizing system", or orgsystem for short.

Let's have another look at the Pc-management, this time supported by an orgsystem. Orgobjects do not circulate between various members of the staff who are to work with them, they stay in the same place together with their history and plans, and are easily accessible to all workers involved.

All planned activities assigned to a given individual appear immediately in his/her personal calendar, so that each worker knows exactly what activities he/she has to complete and when. An orgsystem provides the means to increase the efficiency by:

- assisting workers in executing each activity,
- providing an extremely user-friendly interface.

These two features are a key to successful implementation of an orgsystem. Without them people would not be motivated to use the system, consequently the Pc-management wouldn't work. Let's look at these features in more detail.

Level of Help

All operations needed for executing an activity under the Pc-management belong to one of the two groups:

- external operations-operations that affect the "external world", and
- maintaining operations-operations aimed at maintaining orgobjects.

The character of external operation depends on the type of activity, e.g., packing and shipping for delivery, programming and testing for developing a software module, etc. Maintaining operations are the same for all activities. They include:

- updating the information contained in the relevant orgobject,
- correcting the plan,
- logging the preceding state of the orgobject.

An orgsystem assists a worker to complete both the external operations and the maintaining ones.

1. External operations. Level of help which is possible to offer for completing the external operations depends on the type of activity. For example, programming and testing of a software module are usually performed inside the computer, and they are already fully computerized. Here, an orgsystem should just integrate the existing tools for software development, e.g. editors, debuggers, etc., so that a proper tool is invoked when a user chooses to execute these operations. Packing and shipping are not that easily computerized, not now anyway. But even there, an orgsystem can be helpful to some extent by, e.g., making up a packing list. It's important to give a hand in completing the external operations for each kind of activities. There's a risk otherwise. If some activity is left without the orgsystem's assistance, a worker who completes it can easily forget to make the appropriate changes in the orgobject concerned. In that case, the completed activity will still remain on the list of planned activities and the orgsystem will keep reminding the worker to complete it. There is also a danger that the same activity will be completed several times.
2. Updating. Modification of an orgobject can often be done on the basis of the information collected in the process of executing the external operations. For example, an "order" orgobject contains the information on the quantities of the goods already delivered. This information should be updated after each separate delivery. The new quantities can be easily calculated based on the packing list that was made at the previous step, which permits an orgsystem to update the orgobject without assistance from the users.

3. When correcting a plan, a worker is prompted by the system on the appropriate activities to plan next; in simple cases the plan is corrected by the system itself. This is possible, as an orgsystem possesses two type of knowledge:
   - on the working procedures used in the company, which helps to plan new activities, and
   - on division of responsibilities between different divisions, sections, and workers, which permits to correctly assign new activities.
4. Logging includes two operations:
   - saving the old state of the orgobject, and
   - making a report on the activity completed.

Saving the old state of an orgobject is done by an orgsystem without any user assistance, but an activity report needs a human participation. Even there, an orgsystem helps by automatically supplying the information on what activity has been executed, by whom and when. The rest of the report, e.g., comments, is of course the responsibility of the worker.

User-interface

Conventional computer systems are designed as a set of functions operating on a common database, the main facility of the user-interface being multilevel menus. This type of the user-interface provides the user with a quick access to a function he/she wants to complete. It reflects the objective of a conventional computer system which is to help workers to cope with single activities like updating information, printing a report, etc. An orgsystem objectives are much wider, which brings about the need for a completely different kind of user-interface. An orgsystem's user-interface permits end-users to freely choose between the object-oriented and activity-oriented way of working with orgobjects, as well as easily switch from one to the other. The object-oriented approach is applied when a user wants to work with a particular orgobject for a longer time. In this case, he/she may need to look at the object's current state and its history, as well as to plan and execute various activities involving the orgobject. The activity-oriented approach is applied when a user wants to complete the same activity for a number of orgobjects. In this case, the dialogue designed for a given activity is repeated for all relevant orgobjects. The object-oriented way is particularly useful when one worker is responsible for many activities involving an orgobject. It is also the way that management staff can use when there is a need to evaluate the state of a particular process and to devise a plan for a difficult case. The activity-oriented approach is preferable if a worker is responsible for only one type of activities. It's also the right approach to completing simple activities that do not require much human assistance, e.g., printing an invoice, etc.

Another distinguishing feature of an orgsystem's user-interface is that it maintains personal calendars. A personal calendar is a list of activities assigned to a particular worker. The point is that these activities are included in different orgobjects and the calendar permits a perfect overview of a persons' many tasks. The orgsystem offers a variety of ways to use the calendar. A user can browse through his/her calendar, or some parts of it, e.g., to see all activities planned for a particular day, all activities of a certain type, etc. When browsing, he/she can start the execution of his/her activities (activity-oriented approach), or move to the orgobject where a particular activity belongs and start working with this orgobject in the object-oriented manner.

To maintain its user-friendly character, an orgsystem's user-interface should satisfy a number of general requirements. Most important are the following two:

- easy access to all information required for working with orgobjects. For example, when working with an orgobject representing an order, a user should have access to all information related to the customer who ordered goods: his address, previous contacts with him, etc.;
- consistency. There should be standard procedures for navigating to an orgobject, for getting information (e.g., a company's address), for planning, for starting the execution of activities, etc. These standard procedures

should be the same for all types of orgobjects and activities.

Joys and Hardships of an Orgsystems Developer

There are, naturally, technical problems to solve in the development of an orgsystem. The system requirements discussed in the previous section must be met. However, an orgsystem designer's greatest problem is that he starts the development in an environment initially not based on the Pc-management, which makes both design and implementation of an orgsystem far from trivial tasks.

Orgsystems Design

An orgsystem designer should begin with:

- identifying the company's operational goals,
- figuring out what processes are used to achieve them, and
- designing orgobjects to represent these processes.

His/her next task is to review all the working procedures and tailor them to fit the Pc-management scheme (by adding maintaining operations to each activity).

This is often a tough job, as there are seldom some written descriptions of the working procedures, and if they exist, they are far from complete. The only way to cope with the job is to try and get the missing information from the company's workers. The workers would, naturally, know nothing about orgobjects, but they know their job. The conditions in which an orgsystem designer works are similar to those of a linguist who studies a language that exists only in the spoken form. Linguists have special methods permitting them to get the necessary information from the native speakers without teaching them any linguistic notions. Moreover, it's considered a wrong practice to teach informants linguistics, as it may only spoil them.

An orgsystems designer needs similar methods that would permit him to redesign the company's working procedures without introducing the workers into the world of orgobjects, distributed planning, etc. We believe that rapid prototyping is the right method. As soon as a designer has identified the company's operational goals and processes, and designed the orgobjects to represent them, he/she should make a prototype of the system and let the future users test it. To be able to use prototyping, an orgsystem designer needs appropriate application development tools.

These tools should allow him to quickly produce a sketch of the system that has "look-and-feel" of a real system, but lacks processing routines and database access. It's this sketch that we call the prototype of the system. Working with it, a user can navigate among orgobjects in the same way as he would do that when the orgsystem is ready. He can modify existing orgobjects, create new ones, and see how to start different activities.

But he can't save the information or see the results of the completed activities. After the future users have accepted the prototype, the designer can stepwise add database access and processing routines, which would be also done with the help of the above mentioned application development tools.

Orgsystems Implementation

Implementing an orgsystem means introducing the Pc-management in a non-Pc-management environment. This may be achieved in one of two ways:

- by substituting all the old working procedures in the company at once, or
- by gradual introduction of the new working procedures.

The first approach may suit small companies whose workers often switch from one activity type to another. An orgsystem would help to do these switches very quickly, and it would help the workers, who usually have a lot of different things to do, to preserve the order in their affairs. The staff of a small company would easily understand the advantages of using all facilities provided by an orgsystem: object-and activity-oriented ways of working, personal calendars, easy access to the history, etc. However, in case of large companies, the second approach may be the best choice. Large companies usually, have a lot of workers who are involved only in one or several activities for each process. These workers may believe that an orgsystem is too complex for their simple tasks. It would be difficult for them to see the advantages of the object-oriented user-interface, and their earlier experience of traditional computer systems can only make the things worse.

Luckily, an orgsystem provides a means for working in the activity-oriented manner, which would put the workers competing simple activities at ease. There would be no problem to teach them to use the orgsystem in the activity-oriented way, because it resembles their old manner of doing things. Later, the workers could be taught the object-oriented way as well, which would give them better possibilities to take the initiative and find solutions for difficult cases. But even if most of the office workers continue to use the activity-oriented approach, there would always be some key people who benefit from the object-oriented approach, e.g., management staff.

Concluding Remarks

Orgsystems-What's Been Achieved so Far?

The notion of the Pc-management came into being when the author together with several colleagues developed an application for supporting sales and marketing activities of a trading company. The system was called "DealDriver" to highlight that it helps the workers to "drive" the deals to the end which is receiving payment. Deals were thus the first type of orgobjects designed.

The work on the project started in spring 1989, and the first version of DealDriver was ready in summer 1990. Since then, Dealdriver has been successfully used at our home office to support one of IbisSoft's business activities-reselling of professional software.

The DealDriver project, gave us some valuable insights into the problems of orgsystems development which are summarized in our internal reports. We developed also an experimental version of application development tools to support orgsystems development. These tools were later used for building both prototypes and functioning systems in a number of other application fields, e.g., hospital administration. Next two subsections discuss some theoretical and technical aspects of orgsystems development. The reader who is not interested in such issues is invited to look over these.

What are the Related Research Fields?

Orgsystems development belongs to an application field called groupware. This is a multidisciplinary field where social scientists and computer scientists work together. Some of the computer science fields related to our work are as follows:

- the behaviour of dynamic objects, where the orgobjects belong, is being formalized by the theory of object-oriented systems;
- methods of storing and accessing structured information, which are vital for orgsystems development, are the subject of the database theory. Particularly related to our work are the theories of semantic databases, object-oriented databases, and temporal databases;
- methods of planning for robots are one of AI's (Artificial intelligence) favourite research problems. The results obtained there may in some cases be directly applied to the management field. For example, the difference between classical and reactive planning corresponds to the difference between the pure Pj-and Fn-management.

What Makes our Systems Work?

The main ideas of the Pc-management originate from our previous research work on the CHAOS project (CHAOS stands for Concurrent Human-Assisted Object Systems). The project's objective was to work out a formal model for describing distributed interactive systems. This model is based on the notions of objects and connectors. Objects are used to represent the elements of the "real world", (e.g. people, companies, projects, etc.), whereas connectors are the active elements of the system whose task is to make changes in the objects. A connector may be thought of as a little computer connected to one or several objects. As soon as some of these objects change, the connector changes all the other objects to restore the consistency of the system.. Thus defined, our model has a purely reactive nature, i.e. changes in objects are made as a reaction to changes in other objects. But objects in our model can be complex, i.e. they themselves can contain connectors, which means that a reaction can result in adjusting the system configuration to changes in the environment.

The CHAOS model fitted the management field so well that all we had to do was to use another set of terms. Thus, complex objects became orgobjects, connectors became planned activities, and the principle of reactive reconfiguration of the system was called dynamic and distributed planning. Some of the results of applying the CHAOS model to management field were virtually the same as those from the research works based on the theory of planning. However, being more general than the theory of planning, our model provides a better framework for management automation as it covers all aspects of management not only the issues of planning.

The CHAOS model is abstract, but the approach taken in the DealDriver project was very pragmatic. The objective of the project was to create a working system, not to speculate on the management automation issues. This project differs in many ways from similar research projects. Below we list the most important differences:

1. Computer environment. We worked with PC computers under MS DOS in stand-alone and network versions, whereas research projects are often completed on Unix-based workstations. We used text-based terminals, not a graphic-based windowing environment with a mouse, icons, etc. This environment was chosen because it was the one an average company could easily afford.
2. Development tools. Research workers often choose programming languages popular among computer scientists like Lisp, Prolog, Smalltalk, etc. These languages have a sound theoretical basis (e.g., function theory, logic, etc.), but require a lot of programming when they are used for the development of an application. We made a point of getting the maximum available help with

programming by employing commercially available application development tools. We chose JAM from JYACC as a front-end tool, and Btrieve from Novell as a record manager. These tools were of great help to us, as we had limited resources for completing the project (in terms of time and manpower).

3. Design principles. Researchers are often far too interested in the technical issues, such as methods of software design and programming, etc. We concentrated on user-interface issues instead. Our only principle of programming was: a program should work and permit to easily make necessary changes. All programming was done in C-language, and though our system was object-oriented in a very high degree, we didn't use any object-oriented extension to C.

Thus, two factors contributed to the successful completion of the DealDriver project:

- the use of a powerful abstract model, and
- a pragmatic approach to system development, and we strongly believe that both of them are obligatory for the development of a computer system of a totally new kind.

We are also convinced that there is no need to wait 10-20 years, which it usually takes for new research ideas to be implemented in application systems. New ideas can be implemented today and with the means available now.

5

Management of Indian Best Hotels

Taj Hotels

Taj Hotels Resorts and Palaces is the largest Indian luxury hotel chain. A wholly owned subsidiary of the Tata Group, Taj Hotels Resort and Palaces comprises 57 hotels in 39 locations across India with an additional 18 international hotels in the Maldives, Mauritius, Malaysia, Seychelles, United Kingdom, United States of America, Bhutan, Sri Lanka, Africa, the Middle East and Australia. Their first and most well known property is the Taj Mahal Palace & Tower in Colaba, Mumbai. The Taj Mahal Palace & Tower, Mumbai was opened on December 16, 1903, by the founder of the Tata Group, Jamshetji Nusserwanji Tata. Taj President-a business hotel and Taj Land's End-an ultimate luxury boarding are also located in Mumbai. It operates TajAir, a luxury private jet operation with state-of-the-art Falcon 2000 aircraft designed by Dassault Aviation, France; and Taj Yachts, two 3-bedroom luxury yachts which can be used by guests in Mumbai and Kochi.

Falaknuma Palace

Falaknuma Palace is situated on a hill 650 meters in height, in the Old City of Hyderabad, India. It was built by Nawab Vikar-ul-Umra. It was purchased by the then Nizam VI during 1897 for use as a royal guest house. The palace provides a good view of Hyderabad. The palace is spread out in a scorpion shape with two pincers spread out as wings on the north. The middle part occupies the main building. The Harem quarters and the kitchen stretch towards the south.

The palace was designed by an Italian architect. The palace boasts of lavishly decorated interiors made of the Italian marble, and follows a western architectural style. It took almost nine years to complete. This famous palace houses a large collection of rare treasures, paintings, statues, furniture, manuscripts and books collected by the Nizam. The jade collection displayed here is considered to be unique in the world. Some old models of artillery are also exhibited in the front.

The Palace is being converted into a heritage hotel by the Taj Hotels group.

Hotel Organization in Future

No hotel company operating today can be unaware of the swift pace of global change and its impact on every facet of the hospitality industry. With just five years left in this century, we can expect change to be the only constant. New business practices are evolving virtually as fast as our technologies, while resistance to change has become one of the primary causes of business failure.

The specter of constant change raises fundamental questions as to the creation of shareholder wealth in a capital-constrained, highly competitive environment. How will hotel organizations build shareholder wealth, and what key drivers will result in success? What future products and services will be essential in a technology-driven, global environment marked by rising customer expectations? Moreover, what alternative approaches and skills must organizations develop to ensure market success?

The future success of hotel organizations will be driven in large part by the ability to foresee and capitalize--on change. Beyond this truism, however, there is an urgent need to identify what will be required in the competitive environment of the future with its intense focus on serving customer needs. The hospitality industry–as is the case with business generally--is subject to deep currents of change set in motion as economic and social systems shaped in the industrial era evolve to a knowledge-based era driven by technology advances.

In this period of global transition, it behooves hotel organizations to examine the key factors that will not only define success, but the ability to survive in coming years. Many of these issues were spotlighted in a global study undertaken by the Economist Intelligence Unit and co-sponsored by Arthur Andersen. The Successful Corporation of the Year 2000 surveyed more than 600 senior executives around the world. Its mission was to identify the characteristics needed to lead successful businesses in the next century. These executives offer a number of compelling messages regarding the key success factors of the future.

Customers will have the strongest influence on the corporation in the year 2000. Indeed, these executives believe that the customer will be "king" in the new century. Exceptional leadership was by far the attribute most frequently cited by CEOs and senior executives; the consensus appears to be that successful companies in the year 2000 will be led by corporate visionaries. A strategic planning focus is not only essential, but must embody a concept of planning for the future that anticipates change, rather than being based exclusively on historical models. In structuring organizations for the future, companies must build management capabilities to deal with one of the most critical challenges–diversity in the marketplace. Employing information technology to drive business success in this information-driven era is not only the path of least resistance, but vital to virtually every aspect of operations.

The study's top-line results create an excellent backdrop to address key issues confronting the hotel industry, and what factors will lead to membership–rather than rejection–in the elite club of the world's corporate success stories in the year 2000.

From an Asset to Customer Focus

Recognizing that the hotel industry has a somewhat split personality reflecting the inherent conflicts between its real estate and operational aspects, it is important to understand the industry's real estate origins and how they are shaping the challenges ahead. The origins of the industry's real estate persona are embodied in the classic theory of location-"if we build it, they will come." As a result of this "building" complex, the industry has tended to have a real estate and asset orientation, rather than a customer focus. From the hotel company perspective–especially that of the brand-oriented "chain"–the varied interests of a diffused property ownership group can be quite different than the singular interest of the chain that operates and markets the properties.

Even when the ownership of geographically dispersed hotel properties is controlled by a single hotel organization, the financial structuring tends to be property-specific. Corporate financial strategies are frequently subjugated to the needs of the last property deal brought into the company's fold. Each property in a so-called "chain," is frequently the subject of a unique and distinctive ownership and financial structure. This phenomenon–quite common in the real estate sector, but unusual for business enterprises generally–makes for elusive economies of scale in the structuring and financing of property-driven expansion.

Collectively, these factors have produced low comparative returns in real estate, although criticism levelled at commercial real estate returns is somewhat less germane to the hotel industry, where management and franchise fees can produce high returns for those companies where property ownership is held by third parties. Nevertheless, average returns in the real estate industry in the United States, for example, are just over 10 percent, compared to small company stock returns at almost 20 percent and large company stocks at an average of about 15 percent.

While hotel chains have adopted traditional corporate frameworks, there are a number of predominantly real estate-driven, family-owned businesses in the hotel sector that continue to operate as relatively unstructured organizations. In meeting the future, these businesses will need plans, people and processes in order to establish viable corporate forms that can compete in tomorrow's marketplace and capitalize upon its opportunities.

In today's changed environment, the hotel organization must deal with a number of new realities. Investors in our industry are no longer satisfied with long-term capital appreciation and psychic income that heretofore were often the justification for otherwise seemingly uneconomic investments in hotel property or, indeed, hotel chains. The first reality is that there is a very specific and identifiable relationship between bottom line performance and value. Improvements in business operations raises values. It is not surprising, therefore, that the new owners attracted to this industry in recent years have new sets of demands. This transformation from an old-guard group of investors and owners to income and return-driven newcomers has meant that the once "quiet enjoyment" of operators in their management of hotels for third parties is being disturbed, interrupted and overturned.

These challenges all take place in an environment where capital has become extremely selective in markets that have little stability. A global shortage of capital will not remain a short-term problem, and future hotel organizations must have a stronger alignment to capital providers–a critical "customer" group. Hotel companies will need to compete by offering better returns and performance than in the past. Hotel chains have found their development timetables quashed in recent years, making it difficult to achieve goals of critical mass often required to improve performance. These factors are driving consolidation in the brand "sweepstakes." Capital markets, therefore, continue to favour well-established companies, a reality that must drive entrepreneurial organizations to meet the future now by planning for an evolving corporate context in which to operate.

Key Success Factors-The Future

Within this broad context, hotel developers, owners and management companies will all need to develop new strategies, skills and processes that look forward to the competitive demands of the future. These ultimately must address issues related to vision and planning, as well as organizational skill sets and processes to attract and retain customers. To stake a claim in the future, current business practices should be examined in light of what can be expected to be the key success factors in the year 2000.

Embrace a global change orientation. As the information age produces greater worldwide integration of business activities, a global knowledge base will become invaluable. Success in local and regional hotel markets will be shaped decisively by a global business environment that defines capital movement, customer expectations and applications of new technologies.

Focus on the Customer

If the customer is "king" in the 21st century, hotel organizations will be best served by focusing less on their hotel assets as measures of success, and more on their customers.

This involves a fundamental shift in viewing the real estate asset as the wealth creator--to the customer as the key to building shareholder wealth. A customer focus must imbue business decisions at all levels of developing and operating a hotel organization. Pursuing such a course will inevitably impact shareholder wealth. To accomplish this, however, customers need to participate in the product development process.

Fully realizing a customer focus in the industry poses a significant challenge. The hotel industry must confront problems due to conflicts between operational needs and real estate goals. Quite simply, an operator must remain customer-focused, but the short-term strategies to meet these needs may be inconsistent with the long-term objectives of property owners. Balancing those goals will be essential. A customer focus implies a significant shift in what drives hotel development--placing primary emphasis on the customer with the locations to follow. Nevertheless, a hotel organization with its large investment in fixed assets--the real estate--can never be as nimble as a consumer products company in adjusting products and services to match rapid shifts in the marketplace.

The Japanese taught us that the concept of "zero defects" in products and services can yield tremendous benefits. But today an even more rigorous standard dominates--quality that surprises. In practical terms, the hotel industry finds it extremely difficult to meet the standard of zero defects in service. Hotel services are based primarily on people, not computers or other equipment. Quality that surprises takes the concept of zero defects a step further. Yesterday's surprising product or service is today's status quo. Twenty years ago, a business executive did not expect a consistent and predictable level of service wherever he or she travelled in the world. Today that is a standard--not the exception--as is the expectation for sophisticated technology in hotel rooms to support business needs. With customer discrimination so acute, it is not surprising that brand loyalty is a diminishing "commodity" in the hotel industry.

Find the Ingredients for Visionary Leadership

Today's hotel organizations need to recognize the need for visionary leadership. The ability to forecast the future--to anticipate change rather than react to it--will be one of the single greatest determinants of market dominance in the years ahead. The old "command and control" model of leadership is giving way to a focus on leadership in ideas, information, inspiration, vision and teamwork. Warren Bennis, an authority on leadership in the U.S., puts it this way--"For the most part, failing organizations tend to be over-managed and under-led. The leader sets the tone for the moral character, the vision, the corporate culture and the fiber of the institution."

While visionary leadership is essential, it must be linked to business operations and foster a risk bias, rather than a procedural bias. This will allow the organization to stretch and, in turn, change. And it must be shared by empowered professionals and staff throughout the organization, including those who meet the customer. Overcoming the resistance to change can be a daunting task, particularly in large hotel organizations in which diversions from the status quo may threaten established management lines. It suggests that a culture based on conformance may need to be replaced by an emphasis on flexibility, learning and cooperation. Management competencies will need to be aligned in order to achieve the desired result. For many organizations, this may mean a shift from traditional hierarchies typical of companies in an industrial era to a flatter organization with a more transparent interface between leadership, organizational functions and employees.

Create a defensible position through corporate strategy. For many of the industry's leaders, vision is driven by the strategic planning process, a function which has become critical for success.

Strategic planning, however, has at times been a step-child in the hotel industry, and it is often the first to be cut when organizations are downsized. It is clearly in transition. There also has been a tendency to decentralize and simplify this function--both actions of potential benefit. Strategic planning must be led by the top people in the organization--the CEO and COO. On the other hand, it should be close enough to the customer to ensure that planners can "listen" to and be influenced by customer needs.

Empower Management

Beyond the ability to envision the future, core management capabilities will make the difference--they are essential. A clear vision without the management skills to support it cannot be a recipe for success. First and foremost, hotel management must have strategic development skills and the ability to integrate complex factors affecting success. Market volatility has become the norm, in part caused by the rapidly changing tastes of customers. Customers are increasingly approaching the hotel industry with widely different social, economic and political backgrounds, to say nothing of employees. Being able to deal with these diversities in a positive and constructive fashion that capitalizes on the differences, rather than working to find ways to mitigate them, is the clear path for successful management in the future.

The organization will also need to be imbued with a sense of entrepreneurship that reacts proactively to the market's diversity. Traditional organizations that follow well-documented rules must give way to leaders who can balance a sense of discipline with that of flexibility. Talent and resources must be marshalled and leveraged. In an industry with high fixed costs and labour intensity, the concept of leverage in the hotel business is an all-important one. Improving labour productivity through technology must be a goal for today's forward-looking hotel organization. Management must also be able to narrow the gap between the employer and the employee, forcing a flatter organization in the process. This will put management closer to the customer and speed the two-way communication process up and down the organization.

Be in the Information Fast Lane

The traditional role of information technology (IT) as a back office support for accounting and bookkeeping has clearly moved front and centre stage. IT today influences all aspects of business from corporate strategies to organizational structure--and from the very business processes it is designed to support to performance measurement. In a world where the customer is "king," IT must also deliver in two critical areas: sales and marketing and customer service.

Technology was once viewed as a way to reduce costs by replacing people. That attitude has been firmly supplanted by one that seeks IT support for the creative work that all organizations must pursue. IT must allow organizations to react more speedily to market needs and, of course, produce the fulfilment of customer demands both quickly and accurately. To do this IT must operate on a decentralized basis. IT delivers, but it has to be the right information to the right people, and it needs to be done on a timely basis.

Improving the Management Project

Improving Management of NGO and Privately Owned Nature Reserves and High Biodiversity Islands in Seychelles Project funded by the Global Environment Facility through the World Bank

The Seychelles is known world wide as a storehouse of rare biodiversity. Historically, most of the islands and ecosystems have been severely impacted by human activities. Nevertheless, a few examples of whole island ecosystems have been protected and restored. These islands are Cousin, Cousine, Aride, Fregate and Aldabra, all managed, surprisingly, by civil society organisations. Nevertheless, there are significant barriers to sustainability of conservation efforts by these organisations.

The focus of the project is two islands, Cousin and Cousine, which are host to numerous rare and endemic species, and immense biodiversity. These include shared resources such as 10 species of breeding seabirds, 5 species of endemic land birds, rare floral species, 8 species of reptiles and hundreds species of invertebrates, the most important population of hawksbill turtles in the Western Indian Ocean and the highest biomass of reef fish in the granitic islands of Seychelles. The project is to ensure the islands' function as a reserve for the preservation of globally important biodiversity through understanding processes and changes in sites, species and habitats in the islands for better management and decision-making on activities to preserve this globally important biodiversity.

Cousin and Cousine are adjacent to Praslin-the second most populous island of the Seychelles. Cousin was purchased in the 1960's through a world wide appeal at a time when unique biodiversity in Seychelles was in jeopardy. An international NGO held the title to the island because land tenureship was the only method of securing the island for perpetuity and thereby restoring the ecosystems. This NGOs also assisted the previous owners of Cousine in the early years to conserve its biodiversity. This proved to be a very wise move because the islands are remarkable in that unlike other granitic islands of Seychelles, endemic and globally important fauna and flora have been saved.

They have been protected by NGO/private resources and management, and at least for Cousin, through national legislation and policy. The ownership and management regimes by civil society organisations and the relative remoteness, which are the main reasons why biodiversity has been saved, are now proving to be constraints for not only continuing with established activities but also for initiating new programs; the civil society organisations cannot source adequate resources from the local private sector, governmental or international sources. In addition, anthropogenic impacts and lack of knowledge of ecosystem-level changes, all mean that science and conservation action on each of them cannot move beyond present capacity and limits.

The project assumption is that conservation of island biodiversity can be sustained and at the same time greatly improved through an inter-island integrated and collaborative approach geared to clear management outcomes and also to the development of public education and community buy-in. The project recognises the importance of developing financial sustainability to maintain these conservation programs. The project intends to build long-term capacity for sustainable conservation and use of island biodiversity through program and capacity building, infrastructure acquisition and installation, co-management, and education and advocacy.

The two islands are small, close to each other, and share similar and sensitive ecosystems, associated conservation activities and problems. They are both focused on biodiversity conservation, chiefly concerning globally threatened endemic land birds and internationally important colonies of breeding seabirds. Each island also hosts similar important reptile, botanical and invertebrate species. Both islands have a distinguished conservation history and offer a slightly different model and philosophy for biodiversity conservation. Cousin Island is owned by an international NGO but managed by an independent, locally registered, not-for-profit Association. Cousine Island is owned and managed by a private limited company registered in Seychelles. Management of the islands are supposed to be undertaken with in-country resources.

Project Vision

The project will remove barriers that currently prevent civil society organisations from augmenting and enhancing their capacity to conserve and restore species, sites and habitats.

The project will aims to create partnerships between neighbouring islands which have shared globally important biodiversity and similar environmental issues. This will be done through a substantial number of new and improved linked programs, the creation of a common resource and management center, institutional strengthening and capacity building, and public education and advocacy.

The ultimate aim of this model partnership is to catalyze further collaboration and public buy-in, to remove other barriers and to mitigate negative ecosystem changes. The process set in motion by the project will improve the management of high biodiversity islands as well as increase the number of managed conservation sites in Seychelles. This project will thus have global biodiversity benefits, lead to greater sustainability of biodiversity and permit the sharing of these benefits to be directed principally at local levels. The vision mirrors the three principal objectives of the 1992 Convention of Biological Diversity.

Overall Goal of the Project

The Goal of the project is to improve management of biodiversity-rich islands by installing a shared multi-pronged programme framework and infrastructure for enhanced and sustainable conservation, financing and use of biodiversity.

The project vision and overall goal will be delivered through two principal components namely Small Island Ecosystem Management, and Public Education and Advocacy.:.

Component 1: Small Island Ecosystem Management

A. Improved management of terrestrial and marine habitats and important species.

B. Establish collaborative management and resource center on Praslin

C. Institutional strengthening

D. Capacity building and training

Component 2: Public Education and Advocacy

A. Develop biodiversity awareness and advocacy programs

B. Establish community outreach, partnerships and stakeholder participation programs

Project Partners

Nature Seychelles, formerly known as BirdLife Seychelles, is a local not-for-profit association registered in Seychelles. It is currently the largest independent environment organisation in Seychelles. The association is involved in a suite of activities including species and habit conservation, monitoring, research, island restoration, eco-tourism, education and awareness and advocacy.

Nature Seychelles manages Cousin Island Special Reserve and has a presence on several other islands. It has a multi-stakeholder and result-oriented approach through its programs such as the Seychelles Magpie-robin Recovery Team (SMART) and the Seychelles Seabird Group (SSG) as well with other organisations such as the WildLife Clubs of Seychelles, Ministry of Environment and Ministry of Education.

Its donors and partners include the World Bank/GEF and the Royal Society for Protection of Birds. It is a member of the BirdLife International network, WIOMSA, the African Bird Club and IUCN, works in close collaboration with WWF, the Mauritian WildLife Foundation and many others.

Cousine Island LTD (Owner and Manger of Cousine Island): is a private limited company registered in the Seychelles. The company has built a very small and ecologically friendly luxury hotel. The island is not legally protected and the owner is not obliged to conserve its biodiversity. The company has voluntarily put in a system for biodiversity conservation using its own resources. It delegates management responsibility for the island to a Conservation Warden. The Warden works in close collaboration with the hotel manager. The purpose of setting up the small hotel is to bring in sufficient revenues to maintain the conservation and research programs on the island and to maintain it as a high biodiversity area. The company supports other conservation programs in Seychelles, for example the Magpie Robin Recovery Program and the Seychelles Rare Birds Committee.

Landmarks Achievements

Hotel Association of India, established on 24th October 1996, within a short span of less than a decade of its inception, has successfully provided an integrated hospitality platform produced ground breaking results and recorded several notable 'firsts' for the hospitality industry described in the ensuing pages:-

Export House Status for Tourism and Hospitality Industry

Among the path breaking industry 'first' initiatives of Hotel Association of India is the unique recognition secured for tourism and hospitality sectors in India as 'export industries'. This was an unparelled achievement of the Association which undertook the entire groundwork and created consensus in support of according export status for hospitality industries.

HAI organized series of inter-active meetings with the concerned Ministries of the Government of India, culminating in a high level Conclave presided over by Shri Ramakrishna Hegde, then Hon'ble Minister of Commerce, Government of India, on 16th July 1998 at the Oberoi Hotel, New Delhi which cleared the decks for the action plan blue-printed by HAI receiving the official seal of approval of the Government of India manifested in the a Gazette Notification of November 26th, 1998 declaring Hotels and Tourism Units eligible for the benefits of Service Export House/International Service Export House/International Star Service Export House/International Super Star Service Export House categories on the basis of their quantum of foreign exchange earnings. This extraordinary recognition placed hotels and tourism units on par with industries engaged in export of products for imports of projects and products against their foreign exchange entitlements and facilitated hotels in acquiring competitive edge vis-à-vis hotels overseas in providing world class facilities.

Tourism Export Promotion Council

Another notable first for hospitality and tourism industries, synchronizing with the grant of Export House Status, was notched by the Hotel Association of India by formulating the Constitution of the Tourism Export Promotion Council (TEPC) on 20th November 1998. The approval of the Company Law Board was also secured for the new body under Section 25 of the Companies Act 1956. TEPC represented an unique experiment in bringing together for the first time all constituents of the tourism sector-hotels, travel agents, tour operators, transporters, airlines, tourism finance companies-under a single umbrella on a common platform.

Establishment of SAARC Hotel Association

HAI reached beyond the national boundaries to provide regional co-operation aiming hotels in South Asia and became the prime mover in the formation of the SAARC Hotel Association. This was achieved by developing close synergy between the hospitality industry organizations of Bangladesh, Bhutan, India, Maldives, Nepal, Pakistan and Sri Lanka. The SAARC Hotel Association was formally launched at Mumbai on 7th April 1999 with Nepal being assigned the responsibility of hosting the SAARC body for its initial two years and later by rotation by other member countries.

International Code of Conduct to Govern Relations Between Hoteliers, Travel Agents and Tour Operators

For the first time in the history of travel trade in India on 28.4.2000, HAI successfully evolved consensus among the Travel Agents Association of India (TAAI) and the Indian Association of Tour Operators (IATO) and the Hotel Association of India (HAl) resulting in the signing of the International Code of Practice governing the relations between Hoteliers, Travel Agents and Tour Operators. The code represents a watershed for the tourism and travel industry in India, as protracted negotiations for adopting a code of practice for over three decades had not yielded any results till HAl took the lead and crafted consensus in favour of adopting the global practice. It's signing by the three national bodies signalled to the international travel fraternity and business travellers that India had opted for internationally approved policies of hotel bookings, cancellations, refunds, claims etc.

Legal 'First' For Hotel Industry

The Hotel Association of India took the lead in invoking the intervention of the High Court of Delhi in protecting the interests of hospitality industry in India on a matter of vital importance to the hotels as well as to the foreign and domestic tourist staying in hotels. Hotel Association of India filed a writ in the High Court Delhi against an arbitrary and ad'hoc administrative directive requiring the hotels in approved categories, classified by the Ministry of Tourism, to follow a Single Tariff system. The directive would have proved detrimental and counter productive to national tourism interests. The industry perspective presented by HAI was accepted by the High Court of Delhi which granted a Stay in favour of hotel industry, signifying an unique legal validation of hospitality industry system of operation across the country.

Seeking Repeal of Anti-women Legislation

The Punjab Excise Act enacted during the British rule in India in 1914 contains an archaic and anti-women provision prohibiting the employment of women in licenced premises, i.e., bars and restaurants in hotels. The Hotel Association of India challenged the validity of this ancient legislation before the Hon'ble High Court to protect the interest of women. The HAI's Writ against the constitutional validity of the provisions of the Punjab Excise Act, 1914

Media Centric Initiatives

The large number of foreign correspondents stationed in India, representing powerful and popular foreign publications, newspapers, journals, T. V. Channels, Broadcasters play a major role in making or marring the image of India as a peaceful tourists destination country through their news reports and dispatches. HAI took the lead in organizing the first ever hospitality industry meeting with the foreign correspondent stationed in New Delhi. The event was organized with the objective to discuss adverse the impact of Travel Advisories issued by foreign Governments on the State of Indian hospitality and tourism industry and correct their perspective to restore consumer confidence in travel, tourism and hospitality sectors adversely affected by global events of preceding years. Because of the unique nature of the special event and its potential for future tourists arrivals in India, the Ministry of Tourism fully associated with HAI.

Survey on the Impact of Travel Advisories in Hospitality Industry

Foreign Embassies and Missions are often instrumental in advising their respective countries to issue "Travel Advisories" to caution their citizens from undertaking visits to specific countries owing to adverse conditions of safety and security.

Travel Advisories against visiting India were issued by several countries following global events like the terrorist attacks on 9/11 in USA and 13/12 in New Delhi, War in Afghanistan and tension on Indo-Pak borders etc. The adverse travel advisories affected tourists arrivals to India over a prolonged period.

The Hotel Association of India stepped in by organizing an innovative Survey among foreign tourists staying in hotels to obtain their reactions to such advisories issued by the foreign governments.

The HAI Survey brought out that a preponderant majority of tourists declared India as a safe and peaceful destination and foreign travellers viewed the travel advisories and warnings as "coloured by political considerations" and based on "inadequate knowledge of ground realities". Some of them opined that they found New Delhi "safer than Manhattan". HAI Survey facilitated the Governments of the respective countries in reviewing and withdrawing the adverse travel advisories and re-assured tourists of their safety and security in India.

Setting Up of Confederation of Indian Travel and Tourism Industry

Another first initiative mooted by the Association related to the need for creating a Confederation of Indian Travel and Tourism Industry (CITTI) as an umbrella organization to represent all components of the Travel & Travel industry in India. Unlike other industries, there has never been an umbrella organization in the tourism industry. To fill this gap, HAI proposed the setting up of CITTI which would address the policy issues and concerns of the industry. The Constitution of the proposed new body has been drawn up and made available to all sectoral associations to facilitate its establishment in the future.

Study of Tariff System in Hotels

The first ever 'While Paper' on Tariff Systems in Hotels in India, produced by a Central Government Autonomous Organisation the National Institute of Public Finance and Policy (NIPFP), was undertaken at the behest of the Hotel Association of India.

The NIPFP headed by eminent economists of the standing of Dr. Raja J Chelliah, former Chief Economic Advisor of the Government of India and Dr. C. Rangarajan, former Governor of the Reserve Bank of India, provided the Indian hospitality industry with its most appropriate perspective and authentic study of tariff systems.

First Afro-Asian Infotech Hotels Expo

HAI-led initiative resulted in Afro-Asian Region's first Conference-cum-Exposition on Information Technology being institutionalized as 'an annual event in New Delhi for countries in the South Asian Region.

The first Conference-cum-Expo organized by HAl on April 10-11, 2000 at the ITC Maurya Sheraton Hotel, New Delhi received support from the United Nations Economic and Social Commission for Asia and the Pacific, and the SAARC Tourism Council. The Ministries of Tourism and Information Technology, Government of India, extended official support to HAl as Co-sponsors of the event.

Second Afro-Asian Infotech-hotels Expo

The Second Conference-cum-Exposition on Information Technology in Hotels was organized on March 15-16, 2001 at the Taj Palace Hotel, New Delhi.

This Afro-Asian conference was supported by United Nation Economic and Social Commission for Asia and like the front conference the Pacific (UN-ESCAP); Ministry of Tourism, Ministry of Information Technology, Government of India, SAARC Tourism Council and SAARC Hotel Association, Pacific Asia Travel Association (PATA) and International Hotel & Restaurant Association (IH&RA).

Creating a National Network of HAI Chapters

The Hotel Association of India, established in April 1997, enlisted co-operation on a voluntary basis of professional hoteliers in twenty five State and fifty three cities to monitor hospitality related developments to enable the Association to address the concerns of the hospitality industry at the grass-roots level.

Going Global With Knowledge Exchange Partners

Knowledge Exchange partnerships were formed with international organization such as the World Travel and Tourism Council (WTTC); the Pacific Asia Travel Association (PATA); World Tourism Organisation (WTO); the International Hotel and Restaurant Association (IH&RA); the United Nation Economic and Social Commission for Asia and the Pacific (UN-ESCAP); the South Asia Association of Regional Countries (SAARC), the World Health Organisation (WHO) and the European Union's South Asia Integrated Tourism Human Resource Development Programme (EU-SAITHRDP)

Inter-sectoral Linkages with Apex National Fora

At the National level working partnerships were established with apex industry for a like the Federation of Indian Chamber of Commerce and Industry (FICCI); Associated Chamber of Commerce and Industry of India (ASSOCHAM); Confederation of Indian Industry (CII); to provide hospitality industry perspective in the formation of national industrial policies and development.

Affiliation with World Health Organisation (WHO)

HAI's pioneered the concept of 'Healthy Hotels' in line with WHO's 'Healthy Cities' campaign by initiating programmes for the hospitality industry on 'Hygiene Management in Hotels' at Agra in 1997. The WHO representative in India delivered the keynote address at the First Hygiene Management Seminar.

Innovative-"India Quiz Contest" at ITB Berlin 2002

A new promotional first was scored by the HAI at ITB Berlin, held from 16th to 20th March 2002. This was the first time 25 leading Indian hotels were brought together by HAI on the industry net to sponsor prizes of FAM Holiday Tours to Travel Trade visitors at the ITB.

The India Quiz Contest brochure of HAI provided a high visibility to the Indian hospitality industry products among visitor to the ITB, Berlin. The participating hotels received excellent marketing exposure of their properties in the Quiz brochure. This also offered unique opportunities for prospective agents and operator for the familiarization and experience of the hotels.

Guidelines for Provision of Disabled Friendly Facilities in Hotels

The Association undertook a pioneering role in formulating a comprehensive set of Guidelines for provision of Disabled Friendly facilities in Hotels, especially in parking and Approach Areas, Lobbies, Public Areas, Lifts, Rooms, Bathrooms and to install special Fire Prevention measures for the disabled.

Promoting Public-Private Partnership

The Association in a step towards promoting the public-private partnership called upon its members to extend their full corporation to the Archeological Survey of India in the maintenance of the National monuments, which has translated into following public-private sector partnership:-

- (i) Illumination of Humayun's Tomb at Delhi by the Oberoi Group of Hotels.
- (ii) Development of facilities for visitors at the Agra Fort by the ITC Hotels Ltd.
- (iii) Main entrance of the Jantar Mantar observatory at New Delhi by the Apeejay Surrendra Park Hotels Pvt. Ltd.
- (iv) Illumination of the Safdarjung Tomb, New Delhi by the Grand Group of

Special Promotional Packages in Hotels

A major initiative undertaken by HAI galvanized the entire Indian hospitality industry to come together under the Association's banner to offer for the first time in the history of the industry as many as 62 special promotional packages in hotels for marketing averages in association with Air India.

Memorandum of Undertakings Signed With the Hotel Association of Nepal and the Uganda Investment Authority

The Hotel Association of India signed two Memorandum of Understanding which aimed at fostering and promoting tourism in their respective countries by inter alia agreeing to exchange information in respect to development and trend in the fields of tourism, hospitality and hotel sectors and encourage interaction between their respective hotels and Hospitality Association of India for Tourism Promotion and exploring investment opportunities in these sectors.

India Quiz Contest Brochure at 51st PATA Annual Conference

Encouraged by the overwhelming response received from the ITB Berlin, HAI launched its exclusive India Quiz Contest at the 51st PATA Annual Conference held in New Delhi from 14.04.2002 to 18.04.2002 offering opportunities of FAM Holiday in 14 leading Hotels.

Study Project on Management of Cross-cultural Tourists Movements in Hospitality Sector

HAI initiated a study project on Management of cross-cultural tourism movements in hospitality sector to assess and promote awareness among staff in smaller hotel and upgrade their knowledge and skills for handling of foreign tourists.

Grant of Fiscal Benefits to the Hospitality Industry

For the first time the tourism industry's aspirations elaborated in the Hotel Association of India's various memoranda to the Central Government were translated into "tourism-friendly", measures in the Union Budget of 2003-04. These measures were aimed at making India more affordable destination, fuelling growth of hospitality infrastructure, facilitating business re-organisation, re-structuring hospitality industry and motivating State Governments to rationalize tourism tax regime. The major incentives extended to hospitality industries included and exemption of Service tax in hotels relating to Conference and Banquet business, which have been excluded from the service tax net.

Encouraging Investments

Hotel Association of India orchestrated the strategy leading to announcement in the Union Budget 2003 of benefits under Section 10(23) (g) on loans to hotels (3 star and above categories) for increasing the availability of funds for the hotel industry.

This provision has allowed lending institutions to make available funds to hotel projects at reduced rates of interest. The financial institutions will get a tax break on the interest income they earn on loans extended to such borrowers. Inclusion of finance to the hotel projects of three star category and above for the first time under Section 10 (23)(g) of the Income Tax Act "signals" the positioning of hotels on the threshold of securing full infrastructure status as granted to other industries. HAI is now carrying this agenda forward to securing the wider benefits of infrastructure under Section 84 I/A of Income Tax Act.

Restructuring Hospitality Business

Amalgamation and Merger

It is at the behest of HAI that the Finance Ministry constituted a Working group under Chief Commissioner of Income Tax Mumbai which recommended the grant of benefits under Section 72 A of the Income Tax Act (which relates to the set-off of accumulated losses and depreciation on amalgamation), for the hotel industry to help loss-making hotel companies in re-organising their business.

The facility of mergers and acquisitions was hitherto available only to industrial undertakings and manufacturing units. With its extension to hotel companies, it has facilitated moves towards consolidation with the hospitality industry and releasing of resources blocked in non-performing assets.

This measure has now enabled smaller hotel units to enter into franchisee arrangements with established hotel groups/ chains which in turn has led to improvements in occupancy levels and service standards.

Zero Duty Facility for Imports by Hotels

HAI pursued with the Ministry of Commerce, Government of India for grant of the zero duty import facility to hotels and stand alone restaurants. The Industry has now been granted under the "Served from India Scheme", the zero duty facility to all hotels including one star, two star hotels for import of food items and alcoholic beverages sell which would make India an affordable destination.

HAI Directory of Hotels Going Global

The exclusive HAI Directory of Hotels is an annual publication promoted with a singular aim of fulfilling the promotional need for tourists and visitor coming to India for an authentic compendium of leading Indian hotels recognized by the Ministry of Tourism. For the first time in 2005 the Directory was utilized by the Ministry of Tourism for distribution among foreign travel agents and tour operators in 12 countries through the Government of India's Tourist Offices abroad.

World Tourism Day Celebartion

A new promotional first was scored by HAI for creating awareness about the World Tourism Day on 27th Sept. 2005 amongst not only the member-hotels but also the school children. To encourage and facilitate the member-hotels in celebrating the World Tourism Day on 27th September 2005, HAI outlined a bouquet of activities to be organized by the member-hotels. The member-hotels came forward in large numbers and organized the activities with enthusiasm and excitement. In New Delhi, HAI collaborated with the Sanskriti School to launch a Quiz Contest on Tourism for school children on the World Tourism Day.

Members Services

Variety of professional member-services are provided by HAI to its members these include:-

(i) INFORMATION BULLETINS sent out regularly with updates on latest developments concerning hotel industries, policy changes and pronouncements by

Ministry of Tourism, Ministry of Finance, Ministry of Commerce, CBEC, CBDT, State Governments and affiliate international organizations such as WTTC, IH&RA, WTO etc.;

(ii) HAI TODAY-the first hospitality industry magazine of its kind in India;

(iii) HAI DIRECTORY OF HOTELS-an exclusive high quality reference manual of recognized hotels in India;

(iv) HAI PRIVILEGE CARDS which are offered to members in the Gold and Silver Categories entitling them to discounts on hotel room tariffs and restaurants outlets in all member hotels on reciprocal basis;

(v) HAI LEGAL SERVICES which enables members to avail benefits of highest calibre legal advice on issues of concern them and interventions on their behalf in courts.

Green Weeks of the HAI

HAI has successfully institutionalized the concept of celebrating annual green weeks in hotels to exhibit its commitment to conservation of environment through use of bio-degradable and environment-friendly products by efficient management of waste generated and by adopting measures for efficient utilization of day light to conserve upon electricity etc. HAI has this year celebrated its ninth annual green week, reaching out to large number of tourists, employees, their families, school children and society with its environment message.

Fundamentals Of Revenue Management Will Be Revealed In A Special Report Commissioned By HSMAI Special Interest Group

MCLEAN, VA The Hospitality Sales & Marketing Association International (HSMAI) Revenue Management Special Interest Group has taken on an ambitious project to produce the first-ever comprehensive "Fundamentals of Revenue Management" special report.

The report will be a practitioner-friendly publication that

addresses the fundamentals of revenue management for a broad audience of hospitality professionals. With comprehensive content that is both readable and actionable, it will deliver tools and information for revenue management education, incorporating expert advice from interviews with industry executives and educators, case studies, and practical checklists for implementing successful revenue management strategies at the property level.

"Creating relevance for members and the industry at large through ground-breaking initiatives such as this Revenue Management Special Report is in keeping with HSMAI's mission to be the leading source for sales and marketing information, knowledge and business development for professionals in tourism, travel, and hospitality," states Robert A. Gilbert, CHME, CHA, president and CEO of HSMAI.

"We are very excited about this debut project, and expect it will be a springboard for other initiatives including certification and revenue management research," notes Tim Wiersma, vice president of revenue management for Host Marriott and chair of HSMAI's Revenue Management Tangible Resources Committee.

The publication will be produced in a manner similar to the recent special report produced by HSMAI and TIG Global entitled DeMystifying Distribution, widely praised by the industry for its insight, accuracy and comprehensive coverage of the topic.

The commissioned report, which will be released at the third annual HSMAI Revenue Management Strategy Conference on June 19, 2005 in Minneapolis, will be co-authored by Caryl Helsel and Kathleen Cullen of the Solutionz Group, a business development and strategic consulting group based in Florida. Helsel heads the hospitality practice and previously held executive positions with Kimpton Hotels, Pegasus Solutions and Mandarin Oriental Hotel Group, and is the former president of the Hotel Electronic Distribution Network Association (HEDNA). Cullen is a lead consultant on the hospitality team and is a hospitality revenue management and distribution veteran, holding executive positions with Swissotel and Raffles Hotels, as well as past vice president of HEDNA. Delving deep into the fundamentals, nuances and specifics of revenue management, the special report will address the following:

- Ideas and initiatives to maximize revenue opportunities, optimize profits by managing revenues and develop an infrastructure (strategies, policies, procedures, reports, etc.) to make informed decisions about accepting or rejecting business.
- An overview of the external market such as segmentation, demand forecasting, revenue strategy, operational forecast, interdepartmental integration, strategic pricing, inventory control strategies and internal performance analysis.
- Tactics including rate-level maintenance, inventory management and rate offer assessment (for group and negotiated rates).
- The optimal environment, characteristics and descriptors.

The Revenue Management Special Interest Group is made up of a group of HSMAI members who advance the revenue management discipline through education, certification, participation, resources and guidance, enabling leaders to optimize revenue and performance within their own organizations. The SIG Advisory Board includes corporate revenue management executives from Accor North America, Destination Hotels & Resorts, Host Marriott Corporation, Hilton Hotels, InterContinental Hotels Group, Outrigger Hotels & Resorts, Peabody Hotels, Preferred Hotel Group, and TravelCLICK.

Among the Board's strategic intentions are:

- Provide education on all levels through programs, events, and an annual strategy conference as well as provide education for senior executives through publications, press releases and conference participation.
- Develop and manage a revenue management certification program.
- Develop a sense of community and participation.

- Provide tangible resources through a fundamentals publication that defines the discipline of revenue management and includes a glossary of terms, maintain a website portal, create a self-auditing system and encourage industry internships.

India's Role in the World of Tourism

Tourism in India

Tourism is the largest service industry in India, with a contribution of 6.23% to the national GDP and 8.78% of the total employment in India. India witnesses more than 5 million annual foreign tourist arrivals and 562 million domestic tourism visits. The tourism industry in India generated about US$100 billion in 2008 and that is expected to increase to US$275.5 billion by 2018 at a 9.4% annual growth rate. The Ministry of Tourism is the nodal agency for the development and promotion of tourism in India and maintains the "Incredible India" campaign.

According to *World Travel and Tourism Council,* India will be a tourism hotspot from 2009-2018, having the highest 10-year growth potential. The *Travel & Tourism Competitiveness Report 2007* ranked tourism in India 6th in terms of price competitiveness and 39th in terms of safety and security. Despite short-and medium-term setbacks, such as shortage of hotel rooms, tourism revenues are expected to surge by 42% from 2007 to 2017. India has a growing medical tourism sector. The 2010 Commonwealth Games in Delhi are expected to significantly boost tourism in India.

Tourism by State

Andhra Pradesh

Andhra Pradesh has a rich cultural heritage and a variety of tourist attractions. The state of Andhra Pradesh comprises scenic hills, forests, beaches and temples. Also known as *The City of Nizams* and *The City of Pearls,* Hyderabad is today one of the most developed cities in the country and a modern hub of information technology, ITES, and biotechnology. Hyderabad is known for its rich history, culture and architecture representing its unique character as a meeting point for North and South India, and also its multilingual culture, both geographically and culturally.

Andhra Pradesh is the home of many religious pilgrim centres. Tirupati, the abode of Lord Venkateswara, is the richest and most visited religious centre (of any faith) in the world. Srisailam, the abode of Sri Mallikarjuna, is one of twelve Jyothirlingalu in India, Amaravati's Siva temple is one of the Pancharamams, and Yadagirigutta, the abode of an avatara of Vishnu, Sri Lakshmi Narasimha. The Ramappa temple and Thousand Pillars temple in Warangal are famous for some fine temple carvings. The state has numerous Buddhist centres at Amaravati, Nagarjuna Konda, Bhattiprolu, Ghantasala, Nelakondapalli, Dhulikatta, Bavikonda, Thotlakonda, Shalihundam, Pavuralakonda, Sankaram, Phanigiri and Kolanpaka.

The golden beaches at Visakhapatnam, the one-million-year old limestone caves at Borra, picturesque Araku Valley, hill resorts of Horsley Hills, river Godavari racing through a narrow gorge at Papi Kondalu, waterfalls at Ettipotala, Kuntala and rich biodiversity at Talakona, are some of the natural attractions of the state. Visakhapatnam is home to many tourist attactions such as the INS Karasura Submarine museum (The only one of its kind in India), Yarada Beach, Araku Valley, VUDA Park, Indira Gandhi Zoological Gardens. The weather in Andhra Pradesh is mostly tropical and the best time to visit is in November through to January. The monsoon season commences in June and ends in September, so travel would not be advisable during this period.

Assam

Assam is the central state in the North-East Region of India and serves as the gateway to the rest of the Seven Sister States. Assam boasts of famous wildlife preserves – the Kaziranga National Park (*pictured*) and the Manas National Park, the largest river island Majuli, and tea-estates dating back to time of British Raj. The weather is mostly sub-tropical. Assam experiences the Indian monsoon and has one of the highest forest densities in India. The winter months (October to April) are the best time to visit. Assam has a rich cultural heritage going back to the Ahom Kingdom which governed the region for many centuries before the British occupation.

Other notable features include the Brahmaputra River, the mystery of the bird suicides in Jatinga, numerous temples including Kamakhya of Tantric sect, ruins of palaces, etc. Guwahati, the capital city of Assam, boasts many bazaars, temples, and wildlife sanctuaries.

Bihar

Bihar is one of the oldest continuously inhabited places in the world with history of 3000 years. The rich culture and heritage of Bihar is evident from the innumerable ancient monuments that are dotted all over this state in eastern India. This is the Place of Aryabhatta, Great Ashoka, Chanakya and many more.

Bihar is one of the most sacred places of various religions such as Hinduism, Buddhism, Jainism, Sikhism & Islam. Famous Attraction includes Mahabodhi Temple, a Buddhist shrine and UNESCO World Heritage Site is also situated in Bihar, Barabar Caves the oldest rockcut caves in India, Khuda Bakhsh Oriental Library the Oldest Library of India.

Delhi

Delhi is the capital city of India. A fine blend of old and new, ancient and modern, Delhi is a melting pot of cultures, religions. Delhi has been the capital of numerous empires that ruled India, making it rich in history. The rulers left behind their trademark architectural styles. Delhi currently has many renowned historic monuments and landmarks such as the Tughlaqabad fort, Qutub Minar, Purana Quila, Lodhi Gardens, Jama Masjid, Humayun's tomb, Red Fort, and Safdarjung's Tomb. Modern monuments include Jantar Mantar, India Gate, Rashtrapati Bhavan, Laxminarayan Temple, Lotus temple and Akshardham Temple.

New Delhi is famous for its British colonial architecture, wide roads, and tree-lined boulevards. Delhi is home to numerous political landmarks, national museums, Islamic shrines, Hindu temples, green parks, and trendy malls.

Goa

Goa is one of the most famous tourist destinations in India. A former colony of Portugal, Goa is famous for its excellent beaches, Portuguese churches, Hindu temples, and wildlife sanctuaries. The Basilica of Bom Jesus, Mangueshi Temple, Dudhsagar Falls, and Shantadurga are famous attractions in Goa. Recently a Wax Museum (Wax World) has also opened in Old Goa housing a number of wax personalities of Indian history, culture and heritage.

The Goa Carnival is a world famous event, with coloruful masks and floats, drums and reverberating music, and dance performances. The celebrations run three days culminating in a carnival parade on fat Tuesday.

Himachal Pradesh

Himachal Pradesh is famous for its Himalayan landscapes and popular hill-stations. Many outdoor activities such as rock climbing, mountain biking, paragliding, ice-skating, and heli-skiing are popular tourist attractions in Himachal Pradesh.

Shimla, the state capital, is very popular among tourists. The Kalka-Shimla Railway is a Mountain railway which is a UNESCO World Heritage Site. Shimla is also a famous skiing attraction in India. Other popular hill stations include Manali and Kasauli.

Dharamshala, home of the Dalai Lama, is known for its Tibetan monasteries and Buddhist temples. Many trekking expeditions also begin here.

Jammu and Kashmir

Jammu and Kashmir is the northernmost state of India. Jammu is noted for its scenic landscape, ancient temples, Hindu shrines, castles, gardens, and forts. The Hindu holy shrines of Amarnath and Vaishno Devi attract tens of thousands of Hindu devotees every year. Jammu's natural landscape has made it one of the popular destinations for adventure tourism in South Asia. Jammu's historic monuments feature a unique blend of Islamic and Hindu architecture styles.

Tourism forms an integral part of the Kashmiri economy. Often dubbed "Paradise on Earth", Kashmir's mountainous landscape has attracted tourists for centuries. Notable places are Dal Lake, Srinagar Phalagam, Gulmarg, Yeusmarg and Mughal Gardens etc. However, the tourism industry is severely affected by the insurgency. In recent years, Ladakh has emerged as a major hub for adventure tourism. This part of Greater Himalaya called "moon on earth" comprising of naked peaks and deep gorges was once known for the silk route to High Asia from the subcontinent. Leh is also a growing tourist spot.

Karnataka

Karnataka has been ranked as fourth most popular destination for tourism among states of India. It has the second highest number of protected monuments in India, at 507.

Kannada dynasties like Kadambas, Western Gangas, Chalukyas, Rashtrakutas, Hoysalas and Vijayanagaras, ruled Karnataka particularly North Karnataka. They built great monuments to Buddhism, Jainism, Shaivism.

The monuments are still present at Badami, Aihole, Pattadakal, Hampi, Lakshmeshwar, Sudi, Hooli, Mahadeva Temple (Itagi), Dambal, Lakkundi, Gadag, Hangal, Halasi, Galaganatha, Chaudayyadanapura, Banavasi, Belur, Halebidu, Shravanabelagola, Sannati and many more. Notable Islamic monuments are present at Bijapur, Bidar, Gulbarga, Raichur and other part of the state. Gol Gumbaz at Bijapur, has the second largest pre-modern dome in the world after the Byzantine Hagia Sophia. Karnataka has two World heritage sites, at Hampi and Pattadakal, both are in North Karnataka.

Karnataka is famous for its waterfalls. Jog falls of Shimoga District is one of the highest waterfalls in Asia. This state has 21 wildlife sanctuaries and five National parks and is home to more than 500 species of birds. Karnataka has many beaches at Karwar, Gokarna, Murdeshwara, Surathkal. Karnataka is a rock climbers paradise. Yana in Uttara Kannada, Fort in Chitradurga, Ramnagara near Bangalore district, Shivagange in Tumkur district and tekal in Kolar district are a rock climbers heaven.

Kerala

Kerala is a state on the tropical Malabar Coast of southwestern India. Nicknamed as one of the " *paradises of the world"* by National Geographic, Kerala is famous especially for its ecotourism initiatives. Its unique culture and traditions, coupled with its varied demography, has made it one of the most popular tourist destinations in India. Growing at a rate of 13.31%, the tourism industry significantly contributes to the state's economy. Kerala, a state situated on the tropical Malabar Coast of southwestern India, is one of the most popular tourist destinations in the country. Named as one of the *ten paradises of the world* by the National Geographic Traveller, Kerala is famous especially for its ecotourism initiatives. Its unique culture and traditions, coupled with its varied demography, has made Kerala one of the most popular tourist destinations in the world. Growing at a rate of 13.31%, the tourism industry is a major contributor to the state's economy.

Until the early 1980s, Kerala was a hitherto unknown destination, with most tourism circuits concentrated around the north of the country. Aggressive marketing campaigns launched by the Kerala Tourism Development Corporation—the government agency that oversees tourism prospects of the state—laid the foundation for the growth of the tourism industry.

In the decades that followed, Kerala Tourism was able to transform itself into one of the niche holiday destinations in India. The tag line *Kerala-God's Own Country* was adopted in its tourism promotions and became synonymous with the state. Today, Kerala Tourism is a global superbrand and regarded as one of the destinations with the highest brand recall. In 2006, Kerala attracted 8.5 million tourists–an increase of 23.68% in foreign tourist arrivals compared to the previous year, thus making it one of the fastest growing tourism destination in the world.

Popular attractions in the state include the beaches at Kovalam, Cherai and Varkala; the hill stations of Munnar, Nelliampathi, Ponmudi and Wayanad; and national parks and wildlife sanctuaries at Periyar and Eravikulam National Park.

The "backwaters" region—an extensive network of interlocking rivers, lakes, and canals that centre on Alleppey, Kumarakom, and Punnamada—also see heavy tourist traffic. Heritage sites, such as the Padmanabhapuram Palace, Hill Palace, Mattancherry Palace are also visited. Cities such as Kochi and Thiruvananthapuram are popular centres for shopping and traditional theatrical performances.

The state's tourism agenda promotes ecologically sustained tourism, which focuses on the local culture, wilderness adventures, volunteering and personal growth of the local population. Efforts are taken to minimise the adverse effects of traditional tourism on the natural environment, and enhance the cultural integrity of local people.

Historical Context

Since its incorporation as a state, Kerala's economy largely operated under welfare-based democratic socialist principles. This mode of development, though resulted in a high Human Development Index and standard of living among the people, lead to an economic stagnation in the 1980s (growth rate of 2.3% annually) This apparent paradox – high human development and low economic development – lead to a large number of educated unemployed seeking jobs overseas, especially in the Gulf countries. Due to the large number of expatriates, many travel operators and agencies set shop in the state to felicitate their travel needs. However, the trends soon reciprocated with the travel agencies noticing the undermined potential of the state as a tourist destination.

By 1986, tourism had gained an industry status. Kerala Tourism subsequently adopted the tagline *God's Own Country* in its advertisement campaigns. Aggressive promotion in print and electronic media were able to invite a sizable investment in the hospitality industry. By the early 2000s, tourism had grown into a fully fledged, multi-billion dollar industry in the state. The state was able to carve a niche place for itself in the world tourism industry, thus becoming one of the places with the 'highest brand recall'. In 2003, Kerala, a hitherto unknown tourism destination, became the fastest growing tourism destination in the world. Today, growing at a rate of 13.31%, Kerala is one of the most visited tourism destinations in India.

Major Attractions

Beaches

Kovalam beach near Thiruvananthapuram was among the first beaches in Kerala to attract tourists. Rediscovered by back-packers and tan-seekers in the sixties and followed by hordes of hippies in the seventies, Kovalam is today the most visited tourist destination in the state.

Other popularly visited beaches in the state include those at Alappuzha Beach, Nattika beach [Thrissur], Vadanappilly beach [Thrissur], Cherai Beach, Kappad, Kovalam, Marari beach, Fort Kochi and Varkala. The Muzhappilangad Beach beach at Kannur is the only drive-in beach in India.

Backwaters

The backwaters in Kerala are a chain of brackish lagoons and lakes lying parallel to the Arabian Sea coast (known as the Malabar Coast). Kettuvallam (Kerala houseboats) in the backwaters are one of the prominent tourist attractions in Kerala. Alleppey, known as the "Venice of the East" has a large network of canals that meander through the town. The Vallam Kali (the Snake Boat Race) held every year in August is a major sporting attraction.

The backwater network includes five large lakes (including Ashtamudi Kayal and Vembanad Kayal) linked by 1500 km of canals, both manmade and natural, fed by 38 rivers, and extending virtually the entire length of Kerala state. The backwaters were formed by the action of waves and shore currents creating low barrier islands across the mouths of the many rivers flowing down from the Western Ghats range.

Hill Stations

Eastern Kerala consists of land encroached upon by the Western Ghats; the region thus includes high mountains, gorges, and deep-cut valleys. The wildest lands are covered with dense forests, while other regions lie under tea and coffee plantations (established mainly in the 19th and 20th centuries) or other forms of cultivation. The Western Ghats rises on average to 1500 m elevation above sea level. Certain peaks may reach to 2500 m. Popular hill stations in the region include Devikulam, Munnar, Nelliyampathi, Peermade, Ponmudi, Vagamon, Wayanad and Kottanchery Hills.

Wildlife

Most of Kerala, whose native habitat consists of wet evergreen rainforests at lower elevations and highland deciduous and semi-evergreen forests in the east, is subject to a humid tropical climate, however, significant variations in terrain and elevation have resulted in a land whose biodiversity registers as among the world's most significant. Most of Kerala's significantly biodiverse tracts of wilderness lie in the evergreen forests of its easternmost districts. Kerala also hosts two of the world's Ramsar Convention-listed wetlands: Lake Sasthamkotta and the Vembanad-Kol wetlands are noted as being wetlands of international importance. There are also numerous protected conservation areas, including 1455.4 km² of the vast Nilgiri Biosphere Reserve. In turn, the forests play host to such major fauna as Asian Elephant (*Elephas maximus*), Bengal Tiger (*Panthera tigris tigris*), Leopard (*Panthera pardus*), and Nilgiri Tahr (*Nilgiritragus hylocrius*), and Grizzled Giant Squirrel (*Ratufa macroura*). More remote preserves, including Silent Valley National Park in the Kundali Hills, harbour endangered species such as Lion-tailed Macaque (*Macaca silenus*), Indian Sloth Bear (*Melursus (Ursus) ursinus ursinus*), and Gaur (the so-called "Indian Bison" — *Bos gaurus*). More common species include Indian Porcupine (*Hystrix indica*), Chital (*Axis axis*), Sambar (*Cervus unicolor*), Gray Langur, Flying Squirrel, Swamp Lynx (*Felis chaus kutas*), Boar (*Sus scrofa*), a variety of catarrhine Old World monkey species, Gray Wolf (*Canis lupus*), Common Palm Civet (*Paradoxurus hermaphroditus*). Many reptiles, such as king cobra, viper, python, various turtles and crocodiles are to be found in Kerala — again, disproportionately in the east. Kerala's avifauna include endemics like the Sri Lanka Frogmouth (*Batrachostomus moniliger*), Oriental Bay Owl, large frugivores like the Great Hornbill (*Buceros bicornis*) and Indian

Grey Hornbill, as well as the more widespread birds such as Peafowl, Indian Cormorant, Jungle and Hill Myna, Oriental Darter, Black-hooded Oriole, Greater Racket-tailed and Black Drongoes, bulbul (*Pycnonotidae*), species of Kingfisher and Woodpecker, Jungle Fowl, Alexandrine Parakeet, and assorted ducks and migratory birds. Additionally, freshwater fish such as *kadu* (stinging catfish — *Heteropneustes fossilis*) and brackishwater species such as *Choottachi* (orange chromide — *Etroplus maculatus*; valued as an aquarium specimen) also are native to Kerala's lakes and waterways.

Festivals

The major festival in Kerala is Onam. Kerala has a number of religious festivals. Thrissur Pooram and Chettikulangara Bharani are the major temple festivals in Kerala. The Thrissur Pooram is conducted at the Vadakumnathan temple, Thrissur. The Chettikulangara Bharani is another major attraction. The festival is conducted at the Chettikulangara temple near Mavelikkara. Parumala Perunnal, Manarkadu Perunnal are the major festivals of Christians. Muslims also have many important festivals.

Radiation Tourism

Karunagappally Taluk Karunagappalli, Places of Interest in Kollam District is the world's hottest spot of natural radiation. The radiation is caused by monazite sands which contain the radioactive element, thorium. The people in the area are exposed to radiation which is 10 times greater than the worldwide average. Tourist spots that offer the chance of the Radiation experience are very rare in the world.

Ayurveda

Medical tourism, promoted by traditional systems of medicine like Ayurveda and Siddha are widely popular in the state, and draws increasing numbers of tourists. A combination of many factors has led to the increase in popularity of medical tourism: high costs of healthcare in industrialised nations, ease and affordability of international travel, improving technology and standards of care.

However, rampant recent growth in this sector has made the government apprehensive. The government is now considering introduction of a grading system which would grade hospitals and clinics, thus helping tourists in selecting one for their treatments.

Culture

Kerala's culture is mainly Dravidian in origin, deriving from a greater Tamil-heritage region known as Tamilakam. Later, Kerala's culture was elaborated on through centuries of contact with overseas cultures. Native performing arts include *koodiyattom, kathakali* – from *katha* ("story") and *kali* ("play") – and its offshoot *Kerala natanam, koothu* (akin to stand-up comedy), *mohiniaattam* ("dance of the enchantress"), *thullal, padayani,* and *theyyam.* Other arts are more religion-and tribal-themed. These include *chavittu nadakom, oppana* (originally from Malabar), which combines dance, rhythmic hand clapping, and *ishal* vocalisations. However, many of these artforms largely play to tourists or at youth festivals, and are not as popular among most ordinary Keralites. These people look to more contemporary art and performance styles, including those employing mimicry and parody. Additionally, a substantial Malayalam film industry effectively competes against both Bollywood and Hollywood.

Several ancient ritualised arts are Keralite in origin; these include *kalaripayattu* (*kalari* ("place", "threshing floor", or "battlefield") and *payattu* ("exercise" or "practice")). Among the world's oldest martial arts, oral tradition attributes *kalaripayattu*'s emergence to Parasurama. Other ritual arts include *theyyam, poorakkali* and *Kuthiyottam.*

Kuthiyottam is a ritualistic symbolic representation of human bali (homicide). Folklore exponents see this art form, with enchanting well structured choreography and songs, as one among the rare Adi Dravida folklore traditions still preserved and practiced in Central Kerala in accordance to the true tradition and environment. Typical to the Adi Dravida folk dances and songs, the movements and formations of dancers (clad in white thorthu and banyan) choreographed in Kuthiyottam are quick, peaks at a particular point and ends abruptly. The traditional songs also start in a stylish slow pace, then gain momentum and ends abruptly.

Kuthiyotta Kalaris', run by Kuthiyotta Asans (Teachers or leaders), train the group to perform the dances and songs. Normally, the training starts about one to two months before the season. Young boys between 8 to 14 years are taught Kuthiyottam, a ritual dance in the house amidst a big social gathering before the portrait of the deity. Early in the morning on Bharani, after the feast and other rituals, the boys whose bodies are coiled with silver wires, one end of which is tied around his neck and an arecanut fixed on the tip of a knife held high over his head are taken in procession to the temple with the accompaniment of beating of drums, music, ornamental umbrellas, and other classical folk art forms, and richly caparisoned elephants.

All through the way to the temple tender coconut water will be continually poured on his body. After the circumambulation the boys stands at a position facing the Sreekovil (Sanctum Sanctorum) and begins to dance. This ceremony ends with dragging the coil pierced to the skin whereby a few drops of blood comes out.

On this day just after midday the residents of the locality bring huge decorated effigies of Bhima panchalia, Hanuman and extremely beautiful tall chariots in wheeled platforms, and after having darshan the parties take up their respective position in the paddy fields lying east of the temple.

During the night, the image of Devi will be carried in procession to the effigies stationed in the paddy fields. On the next day these structures will be taken back. A big bazaar is also held at Chetikulangara as part of this festival. Kuthiyottam is the main vazipadu of the Chettikulangara temple, Mavelikkara.

In respect of Fine Arts, the State has an abounding tradition of both ancient and contemporary art and artists. The traditional Kerala murals are found in ancient temples, churches and palaces across the State. These paintings, mostly dating back between the 9th to 12th centuries AD, display a distinct style, and a colour code which is predominantly ochre and green.

Like the rest of India, religious diversity is very prominent in Kerala. The principal religions are Hinduism, Christianity, and Islam; Jainism, Judaism, Sikhism, and Buddhism have smaller followings. The states historic ties with the rest of the world has resulted in the state having many famous temples, churches, and mosques. The Paradesi Synagogue in Kochi is the oldest in the Commonwealth of Nations.

Recognising the potential of tourism in the diversity of religious faiths, related festivals and structures, the tourism department launched a *Pilgrimage tourism* project.

Major pilgrim tourism attractions include Guruvayur, Sabarimala, Malayatoor, Paradesi Synagogue, St. Mary's Forane (Martha Mariam) Church Kuravilangad built in 105 A.D, Attukal Ponkal and Chettikulangara Bharani.

Advertising Campaigns

Kerala Tourism is noted for its innovative and market-focused ad campaigns. These campaigns have won the tourism department numerous awards, including the *Das Golden Stadttor Award for Best Commercial, 2006, Pacific Asia Travel Association-Gold Award for Marketing, 2003* and the Government of India's *Best Promotion Literature, 2004, Best Publishing, 2004* and *Best Tourism Film, 2001.*

Catchy slogans and innovative designs are considered a trademark of brand Kerala Tourism. Celebrity promotions are also used to attract more tourists to the state. The Kerala tourism website is widely visited, and has been the recipient of many awards. Recently, the tourism department has also engaged in advertising via mobiles, by setting up a WAP portal, and distributing wallpapers and ringtones related to Kerala through it.

Threats to the Tourism Industry

With increasing threats posed by global warming and changing weather patterns, it is feared that much of Kerala's low lying areas might be susceptible to beach erosions and coastal flooding. The differing monsoon patterns also suggest possible tropical cyclones in the future.

Awards

The state has won numerous awards for its tourism initiatives. These include:

- 2005-Nominated as one among the three finalists at the World Travel and Tourism Council's 'Tourism for Tomorrow' awards in the destination category.
- Das Golden Stadttor Award for Best Commercial, 2006

Pacific Asia Travel Association;

- Grand award for Environment, 2006
- Gold award for Ecotourism, 2006
- Gold award for Publication, 2006
- Gold Award for E-Newsletter, 2005
- Honourable Mention for Culture, 2005
- Gold Award for Culture, 2004
- Gold Award for Ecotourism, 2004
- Gold Award for CD-ROM, 2004 and 2003
- Gold Award for Marketing, 2003
- Grand Award for Heritage, 2002

Pacific Asia Travel Writers Association;

- International Award for Leisure Tourism, 2000–2001.

Government of India;

- Best Performing Tourism State, 2005
- Best Maintained Tourist-friendly Monument, 2005
- Best Publishing, 2005
- Best Marketed and Promoted State, 2004.
- Best Maintained Tourist-friendly Monument, 2004
- Best Innovative Tourism Project, 2004
- Best Promotion Literature, 2004
- Best Publishing, 2004
- Best Performing State for 2003, 2001, 2000 and 1999- Award for Excellence in Tourism.

- Best Practices by a State Government, 2003
- Best Eco-tourism Product, 2003
- Best Wildlife Sanctuary, 2003
- Most Innovative Use of Information Technology, 2003 and 2001
- Most Tourist-friendly International Airport, 2002
- Most Eco-friendly Destination, 2002
- Best Tourism Film, 2001.

Outlook Traveller – TAAI;

- Best State that promoted Travel & Tourism, 2000–2001.

Federation of Indian Chambers of Commerce and Industry;

- Award for Best Marketing, 2003
- Award for Best Use of IT in Tourism, 2003.

Galileo-Express Travel & Tourism;

- Award for the Best Tourism Board, 2006
- Award for the Best State Tourism Board, 2003.

Madhya Pradesh

Madhya Pradesh is called the "*Heart of India*" because of its location in the centre of the country. It has been home to the cultural heritage of Hinduism, Islam, Buddhism, Sikhism, Jainism. Innumerable monuments, exquisitely carved temples, stupas, forts and palaces are dotted all over the State.

The temples of Khajuraho are world-famous for their erotic sculptures, and are a UNESCO World Heritage Site. Gwalior is famous for its forts, the Tomb of Rani Lakshmibai, and the Palace of Tansen.

Madhya Pradesh is also known as *Tiger State* because of the tiger population. Famous national parks like Kanha, Bandhavgadh, Shivpuri, Sanjay, Pench are located in MP. Spectacular mountain ranges, meandering rivers and miles and miles of dense forests offering a unique and exciting panorama of wildlife in sylvan surroundings.

Maharashtra

Maharashtra is the second most visited state in India by foreign tourists, with more than 2 million foreign tourists arrivals annually. Maharashtra boasts of a large number of popular and revered religious venues that are heavily frequented by locals as well as out-of-state visitors.

Ajanta Caves, Ellora Caves and Victoria Terminus are the three UNESCO World Heritage sites in Maharashtra and are highly responsible for the development of Tourism in the state. Mumbai is the most cosmopolitan city in India, and a great place to experience modern India.

Mumbai famous for Bollywood, the world's largest film industry. In addition, Mumbai is famous for its clubs, shopping, and upscale gastronomy. The city is known for its architecture, from the ancient Elephanta Caves, to the Islamic Haji Ali Mosque, to the colonial architecture of Bombay High Court and Victoria Terminus.

Maharashtra also has numerous adventure tourism destinations, including paragliding, rock climbing, canoeing, kayaking, snorkelling, and scuba diving. Maharashtra also has several pristine national parks and reserves. The Bibi Ka Maqbara at Aurangabad the Mahalakshmi temple at Kolhapur, the cities of Nashik, Trimbak famous for religious importance and the city of Pune the seat of the Maratha Empire and the fantastic Ganesh Chaturthi celebrations together contribute for the Tourism sector of Mahrashtra.

Orissa

Orissa has been a preferred destination from ancient days for people who have an interest in spirituality, religion, culture, art and natural beauty. Ancient and medieval architecture, pristine sea beaches, the classical and ethnic dance forms and a variety of festivals.

Orissa has kept the religion of Buddhism alive. Rock-edicts that have challenged time stand huge and over-powering by the banks of the river Daya. The torch of Buddhism is still ablaze in the sublime triangle at Udayagiri and Khandagiri Caves, on the banks of river Birupa. Precious fragments of a glorious past come alive in the shape of stupas, rock-cut caves, rock-edicts, excavated monasteries, viharas, chaityas and sacred relics in caskets and the Rock-edicts of Ashoka. Orissa is also famous for its well-preserved Hindu Temples, especially the Konark Sun Temple.

Orissa is the home for various tribal communities who have contributed uniquely to the multicultural and multilingual character of the state. Their handicrafts, different dance forms, jungle products and their unique life style blended with their healing practices have got world wide attention.

Puducherry

The Union Territory of Puducherry comprises four coastal regions viz-Puducherry, Karaikal, Mahe and Yanam. Puducherry is the Capital of this Union Territory and one of the most popular tourist destinations in South India. Puducherry has been described by National Geographic as "a glowing highlight of subcontinental sojourn". The city has many beautiful colonial buildings, churches, temples, and statues, which, combined with the systematic town planning and the well planned French style avenues, still preserve much of the colonial ambience.

Punjab

Punjab is one of India's most beautiful states. The state of Punjab is renowned for its cuisine, culture and history. Punjab has a vast public transportation and communication network. Some of the main cities in Punjab are Amritsar, Chandigarh, and Ludhiana. Punjab also has a rich religious history incorporating Sikhism and Hinduism. Tourism in Punjab is principally suited for the tourists interested in culture, ancient civilization, spirituality and epic history. Some of the villages in Punjab are also a must see for the person who wants to see the true Punjab, with their beautiful traditional Indian homes, farms and temples, this is a must see for any visitor that goes to Punjab.

Rajasthan

Rajasthan, literally meaning *"Land of the Kings"*, is one of the most attractive tourist destinations in Northern India. The vast sand dunes of the Thar Desert attract millions of tourists from around the globe every year.

Attractions:

- Jaipur-The capital of Rajasthan, famous for its rich history and royal architecture.
- Jodhpur-Fortress-city at the edge of the Thar Desert, famous for its blue homes and architecture.
- Udaipur-Known as the "Venice" of India.
- Jaisalmer-Famous for its golden fortress.
- Barmer-Barmer and surrounding areas offer perfect picture of typical Rajasthani villages.
- Bikaner-Famous for its medieval history as a trade route outpost.
- Mount Abu-Is the highest peak in the Aravalii Range of Rajasthan.
- Pushkar-It has the first and one of the very Brahma temples in the world.
- Nathdwara-This town near Udaipur hosts the famous temple of Shrinathji.
- Ranthambore-Situated near Sawai Madhopur, this town has one of the largest and most famous national parks in India.

Sikkim

Originally known as Suk-Heem, which in the local language means "peaceful home", Sikkim was an independent kingdom till the year 1974, when it became a part of the Republic of India. The capital of Sikkim is Gangtok, located approximately 185 kilometers from New Jalpaiguri, the nearest railway station to Sikkim.

Although, an airport is under construction at Dekiling in East Sikkim, the nearest airport to Sikkim would be Bagdogra. Sikkim is considered as the land of Orchids and mystic cultures and colorful traditions. Sikkim is well known among trekkers and adventure lovers, as West Sikkim has a lot to give them.

Places near Sikkim include Darjeeling also known as the Queen of hills and Kalimpong. Darjeeling, other than its world famous "Darjeeling tea" is also famous for its refined "Prep schools" founded during the British Raj. Kalimpong is also famous for its flora cultivation and is home to many internationally known Nurseries.

Tamil Nadu

Tamil Nadu lies in the southern Indian peninsula, on the shores of the Bay of Bengal. Many great rulers including the Cholas, Pallavas, Pandyas and the Vijayanagara Empire ruled over parts of Tamil Nadu. The state is known for its cultural heritage and temple architecture.

Attractions include Mahabalipuram, famous for its Shore Temple, Kanyakumari, the southernmost tip of India, Auroville, an International Utopian city, Mudumalai Wildlife Sanctuary, Ooty and Kodaikanal, two famous hill stations.

Uttarakhand

Uttaranchal is the 27th state of the Republic of India. It contains glaciers, snow-clad mountains, valley of flowers, skiing slopes and dense forests, and many shrines and places of pilgrimage. *Char-dhams*, the four most sacred and revered Hindu temples: Badrinath, Kedarnath, Gangotri and Yamunotri are nestled in the Himalayas. Haridwar which means *Gateway to God* is the only place on the plains.

It holds the watershed for Gangetic River System spanning 300 km from Satluj in the west to Kali river in the east. Nanda Devi (25640 Ft) is the second highest peak in India after Kanchenjunga (28160 Ft).

Dunagiri, Neelkanth, Chaukhamba, Panchachuli, Trisul are other peaks above 23000 Ft. It is considered the abode of *Devtas, Yakashyas, Kinners,* Fairies and Sages. It boasts of some old hill-stations developed during British era like Mussoorie, Almora and Nainital.

Glaciers Pindari Glacier, Milam Glacier, Gangotri Glacier, Bunder Punch Glacier, Khatling Glacier, Doonagiri Glacier,

Dokrani Glacier, Kaphini Glacier, Ralam Glacier Wildlife Reserves Corbett National Park, Rajaji National Park, Asan Conservation Reserve, Nanda Devi National Park, Govind Wildlife Sanctuary, Askot Musk Deer Sanctuary (Askot), Valley of Flowers Adventure Sports Skiing at Mundali, Auli, Dayara Bagyal and Munsiyari. Trekking at Mussoorie, Uttarkashi, Joshimath, Munsiyari, Chaukori, Pauri, Almora, Nainital.

Uttar Pradesh

Situated in the northern part of India, Uttar Pradesh is important with its wealth of monuments and religious fervour. Geographically, Uttar Pradesh is very diverse, with Himalayan foothills in the extreme north, the Gangetic Plain in the centre, and the Vindhya Mountain Range towards the South. It is also home of India's most visited site, the Taj Mahal, and Hinduism's holiest city, Varanasi. The most populous state of the Indian Union also has a rich cultural heritage, and at the heart of North India, Uttar Pradesh has much to offer. Places of interest include Varanasi, Agra, Mathura, Jhansi, Prayag, Sarnath, Ayodhya, Dudhwa National Park and Fatehpur Sikri.

West Bengal

Kolkata, one of the many cities in the state of West Bengal has been nicknamed the City of Palaces. This comes from the numerous palatial mansions built all over the city. Unlike many north Indian cities, whose construction stresses minimalism, the layout of much of the architectural variety in Kolkata owes its origins to European styles and tastes imported by the British and, to a much lesser extent, the Portuguese and French.

The buildings were designed and inspired by the tastes of the English gentleman around and the aspiring Bengali Babu (literally, a *nouveau riche* Bengali who aspired to cultivation of English etiquette, manners and custom, as such practices were favourable to monetary gains from the British).

Today, many of these structures are in various stages of decay. Some of the major buildings of this period are well maintained and several buildings have been declared as heritage structures.

From historical point of view, the story of West Bengal begins from Gour and Pandua situated close to the present district town of Malda.

The twin medieval cities had been sacked at least once by changing powers in the 15th century. However, ruins from the period still remain, and several architectural specimens still retain the glory and shin of those times.

The Hindu architecture of Bishnupur in terracotta and laterite sandstone are renowned world over. Towards the British colonial period came the architecture of Murshidabad and Coochbehar.

6

Present Status of Hospitality Industry

The hospitality industry is growing at a faster rate than ever envisaged and today it has no boundaries.

So high is the confidence in this industry that the only restriction is ambition. Over 250 million people around the world are estimated to be employed in this sector alone and the statistics indicate that one job is created in every two and a half seconds by the hospitality industry. Being a trade that encompasses industries like aviation, shipping, entertainment, catering, multiplexes, shopping malls, call centers and of course hotels and restaurants, the opportunities are pouring in with exciting career, assured job, handsome pay packets and above all international recognition and job satisfaction.

Why Hotel Management ?

For a professional this is a very lucrative segment capable of offering a long growth oriented career. The hotel sector itself requires a large amount of well trained manpower with excellent skill in housekeeping, food & beverage service and production, marketing, accounting, security, engineering, fire fighting, public relations and so on. A hospitality professional can find job opportunity in customer relations, sales and marketing and event management.

In this fast changing world, the hospitality industry has become the ideal place for those having an inborn talent to mingle with people, work with them and serve them. The young entrants have to come up with an open mind to explore the challenging world of hospitality business. They shall need to be multi skilled, talented and proactive not only to stay afloat but also to stay in demand in the challenging times that lie ahead.

Royal Group and Hospitality Industry

Hotel Division

The entry of Royal Group into the hospitality industry was by opening an ethnic village resort namely Royal Village in close harmony with the nature in the suburbs of Cochin. The century old traditional Farm House which stands as a testimony of ancient Kerala lifestyle attracting domestic and international tourists alike symbolizes the desire of the group to preserve and protect the culture and heritage of our country.

Munnar is best known for its personalized and intimate services offered. This luxury hotel with its exceptional five star facilities may be perhaps the only one of its kind in the state with state of the art Discotheque, star gaze gallery and many more making once stay highly enjoyable. All the above properties and their upcoming new proprieties in prime tourist locations in the state are together known as Royal Group of Hotels-for the rich and famous-which is well known in the fields of hotel, travel and tourism all over India and abroad.

Education

For Royal Group the field of education is not new. By the end of eighties before the policy of liberalization and globalization was heard, at a time when new products and technology with foreign tie ups were all poised to enter the Indian market and when there was acute shortage of trained manpower, Royal Group was quick to take initiative in establishing job oriented courses in the state. Thus was born School of Engineering. By conducting Kerala Government Engineering courses in different streams at Trivandrum over a decade, the education division of Royal Group has marked their presence in the field of Technical Education. Catering College, with its different divisions is functioning in a multi level operating system imparting courses in Hotel Management at various levels. The college has got approval from the All India Council for Technical Education (AICTE) New Delhi and the Government of Kerala for conducting 3 year Diploma course in Hotel Management and Catering Technology at Munnar. In association with the largest educational chain in the world-the Educational Institute of American Hotel & Lodging Association (AH&LA) USA the college offers specialized courses in Front Office Management, Housekeeping Management, Principles of Food Production, Food & Beverage Service and International Hotel Management in addition to Professional Cookery at their branches at Cochin, Calicut and Trivandrum also.

As a recognition of the facilities and the reputation, the renowned Punjab Technical University has approved Munnar Catering College as their outside study centre in conducting different Hotel Management courses at Diploma, Postgraduate Diploma, Degree and Postgraduate Degree level at their Cochin and Trivandrum branches.

The educational division of the Royal Group also conducts courses in Pharmaceutical Sciences with approval from the Government of Kerala, the Pharmacy Council of India and AICTE and Para Medical Courses in association with The Punjab Technical University under Distance Education Programme. The Institute of Pharmaceutical Sciences established in the capital city of the state is now offering Diploma in Pharmacy for eligible candidate selected as per specified norms fixed for the purpose, whereas the Institute of Para Medical Sciences, Trivandrum offers courses for Diploma in Hospital Management, Diploma, P.G Diploma, B.Sc & M.Sc. degrees in Medical Laboratory Technology.

By conducting Kerala Government Engineering courses in different streams at Trivandrum over a decade, the education division of Royal Group has marked their presence in the field of Technical Education also.

On the Job Training

For developing competence in the operation of all departments of a hotel an unmatched opportunity is wide open for the students of Munnar Catering College to get trained at own hotel and resort which many other institutions cannot offer. Students of Munnar Catering College are offered on the job training in all the departments of own hotels under guidance and supervision of experienced and talented professionals exclusively appointed for the purpose. In addition to this, to get a better understanding and first hand information of what is happening around in the hospitality industry the students are also sent for practical training during their course of study to other reputed hotels too, as part of their curriculum in Hotel Management.

Hotels and Catering Sector-Visions of the Future

This second article in the Sector Futures series on the hotels and catering sector looks at the trends and drivers affecting the sector, presents a framework to link them together and assesses their impact. The article also reviews some scenario work relating to the sector before concluding with an examination of the implications on the sector of the drivers and scenarios. Examples of the implications include better working conditions, consolidation and more consumer protection. Following the overview of the sector and initial look at trends and drivers in the first article of this series, this article now examines these trends and drivers in more detail and reviews existing foresight research on the hotels and catering sector.

Trends and Drivers of Change

The discussion above identified and introduced several trends and drivers that are shaping the sector. In a STEEP (social, technological, economic, environmental and political) breakdown, the key social drivers were identified as ageing populations and changing lifestyles and tastes. Information technologies, along with new production and kitchen technologies, were identified as the key technological drivers. Economic drivers included globalisation and low-cost travel, which in part raise issues about skill levels, migration and competition. Regarding environmental drivers, the main issues were identified as the direct impact of climate change on the sector as part of the tourist industry and the political desire to improve energy and resource efficiency across the economy. The key political drivers are likely to be legislation to improve consumer and worker rights, along with the quality and labelling of food. Beyond that, the sector, as part of the tourist industry, remains sensitive to the impact of international relations on consumer behaviour. The links and interactions between these forces are shown in the schematic diagram below.

STEEP Analysis

The following table summarises the STEEP factors affecting, or expected to affect, the industry along with their possible impacts.

Table 1: STEEP analysis and possible future of hotels and catering industry

Trends and drivers	Possible future of hotels and catering industry
Social	
Ageing population	Ageing consumers create a new type of demand. Older workers push harder for better conditions and better-qualified young workers choose other careers. These pressures lead to more social dialogue and an improvement in working conditions.
Change in tastes and demands	More informed and flexible consumers demand more value and more personal service. Increase in niche markets, e.g. organic/ethical restaurants, health hotels, etc.; expansion of budget hotels.
Technological	
Information technologies	Leads to better resource management and more flexible service delivery. Consequently, creates demand for new IT skills and less demand for traditional skills. This may shift gender balance in the work-force.
New kitchen technology	Outsourcing and simplification of kitchen operations expected to turn kitchens into assembly lines, deskill staff and bring about lower wages. This may lead to higher margins for companies.

Internet	Expands the range of information providers and establishments on offer to consumers and leads to changes in shopping behaviour. For firms, it expands the customer base and creates new competition, raises the importance of presentation and quality of service and demands new marketing strategies.
Economic	
Low-cost air travel	More tourists and more trips taken, but expenditure patterns are unclear; expansion of services in new destinations. Long-term growth may be curbed by environmental concerns.
Globalisation	New geographic and consumer markets pose threats and opportunities to the sector. Likely to favour large enterprises and promote consolidation. Likely to stimulate debate on skill levels and migration.
Environmental	
Climate change	Negative impact on the industry in affected tourist areas. Policy on use of energy resources might bring about cultural and hardware changes.
Environmental awareness`	Increased focus on dealing with pollution and waste management results in more environmentally friendly resource use, which may raise costs.
Political	
Legislation	Improvements in working conditions, consumer protection and product information increase costs for businesses. Small businesses are the most affected, because the improvements encourage consolidation. Effects filter down the supply chain and could alter the products on offer.
EU enlargement	Within the EU, increased tourist demand, migration and competition.
Social dialogue	Better industrial relations and working conditions, with higher skill levels. Potential to reduce labour turnover.

Assessment of the Trends and Drivers

Sociological Drivers

Sociological changes, such as changes in lifestyles, are driven by and affect consumers, and directly affect businesses. The temporal impact varies, but some changes, such as the increased use of the Internet for shopping, have had a profound impact on the industry. Such drivers require businesses to adapt in order to survive, for example, by reviewing their relationship with the customer and their marketing strategy.

An ageing population will affect the composition of the work-force (as outlined in the first article) and may help improve working conditions; it is also likely to lead to a change in the composition of consumer demand. In addition, growing interest from consumers in the production and health aspects of food is increasing pressure on caterers to supply better-quality food, produced in socially responsible ways, and with information on its origins. Reluctance by the industry to act on these issues is leading to increased governmental involvement. Changes to the supply chain in response to these trends are likely to be long-lasting.

Technological Drivers

Technology has been a primary driving force of change among consumers and in the sector, thereby helping to globalise it. While it creates opportunities, technology is also a major threat to small enterprises in the sector. Because of their small size, it is much harder for them to generate economies of scale and recover the cost of investment in new technologies. However, if they do not invest in new technologies, they are likely to lose out to those who have. The increasing use of technology has led to a need to retrain existing staff. Some industry bodies have argued that technology poses a threat to employment by reducing staff hours (as seen in the fall in full-time employment) and thus will exert downward pressure on wages. The initial boom in the use of information technologies appears to be slowing, and while its use will continue to increase, it is likely to be at a more gradual pace.

Economic Drivers

Globalisation has affected all parties. It has pushed governments to cooperate and integrate more, and in doing so has made the world more accessible to all parties. Economically, it has reduced restrictions on the movement of capital, labour and resources.

For the consumer, it has opened up new parts of the world, thus the hotels and restaurants most dependent on tourism face stiffer competition for their services, but they may also benefit from tourist visits from newly accessible regions. For companies, it opens up a larger market and offers the possibility of greater economies of scale that benefit larger chain groups and encourage consolidation. Recent trends show that many companies in the sector have chosen to expand by means of mergers or acquisitions as they become more aware of the need to pool resources in order to compete effectively in an expanding market.

The rise in low-cost air travel has above all benefited consumers, offering them more choice, flexibility and pricing options. While establishments are receiving increased numbers of visitors, it is not clear that the increase in visitor spending has been commensurate with the increase in numbers.

Many tourists have become far more cost conscious, leading to a growing demand for budget, no-frills hotels. The EU market for low-cost travel still has some way to go before it reaches maturity, so the effects have probably not yet reached a plateau.

However, with governments looking increasingly set to levy environmental taxes on air travel and with oil prices rising and staying high, ticket prices can be expected to rise also. The impact of this on consumer demand is uncertain, as it is not yet clear how sensitive consumers are to the pricing of budget air travel.

Environmental Drivers

In general, environmental drivers are likely to have a less immediate impact on the sector than the other drivers discussed. The most direct impact is likely to be felt by establishments that form part of the tourist industry in areas affected by climate change (coastal and ski resorts) and areas of environmental interest. However, the timeframe for such effects is likely to be further in the future than for other drivers.

Although freak changes or storms may wreak havoc, the resultant damage they cause is often temporary, but the permanent damage, as from rising sea levels, is taking place as a slow, gradual process. Nevertheless, the net impact on businesses in affected areas can be expected to be negative as the features that made them attractive in the first place are eroded. While some may be able to adapt to the new environment, their success is likely to depend on how consumers react. In other respects the impact of environmental changes is likely to be felt through policies to reduce emissions, to improve the use of all resources, especially energy resources, and to reduce pollution by improving waste management.

Although much of the focus has been on power generation plants, all companies are under pressure to be more energy efficient and such pressures are likely to increase in the medium term. Furthermore, the timeframe for these drivers may be longer than for others, as environmental concerns are often low on the political agenda, and it is not easy to reach political consensus on environment-energy policies when these are believed to curb growth. Any costs created by environmental policy can be expected to affect enterprises in the first place, and it will be up to them how to deal with this. The obvious choice is to pass it on to customers, but regardless of whether this is done or not, any additional costs are likely to favour larger enterprises that enjoy greater economies of scale and have more flexibility in absorbing costs.

Political Drivers

New legislation, such as smoking bans, changes to licensing laws and new regulations governing food safety, is partly a response to changes in people's tastes and lifestyles. However, new laws can bring great costs to businesses. The smoking ban, for example, has improved conditions for workers and customers, but at the same time there is evidence that it has reduced turnover and that this has translated into job losses.

Over the medium term, firms are likely to face increased demands from consumers for more informative marking and higher-quality standards for food. How governments will respond to such pressure from consumers is unclear. In the UK, for example, the quality of catered school meals became a hot topic in 2005 after the poor quality of such meals was highlighted by a high-profile chef on TV. One company supplying such meals (Compass) has suffered as a result, and the UK government is taking action to improve the quality of school meals. On the other hand, among the proposed EU laws recently scrapped by the EC president, José Barroso, there was one on food labelling. Nevertheless, governments may still be willing to take initiatives independently of EU legislation in order to satisfy their electorates.

The enlargement of the EU has positively impacted on the hotels and catering sector because the new Member States provide a new source of demand. However, migration from the new to the old Member States in pursuit of higher wages and a better standard of living is turning out to be lower than had been expected before accession. Moreover, because economic growth in the new Member States is expected to accelerate now that they are in the EU, rising wage levels and improved standards of living will probably make migration to EU15 countries less attractive.

New policies are helping to expand the scope of social dialogue within the hotels and catering sector. Social dialogue is becoming a major part of good governance because it allows all stakeholders to be part of policymaking within the firm and industry. On the other hand, union membership in this sector is comparatively low, making it difficult for workers to agree on objectives and to present a united front.

Scenarios for the Hotels and Catering Sector

In contrast to STEEP analysis, scenario work allows us to look beyond the familiar environment. It helps the industry to prepare for the consequences of unexpected events by asking the following questions:

- What if (X) happens?

- What would be the effects on the industry if (X) were to happen?
- What are the best ways of counteracting adverse effects?

The search for scenario work on hotels and restaurants failed to discover work related solely to hotels and restaurants. It was only as part of the tourist industry that hotels and catering received attention, and so the scenario analysis here is based primarily on foresight work related to tourism. Although hotels and restaurants are part of and rely on the tourist industry, their market is not confined just to tourists. Furthermore, the published scenario work was reactive, in that it was based on dramatic events in their immediate aftermath. It did not analyse the possible effects of hypothetical events or look at observable and more prosaic trends. In recent years, there have been several unexpected events that have affected the hotels and catering industry, such as the 9/11 terrorist attacks, the outbreak of SARS, the foot and mouth epidemic in the UK and the bombings in Madrid and London. Such shocks have a low probability of occurrence, but their impact is high. Recently, however, such shocks have become more frequent and hence people are more inclined to believe that they will happen again. It is extremely difficult to predict these shocks, but good policies at all levels (European, national or firm) or any foresight work must not ignore their possible reoccurrence. Petersen (1997) refers to these shocks as 'wild cards'. He suggests that some shocks are imaginable, and if agents are well prepared, they could be turned into manageable events:

There is a general assumption that there is nothing to do about these huge surprises. However, not all wild cards are unimaginable and by identifying wild card events that may possibly occur in the future on a proactive rather than reactive matter, these can sometimes be converted into anticipated manageable events. The chance alone of averting a future catastrophe or at least preparing strategies to handle it may be reason enough to examine wild card possibilities. If not dealt with wild cards can trigger a chain of events much worse than the initial happening. A major natural disaster can for instance cause a global epidemic, which may lead to nations closing their borders in turn leading to a collapse of the airline industry and so forth. (1997, pp. 43-47)

Post-9/11 Scenarios

One topic that scenario work could not ignore was the impact of 9/11 on the travel and tourism industry. Two major scenarios were published shortly after the attack on New York. The World Travel and Tourism Council (WTTC) estimated at that time that there were 207 million people employed worldwide in the travel and tourism economy. Its 'best guess' was that the attacks would lead to 8.8 million job losses worldwide, of which 1.2 million would be in the EU. Within six weeks of 11 September 2001, the International Labour Organisation (ILO) published the report The social impact on the hotel and tourism sector of events subsequent to 11 September 2001 (136kb), which outlined two possible scenarios:

The Best-case Scenario

Assumptions:

- 9/11 is a one-off;
- there are no other attacks in the United States (US);
- there are no other attacks in other parts of the world.

Travel to Europe, which before the attack was showing recovery from recession, would not be badly affected. Europeans would continue to travel within the continent, while travel to the Middle East was unlikely to revive in the short term. The European tourism industry would benefit as a substitute destination choice. However, US tourists, who account for a significant part of the demand in the industry, would not return to Europe for some time. The reduction in US tourists, who are recognised as big spenders, would affect upmarket restaurants and hotels the most.

The Worst-case Scenario

Assumptions:

- there are other major terrorist attacks in the US;

- there are outbreaks of terrorism in other countries;
- the ongoing war in Afghanistan spreads to other regions.

In this scenario, the tourist demand from Asia and North America would plummet. Within Europe, the travel pattern would also change depending on the scale and location of any attacks. Domestic travel would probably benefit, with demand shifting from the location of an attack to an alternative location. In the extreme position, personal or business holidays would come to a halt.

In the ILO's best-case scenario, the WTTC predictions were pessimistic. In the ILO's worst-case scenario, the consequences are far worse than the WTTC's predictions.

Iraq War Scenarios

When the US and the UK decided to invade Iraq in 2003, WTTC looked at the possible outcomes of the Iraq war and their consequences for the US tourist industry in its 2003 research on the United States-Travel and tourism, a world of opportunity (526kb, pp.18-21). The WTTC's scenario was informed by the experience of the 1991 Gulf war, the effects of which, according to the WTTC, were to limit economic growth through three main channels: higher oil prices, shattered consumer and business confidence and lower equity prices.

The base scenario: diplomatic solution or victory after a short, contained war

In the base case, the war is assumed to be short, contained and successful, and to remove global uncertainty. The effects on oil prices, confidence and equity prices are assumed to be very similar to what they would have been had there been a diplomatic solution to the crisis. In the short term, economic growth is assumed to be higher due to increased government spending. The difference in the effects on travel and tourism between no war and a speedy, contained war is therefore predicted to be small. However, the threat of war was assumed to undermine confidence and to reduce international travel, and this would affect the travel and tourism industry more than the rest of the economy.

Assumptions:

- quick, decisive victory or diplomatic solution;
- no use of weapons of mass destruction (WMD) against US troops, Israel or region;
- no reduction in OPEC oil production and exports;
- no challenges to Arab governments in region;
- new Iraqi government installed and in control;
- no damage to oil-producing capacity in Iraq or elsewhere.

The war scenario: victory with regional disruption

Under this scenario, a longer-lasting war results in persistently higher oil prices, with a deeper and longer fall in confidence and equity markets. The effects on the travel and tourism industry are expected to be more severe.

Assumptions:

- Iraq attacks oil facilities in region, with limited damage but political and economic knock-on effects;
- Iraq attacks Israel and US troops but not with WMD effective enough to trigger a major response or to have highly lethal effects;
- unexpected protracted Iraqi military resistance;
- limited Israeli intervention in war; rising political unrest in region;
- low-level civil tensions and clashes in Iraq after military conflict is over;
- some terrorist attacks on US interests.

These pressures were predicted to lead to a slowing of between 1% and 2% in GDP growth in the US and UK. The effects on the travel and tourism industry are more severe under the war scenario. In the US, under this scenario, in 2003 the travel and tourism industry would experience:

- 0.9% fall in industry demand;
- 3.7% fall in industry GDP;
- 8.9% fall in exports;

- loss of 449,100 jobs.

Climate Change Scenarios

Although the global climate has been changing for some time, there is uncertainty about its future path and patterns as well as the consequences. Research commissioned by the World Tourism Organisation (WTO) suggests two possible scenarios on global climate change, relating specifically to the tourist industry in Hungary, The responses of Lake Balaton to global cliamte change (299kb, Rátz, 2003).

Climate Zone Shift Scenario

Assumptions:

- The temperate climate zone covering Hungary shifts northward and is replaced by a warmer climate.

This would be expected to lead to a longer summer season with much higher temperatures. This could have benefits for the tourist industry, assuming the temperatures are not too high and droughts are infrequent. In contrast, winter sports tourism is likely to disappear under such a scenario.

Ice Caps Melt Scenario

Assumptions:

- Ice caps melt due to global warming.

Under this scenario, the Gulf Stream cools down and changes the climate in Europe. The Hungarian climate becomes colder and wetter. This would have a mainly negative impact on the tourism industry, as the summer season becomes shorter and wetter. However, it could lead to the further development of winter sports tourism.

Scenario Summary

Some scenario work relevant to the hotels and catering industry tends to focus on dramatic events. In some cases, the work is done after the shocks have occurred, with a best-case scenario assuming that these shocks are unique and the worst-case scenario assuming that they are not. In hindsight, it is easy to say that it is a pity such analysis was not conducted before the events occurred and that there were no plans to deal with the consequences of such events. Regarding the climate change scenario, it should be emphasised that it related to Hungary only. Furthermore, the study's primary focus was not the effect of climate change on the hotels and catering sector; instead, it formed part of a wider discussion on the overall impact of climate change on the region. Since the concern here is the European hotels and catering sector, the major drawback of the Iraq war scenario is its focus on the US tourist industry.

Moreover, to date there appears to have been little work done on exploring the future of the industry through scenario planning in the light of the various current influences identified in the first two articles of this series. It may be more useful to project these current trends and drivers and identify possible outcomes and responses.

Possible scenarios to consider are:

- What if the current weakness of the EU economy persists for much longer than expected?
- What if there is a collapse in the world financial market?
- What if there are more outbreaks of deadly viruses?
- What are the implications of developing countries becoming developed over the next 10 years?
- What would happen if the Internet ceased to exist, e.g. because of political censorship?
- What if the current skills gaps remain in 10 or 15 years' time?
- What will the role of information technologies be in the industry in the future, and how will this affect labour demand?
- What are the implications if the European Union breaks up?
- What are the implications of a Europe-wide zero immigration policy?
- What are the implications for labour supply if there are no government pensions?

Implications

As younger workers increasingly become more qualified, they are less likely to consider the hotels and catering industry, with its poorer working conditions, as a career option. This and the ageing of the population are likely to persuade businesses to employ older workers. Because of their circumstances, older workers are often less mobile and have other commitments. Consequently, they are likely to be more demanding about working conditions, to be more favourable to union membership and to become more involved in social dialogue.

Changing lifestyles and more demanding consumers are likely to promote the development of more specialised enterprises and broaden competition among hotels and restaurants. The more specialised nature of services should allow firms to charge a premium.

These niche markets are likely to attract multinationals as other parts of the hotels and catering industry become commoditised and less profitable. Commoditisation exerts downward pressure on premiums and profits. In order to survive and make a profit, firms offering commoditised services can be expected to cut costs and homogenise the service/experience on offer.

On the supply side, the increasing use of technology will continue to help establishments better manage their resources and reduce spare capacity. A better knowledge of future demands has implications for staff, in that establishments are likely to seek more flexible working patterns to match demands.

This in turn has implications for lifestyle and for where the savings go. On the demand side, the Internet, wireless computing and 3G mobile telephony all make it easier for consumers to obtain information, compare prices and value for money and shop around.

This trend and the increasing use of the Internet as a marketing device by businesses will lead to more intense competition and make it harder to close a sale. Firms are increasingly likely to respond by seeking staff with skills in information and communication technologies (ICT), including marketing, sales and web design.

Any increase in outsourcing in the catering industry further separates the consumer from food producers, making it harder to check the origin of food. This implies a possible widening of the information gap and is likely to increase pressure on catering companies to provide information about the food they serve. Businesses can be expected to resist this because of the cost implications, so governments may intervene.

The use of technology in the kitchen can be expected to raise productivity and lower labour demand. This again has implications for where the savings go. Increased productivity should see wages rise, but lower reliance on chefs' food preparation skills would have the opposite effect.

In the context of globalisation, EU enlargement offers a larger labour pool and facilitates migration. It is unclear to what extent this will help to fill the skills gap, as the tourist industry in most new Member States is small in comparison to that in France or the UK, for example.

However, as long as relative wage differentials between regions are large enough, workers in poorer regions can be expected to move to richer regions for work. This can be expected to lower employment costs in the hotels and catering industry in richer regions.

Furthermore, this is likely to attract the most skilled from the poorer regions, thus hindering the development of the industry there. At the same time, in enlarging the EU hotel and catering market and making it more accessible, globalisation has created an opportunity for companies to exploit substantial economies of scale.

To what extent this could approach the scale seen in the US, for example, is unclear given the much wider cultural and language differences that exist in the EU. Nevertheless, it is still likely to lead to the increased presence of larger multinational hotel and catering chains, which is likely to fuel the demand for migrant labour in order to reduce employment costs.

Customers may suffer if this leads to a homogenisation of service on offer, but brand names and reputations should ensure a higher-quality product. In order to maintain this, companies can be expected to recruit the best-skilled staff and improve working conditions in order to retain them.

The skills gap in the industry adversely affects the quality of service in the industry and damages the industry's reputation among travellers.

This lessens establishments' pricing power and makes it harder to attract customers. This implies handsome rewards for companies that fill the gap (with good practice putting firms on a virtuous cycle) and premium wages for those with the necessary skills. The existence of the gap suggests that firms are unwilling to undertake training themselves and that working conditions need to be improved in order to attract and retain skilled staff. Establishments therefore have to take a more proactive and united approach.

Although low-cost airlines have increased the frequency of trips made by travellers, they often stay for a shorter duration and tend to be more cost-conscious. Furthermore, as profit-maximising companies independent of political or national influence, low-cost carriers will not hesitate to scrap unprofitable services. This has implications for policy as well as the hotels and catering industry's marketing strategy at a local level. In some regions, the rapid growth in the tourism and leisure industry is likely to work against raising levels of education or skills, while its effect on wages will depend on the industrial structure of the locality.

Legislation to improve the working environment, e.g. smoking bans in bars and restaurants and working time regulations, has negative implications for firms' margins and labour demand. In response, firms are likely to push for productivity gains and seek more cost-effective labour and a greater application of technology.

Political concern over consumer health and the content of food is increasing pressure on catering firms to reduce sugar and salt levels, for example, in prepared food. If catering firms respond to such concerns, this could create new demands for new tastes in food.

If health problems such as diabetes and obesity become greater public health issues, then the prospect of health-related taxes on food must surely draw closer. Growing concern among consumers about the origin of their food and the production methods involved is largely a social trend, but it, too, is generating political pressure for more information and increased food labelling.

This raises the prospect of legislation forcing the industry to inform consumers. The disclosure of more information and the demand for food produced in more socially responsible ways is likely to promote good practice in the food supply chain, and may lead to a shift away from low-end food establishments.

In the wake of the 9/11 attacks, the EU hotels and catering sector saw turnover growth slow dramatically. US visitor numbers to the EU are only now returning to the pre-9/11 levels.

International relations remain fractured because of the US-led 'war on terror' and the Iraq war. The continuation of political and military hostilities and the continued involvement of EU nations mean that some EU Member States remain targets for terrorism, as seen in the Madrid and London bombings. US tourist confidence is therefore likely to remain fragile. High-profile marketing campaigns may be needed in the US to bolster confidence.

That US visitor levels are recovering suggests terrorism has not inflicted long-lasting damage on the industry. Such damage could be caused, however, if one location were to suffer multiple attacks within a space of two or three years. While the industry is likely to be able to recover from this on an EU level, the impact on the affected region is likely to last longer. Heavy discounting in response, as employed in London in recent years, whether successful or not, would probably lead to lower levels of employment and investment, and a deterioration in working conditions. Such a downward spiral would take years to reverse.

Conclusion

This concludes the review of the key trends and drivers affecting the sector, and of scenario work relating to the sector. The reader should have a better idea of what issues are driving the sector and of the paucity of scenario work relating to the sector. Having looked at the trends and scenarios and their implications, the third and last article in this series, Hotels and catering-policies, issues and the future, carries the discussion forward to look at major policy issues and challenges facing the sector. Consideration is given to their timeframe and the agents and regions affected.

7

Future of Hospitality Organization

Introduction

No hotel company operating today can be unaware of the swift pace of global change and its impact on every facet of the hospitality industry. With just five years left in this century, we can expect change to be the only constant. New business practices are evolving virtually as fast as our technologies, while resistance to change has become one of the primary causes of business failure. The specter of constant change raises fundamental questions as to the creation of shareholder wealth in a capital-constrained, highly competitive environment. How will hotel organizations build shareholder wealth, and what key drivers will result in success? What future products and services will be essential in a technology-driven, global environment marked by rising customer expectations? Moreover, what alternative approaches and skills must organizations develop to ensure market success?

The future success of hotel organizations will be driven in large part by the ability to foresee-and capitalize-on change. Beyond this truism, however, there is an urgent need to identify what will be required in the competitive environment of the future with its intense focus on serving customer needs. The hospitality industry-as is the case with business generally–is subject to deep currents of change set in motion as economic and social systems shaped in the industrial era evolve to a knowledge-based era driven by technology advances. In this period of global transition, it behooves hotel organizations to examine the key factors that will not only define success, but the ability to survive in coming years. Many of these issues were spotlighted in a global study undertaken by the Economist Intelligence Unit and co-sponsored by Arthur Andersen. The Successful Corporation of the Year 2000 surveyed more than 600 senior executives around the world. Its mission was to identify the characteristics needed to lead successful businesses in the next century. These executives offer a number of compelling messages regarding the key success factors of the future.

Customers will have the strongest influence on the corporation in the year 2000. Indeed, these executives believe that the customer will be "king" in the new century. Exceptional leadership was by far the attribute most frequently cited by CEOs and senior executives; the consensus appears to be that successful companies in the year 2000 will be led by corporate visionaries. A strategic planning focus is not only essential, but must embody a concept of planning for the future that anticipates change, rather than being based exclusively on historical models. In structuring organizations for the future, companies must build management capabilities to deal with one of the most critical challenges–diversity in the marketplace. Employing information technology to drive business success in this information-driven era is not only the path of least resistance, but vital to virtually every aspect of operations.

The study's top-line results create an excellent backdrop to address key issues confronting the hotel industry, and what factors will lead to membership–rather than rejection–in the elite club of the world's corporate success stories in the year 2000.

From an Asset to Customer Focus

Recognizing that the hotel industry has a somewhat split personality reflecting the inherent conflicts between its real estate and operational aspects, it is important to understand the industry's real estate origins and how they are shaping the challenges ahead.

The origins of the industry's real estate persona are embodied in the classic theory of location-"if we build it, they will come." As a result of this "building" complex, the industry has tended to have a real estate and asset orientation, rather than a customer focus. From the hotel company perspective–especially that of the brand-oriented "chain"–the varied interests of a diffused property ownership group can be quite different than the singular interest of the chain that operates and markets the properties.

Even when the ownership of geographically dispersed hotel properties is controlled by a single hotel organization, the financial structuring tends to be property-specific. Corporate financial strategies are frequently subjugated to the needs of the last property deal brought into the company's fold. Each property in a so-called "chain," is frequently the subject of a unique and distinctive ownership and financial structure. This phenomenon–quite common in the real estate sector, but unusual for business enterprises generally–makes for elusive economies of scale in the structuring and financing of property-driven expansion.

Collectively, these factors have produced low comparative returns in real estate, although criticism levelled at commercial real estate returns is somewhat less germane to the hotel industry, where management and franchise fees can produce high returns for those companies where property ownership is held by third parties. Nevertheless, average returns in the real estate industry in the United States, for example, are just over 10 percent, compared to small company stock returns at almost 20 percent and large company stocks at an average of about 15 percent.

While hotel chains have adopted traditional corporate frameworks, there are a number of predominantly real estate-driven, family-owned businesses in the hotel sector that continue to operate as relatively unstructured organizations. In meeting the future, these businesses will need plans, people and processes in order to establish viable corporate forms that can compete in tomorrow's marketplace and capitalize upon its opportunities.

In today's changed environment, the hotel organization must deal with a number of new realities. Investors in our industry are no longer satisfied with long-term capital appreciation and psychic income that heretofore were often the justification for otherwise seemingly uneconomic investments in hotel property or, indeed, hotel chains. The first reality is that there is a very specific and identifiable relationship between bottom line performance and value. Improvements in business operations raises values. It is not surprising, therefore, that the new owners attracted to this industry in recent years have new sets of demands. This transformation from an old-guard group of investors and owners to income and return-driven newcomers has meant that the once "quiet enjoyment" of operators in their management of hotels for third parties is being disturbed, interrupted and overturned.

These challenges all take place in an environment where capital has become extremely selective in markets that have little stability. A global shortage of capital will not remain a short-term problem, and future hotel organizations must have a stronger alignment to capital providers–a critical "customer" group. Hotel companies will need to compete by offering better returns and performance than in the past. Hotel chains have found their development timetables quashed in recent years, making it difficult to achieve goals of critical mass often required to improve performance.

These factors are driving consolidation in the brand "sweepstakes." Capital markets, therefore, continue to favour well-established companies, a reality that must drive entrepreneurial organizations to meet the future now by planning for an evolving corporate context in which to operate.

Key Success Factors-The Future

Within this broad context, hotel developers, owners and management companies will all need to develop new strategies, skills and processes that look forward to the competitive demands of the future. These ultimately must address issues related to vision and planning, as well as organizational skill sets and processes to attract and retain customers. To stake a claim in the future, current business practices should be examined in light of what can be expected to be the key success factors in the year

2000. Embrace a global change orientation. As the information age produces greater worldwide integration of business activities, a global knowledge base will become invaluable. Success in local and regional hotel markets will be shaped decisively by a global business environment that defines capital movement, customer expectations and applications of new technologies.

Focus on the Customer. If the customer is "king" in the 21st century, hotel organizations will be best served by focusing less on their hotel assets as measures of success, and more on their customers. This involves a fundamental shift in viewing the real estate asset as the wealth creator–to the customer as the key to building shareholder wealth. A customer focus must imbue business decisions at all levels of developing and operating a hotel organization. Pursuing such a course will inevitably impact shareholder wealth. To accomplish this, however, customers need to participate in the product development process.

Fully realizing a customer focus in the industry poses a significant challenge. The hotel industry must confront problems due to conflicts between operational needs and real estate goals. Quite simply, an operator must remain customer-focused, but the short-term strategies to meet these needs may be inconsistent with the long-term objectives of property owners. Balancing those goals will be essential. A customer focus implies a significant shift in what drives hotel development–placing primary emphasis on the customer with the locations to follow. Nevertheless, a hotel organization with its large investment in fixed assets–the real estate–can never be as nimble as a consumer products company in adjusting products and services to match rapid shifts in the marketplace.

The Japanese taught us that the concept of "zero defects" in products and services can yield tremendous benefits. But today an even more rigorous standard dominates–quality that surprises. In practical terms, the hotel industry finds it extremely difficult to meet the standard of zero defects in service. Hotel services are based primarily on people, not computers or other equipment. Quality that surprises takes the concept of zero defects a step further. Yesterday's surprising product or service is today's status quo. Twenty years ago, a business executive did not expect a consistent and predictable level of service wherever he or she travelled in the world. Today that is a standard–not the exception–as is the expectation for sophisticated technology in hotel rooms to support business needs. With customer discrimination so acute, it is not surprising that brand loyalty is a diminishing "commodity" in the hotel industry.

Find the ingredients for visionary leadership. Today's hotel organizations need to recognize the need for visionary leadership. The ability to forecast the future–to anticipate change rather than react to it–will be one of the single greatest determinants of market dominance in the years ahead. The old "command and control" model of leadership is giving way to a focus on leadership in ideas, information, inspiration, vision and teamwork. Warren Bennis, an authority on leadership in the U.S., puts it this way–"For the most part, failing organizations tend to be over-managed and under-led. The leader sets the tone for the moral character, the vision, the corporate culture and the fiber of the institution."

While visionary leadership is essential, it must be linked to business operations and foster a risk bias, rather than a procedural bias. This will allow the organization to stretch and, in turn, change. And it must be shared by empowered professionals and staff throughout the organization, including those who meet the customer. Overcoming the resistance to change can be a daunting task, particularly in large hotel organizations in which diversions from the status quo may threaten established management lines. It suggests that a culture based on conformance may need to be replaced by an emphasis on flexibility, learning and cooperation. Management competencies will need to be aligned in order to achieve the desired result. For many organizations, this may mean a shift from traditional hierarchies typical of companies in an industrial era to a flatter organization with a more transparent interface between leadership, organizational functions and employees.

Create a defensible position through corporate strategy. For many of the industry's leaders, vision is driven by the strategic planning process, a function which has become critical for success.

Strategic planning, however, has at times been a step-child in the hotel industry, and it is often the first to be cut when organizations are downsized. It is clearly in transition. There also has been a tendency to decentralize and simplify this function–both actions of potential benefit. Strategic planning must be led by the top people in the organization–the CEO and COO. On the other hand, it should be close enough to the customer to ensure that planners can "listen" to and be influenced by customer needs.

Empower Management. Beyond the ability to envision the future, core management capabilities will make the difference–they are essential. A clear vision without the management skills to support it cannot be a recipe for success. First and foremost, hotel management must have strategic development skills and the ability to integrate complex factors affecting success. Market volatility has become the norm, in part caused by the rapidly changing tastes of customers. Customers are increasingly approaching the hotel industry with widely different social, economic and political backgrounds, to say nothing of employees. Being able to deal with these diversities in a positive and constructive fashion that capitalizes on the differences, rather than working to find ways to mitigate them, is the clear path for successful management in the future.

The organization will also need to be imbued with a sense of entrepreneurship that reacts proactively to the market's diversity. Traditional organizations that follow well-documented rules must give way to leaders who can balance a sense of discipline with that of flexibility. Talent and resources must be marshalled and leveraged.

In an industry with high fixed costs and labour intensity, the concept of leverage in the hotel business is an all-important one. Improving labour productivity through technology must be a goal for today's forward-looking hotel organization. Management must also be able to narrow the gap between the employer and the employee, forcing a flatter organization in the process. This will put management closer to the customer and speed the two-way communication process up and down the organization.

Be in the information fast lane. The traditional role of information technology (IT) as a back office support for accounting and bookkeeping has clearly moved front and centre stage. IT today influences all aspects of business from corporate strategies to organizational structure–and from the very business processes it is designed to support to performance measurement. In a world where the customer is "king," IT must also deliver in two critical areas: sales and marketing and customer service.

Technology was once viewed as a way to reduce costs by replacing people. That attitude has been firmly supplanted by one that seeks IT support for the creative work that all organizations must pursue. IT must allow organizations to react more speedily to market needs and, of course, produce the fulfilment of customer demands both quickly and accurately. To do this IT must operate on a decentralized basis. IT delivers, but it has to be the right information to the right people, and it needs to be done on a timely basis.

Hospitality e-Procurement

Models and Strategies

The hospitality industry has historically struggled under the weight of fragmented supply chains, made even more unwieldy by complex and inefficient business processes in distribution and procurement. Now that fragmentation may be put right as old economy hospitality companies turn to e-Business startups to move procurement and distribution processes online. In short, e-Procurement offers the potential for improving both ends of the equation to reduce costs, generate new revenue streams and improve audit control.

The Internet has not only fired the first shot of this revolution, it continues to be reinvented as a way for buyers to meet suppliers, and competitors to compete or partner online in efficient and cost-effective ways. As a ubiquitous global network, the Internet makes it possible to package, distribute and consume information in digital form, breaking the economic bottle-neck imposed by the production, market exchange and distribution of goods.

Digital marketplaces furnishing diverse products and services are breaking down trade barriers and offering access to hospitality companies of all sizes. Deutsche Bank currently estimates a $60 billion domestic and $100 billion international market for hospitality e-Procurement, including furniture, fixtures and equipment (FF&E), renovation and construction, service contracts, operating supplies and food and beverage (F&B). Cost savings from more efficient supply chain transactions are currently estimated to be at $3.5 billion to $4 billion in the United States alone, and $7 billion globally. Hospitality procurement of more than $20 billion domestically and $10 billion internationally is forecast to be on-line in the next 12 to 18 months

Growth in hospitality e-Procurement is clearly explosive in its potential, and our view is that hotel organizations will need to respond to this new market to remain competitive. Nevertheless, there are major obstacles to the industry seizing the advantages of e-Procurement and realizing improvements in the supply chain. This article examines marketplace models and strategies for e-Procurement as part of our series in the Hospitality and Leisure Executive Report on eBusiness opportunities.

The Internet and e-Procurement

The Internet's ability to deliver information in a common format to a wide array of computers enables businesses to access and share information from many sources-including their customers, financial institutions and suppliers. e-Procurement is a direct outgrowth of that capability. As a global network using standardized protocols and universal connectivity, the Internet opens the door for businesses to develop international marketplaces for their products and services.

Not only does the Internet facilitate the sharing of information, it simplifies the process for the end-user as well, and reduces infrastructure and transaction costs. The shared nature of the Internet distributes the infrastructure costs across large groups of potential customers, suppliers and others. That means businesses of any size can gain access for a variety of purposes. Distributors or suppliers can build revenue while also realizing reduced customer contact costs. Rather than maintaining multiple sales contact systems, suppliers need to have just one connection to the Internet.

What is the real potential for hospitality companies? e-Procurement will have a positive impact on business functions and processes for those organizations that fully take advantage of these capabilities. Buyers, for example, have a growing amount of information available to identify the suppliers with whom they want to do business. e-Procurement facilitates the aggregation of small purchases, thereby making the order process more efficient and cost effective. And it minimizes the need for intermediaries between the supplier and buyer. Traditional supply chain distributors, as a result, are being forced to provide value-added services to remain viable in the chain.

The Next Generation

We begin by defining e-Procurement. Using digitized processes, the procurement process is engineered in concert with an all-electronic design and implementation of the infrastructure required to source, supply, manage and control services. It is one of the most important of business-to-business (B2B) functions.

e-Procurement solutions were initially launched by companies such as Ariba, Inc., which developed corporate procurement systems for global 2000 companies to give their employees access to vendors electronically. Though effective, these applications centering on "buy-side" solutions were inherently expensive and time-consuming to implement.

The new generation of e-Procurement is more revolutionary. Today, digital marketplaces create Internet portals to serve multiple buyers and sellers in the exchange of goods and services.

These new ventures are levelling the playing field for both buyers and suppliers, giving smaller companies and those around the world ready access, using a Web browser, to opportunities once available primarily to larger companies in North America. Large up-front investments in hardware and software are unnecessary.

Emerging Marketplace Models

To participate in the development of e-Procurement offerings, hospitality companies will benefit by understanding the emerging digital marketplace models. Our firm's analysis indicates that there are currently two dominant models:

Industry-specific Marketplaces

Organizations with domain expertise in a particular industry-or industry "vertical" in the language of the new economy-launch these exchanges. These market-places support commerce specific to an industry as they seek to aggregate buyers and sellers to reduce transaction costs. Their competitive advantage is based on a unique understanding of industry inefficiencies.

Examples can be seen in Marriott International's and Hyatt's P-Co-a joint, independent electronic purchasing network powered by GoCo-op's eCommerce engine-that leverages economies of scale to reduce prices on product and services. Or consider Instill Corporation, which links food service operators and food service product distributors/manufacturers.

Instill bundles e-Procurement services to improve control and management of foodservice purchasing, offers a consolidated purchase information service for monitoring contract compliance and capturing rebates, provides market intelligence to manufacturers, and creates an online community and marketplace for small chains and independent operators to improve their operating and financial performance.

Horizontal Marketplaces

These exchanges provide a vehicle for many types of buyers and sellers to advertise, share content, bid on products, participate in auctions and manage their supply chains. Such marketplace sites serve a wide range of disparate industries and/or provide them with access to horizontal applications.

Unlike the original e-Procurement systems, which generally provided static catalogues and limited sourcing capability, these new digital marketplaces use dynamic pricing models-primarily auctions or exchanges-which are based on demand. Horizontal marketplaces have multiple revenue streams, the most common of which come from advertising on sites. Many of these marketplaces also generate revenues in the form of commissions charged to sellers participating in auctions. Storefront sales to sellers can be an additional source of revenue for such marketplaces. Tradeout.com, one such example of a horizontal marketplace, categorizes its services to multiple industries by product type. Its services include the hosting of seller-driven auctions for excess inventory resale. In such auctions, sellers list their products and receive price bids from multiple buyers for individual products, thereby enabling the seller to potentially receive the highest price for their products, including any excess inventory that ordinarily would have to be written off. Vertical marketplaces have similar revenue sources, although they are able to command higher advertising fees due to the detailed information they can collect on concentrated groups of members and subscribers. Additionally, some of them also generate revenues by charging subscription fees to access their focused content and product data.

In contrast to vertical marketplaces, horizontal marketplaces face challenges specific to their broad mission. Based on the need to appeal to diverse industries, these marketplaces must satisfy the product, service and content needs of their varied buyers and members, and may be fighting an uphill battle in doing so. Some companies have been successful using this model, but they have had to invest in expensive domain experts to develop the compelling offerings typically available in a vertical marketplace. The diversity of the industries served by horizontal marketplaces, however, can be useful in reducing risk in the event of limited penetration in a particular vertical.

A hybrid marketplace model is beginning to emerge with the advantage of leveraging the strengths of both models. In this model several contiguous verticals are represented in a marketplace. These contiguous verticals can be grouped according to the similar products and services used by all, yet still maintain the content and other offerings unique to each. A hybrid market-place, for example, might provide an exchange for food service, hospitality and grocery industry members, which could be grouped together to access food and beverage suppliers. In contrast, hospitality industry member sites might feature only FF&E items, such as beds. Buyers can benefit from hybrid models of digital marketplaces because they can potentially access more sellers and therefore have more bargaining power.

Similarly, marketplaces are expanding internationally, according to Forrester Research, despite barriers in some countries to Internet adoption, including public policies impeding imports and exports. Global expansion boosts supplier access to new markets and exposes new buyers to eBusiness. Although North America will own half of all online sales in 2004, reports Forrester, eBusiness in Western Europe will grow to $1.5 trillion, followed by Latin America, which is projected to reach $82 billion in 2004. Developing countries such as Zimbabwe are not projected to have eBusiness begin to take off until after 2010.

The Implications of e-Procurement

e-Procurement clearly offers significant opportunities for hospitality industry players to improve their supply chains, and those companies that ignore the potential may suffer in the long run. During these early stages of the e-Procurement revolution, relationships among buyers, sellers and competitors will be redefined. Additionally, global eBusiness will be fuelled by the ability to track the movement of trade goods at any point along the supply chain. Ships transporting goods from Latin America to North America, for example, might be quickly redirected to Europe in the event that bids were greater in other locations. Such flexibility in real-time pricing would greatly minimize reliance on fixed prices. We can summarize the implications for various segments of the hospitality industry in the following points:

Brand Parents

- Established brands can leverage their relationships, experience, knowledge and purchasing power to reengineer corporate purchasing efforts for improved efficiency.

- These players can develop (or partner with vendors and/or with competitors) private, secure, customized sites for employees to purchase products and services from approved vendors. Real-time inventory management and accounting then becomes possible.
- The major brands can also take control of the procurement process by minimizing "maverick" purchases and monitoring adherence to approved vendor lists, ensuring their employees adhere to quality standards.

Management Companies and Independents

- These companies will gain access to rebates traditionally only available to larger companies based on aggregated demand.
- The buying power of hotels outside North America, which have had little clout historically, should be increased.
- Management will be able to leverage public access applications that provide access to extensive vendor networks and their products in horizontal or vertical marketplaces.
- Moving processes online should result in labour cost savings.

Outlook for the Future

To fully leverage the benefits of end-to-end e-Procurement, hospitality companies need to position procurement more strategically and demand value-added services from providers to manage the entire supply chain from requisition to payment. Customer care services-a critical component of these solutions-must be situated throughout the supply chain to enable hospitality companies to realize the full benefits. Consolidated reporting will also be important.

Market forces are promoting marketplaces that encompass several contiguous verticals, rather than a single vertical focus of products or services. In hybrid market-place exchanges, managers of individual verticals will continue to need a great deal of domain expertise. However, they will also be able to cross-pollinate and leverage the capabilities of other marketplaces to benefit each one of their industries individually. This will promote e-Procurement offerings that are moving toward one-stop shopping, while providing vertical-specific services.

In the medium-term we anticipate that eBusiness ecosystems will emerge as the next wave of e-Procurement solutions. These interconnected worlds will allow organizations (employees, suppliers and customers) to transact via a single point for commerce and information, creating a global web of digital markets and corporate exchanges. This new wave of development will provide hospitality companies with clear benefits:

- Competitive and dynamic pricing.
- Ability to customize marketplaces. This will result in minimized searching costs through vendor-specific interfaces to facilitate adherence to quality standards and vendor comparison.
- Consolidated reporting and accounting to monitor supply chain performance and improve budgeting.
- Single point of contact for customer care.
- Access to international distribution networks.
- Process improvements in handling purchase orders.
- Customized online order-flow-tracking capability that is based on a company's internal workflow routing process.
- Streamlined buyer and supplier commerce processes.
- Shared network of commerce services.
- New methods of dynamic sourcing and trade.
- Aggregated purchasing and expanded sales channels.
- Extended customer reach and enhanced customer service.
- Meaningful tools to facilitate marketplace interaction.

To fully leverage the benefits of end-to-end e-Procurement, hospitality companies need to position procurement, hospitality companies need to position procurement more strategically and demand value-added services from providers to manage the entire supply chain from requisition to payment.

Conclusion

Despite the benefits promoted by e-Procurement marketplaces, the industry may be slow to adopt full-fledged solutions. The reasons for that are varied, but they include the large investments in legacy systems; bandwidth scalability and reliability issues associated with the Internet; and resistance to changing procedures and learning new systems. Deutsche Bank warns that e-Procurement cost savings may not be fully realized by the industry for another reason. An increase in e-Procurement marketplaces may decrease the likelihood of an industry platform standard for electronic commerce, thereby reducing the ability of suppliers and buyers to interact on multiple platforms and potentially minimizing cost savings.

Privacy and security issues will also be major issues, particularly in the case of market-places developed by industry leaders. Those hospitality companies interested in such solutions will most likely be wary about exposing their key business functions to competitors. Solution providers will also have to protect against vulnerability to hackers and competitors. To fully realize the benefits of eBusiness in general and e-Procurement in particular, hospitality organizations will need to:

- Determine how to integrate their overall business strategy with the eBusiness ecosystem.
- Identify and weigh the impact on the organization (traditional processes will be affected significantly).
  - * How will our traditional "requisition-to-pay" process be affected?
- Ask the following questions to determine how to best integrate eBusiness systems/solutions with existing legacy/back-office/front-office systems.

* What systems are still necessary?
* What skill sets do we need to acquire?

- Ask for answers in key areas as part of evaluating whether to leverage the Application Service Provider model:
  * Does your company have a shortage in internal IT skills?
  * Are there any upfront costs to buyer (subscription fee model)?
  * Will the ASP partner assume responsibility for managing the application?
  * Will the ASP services free resources to be focused on other areas deemed more critical to your core business?

e-Procurement offers a bright promise of reduced transaction costs and greater efficiencies for hospitality companies. While there are obstacles, it's clear that the success stories of the new economy will increasingly involve companies that use e-Procurement to their own competitive advantage on the global stage.

Hotel Markets-Diverse Strengths Changing Demand

Tokyo

	1993	1994	1995	1996	1997
No. of Hotels	17	19	20	21	21
No. of Rooms	12,079	12,769	13,108	13,557	13,557
A Year Rooms Supply	4,408,835	4,500,059	4,702,043	4,929,699	4,948,305
A Year Rooms Demand	2,968,799	3,101,397	3,165,160	3,632,409	3,751,583
Occupancy	67.3%	68.9%	67.3%	73.7%	75.8%
Average Daily Rate (yen)	24,610	22,590	21,917	21,565	22,198

Japan's hotel markets are diverse as they span the country's four main islands that extend in a crescent shaped archipelago in the north Pacific. The following summarizes characteristics of eight hotel markets, the largest in Japan, beginning with the nation's capital, Tokyo. One of the world's largest cities, Tokyo stands as the centre for Japan's economic and administrative functions, as well as affairs related to political, government, finance, international trade and corporate headquarters. As a result, the Tokyo hotel market is most resilient for every segment, including out-bound, in-bound and regional travellers and consumers. Even with a distressed economy, room demand has surpassed rooms supply. Tokyo also enjoys a double-digit share of the foreigner guests. In the upper-tier properties in Tokyo, room night demand generated by foreign guests exceeds 50 percent of total demand.

A bullish economy in the late 1980s motivated investments in major additions to the high-end hotel market, which came online in the 1990s. Four Seasons Tokyo (1992, 283 rooms); The Westin Tokyo (1994, 444 rooms); Hotel Inter-Continental Tokyo Bay, (1995, 339 rooms); Hotel Nikko Tokyo (1996, 453 rooms); and Park Hyatt (1994, 178 rooms); and Le Meridien Grand Pacific Tokyo (1998, 884 rooms) are good examples of these developments. These new luxury entries increased Tokyo's rooms inventory in the first-tier market 15.9 percent between 1993 and 1998, while demand increased by 26.9 percent during the same period.

Tokyo hotels, however, have not avoided all of the downside of the current economy where losses are seen in the high-volume banquet and restaurant business.

The rooms revenue of the typical full-service first class hotels of 200 rooms or more is typically less than 30 percent of the Gross Operating Revenue (GOR), while at the same time the banquet and F&B can easily sell 60 percent or more of GOR. The shrinkage of the gross market size in Tokyo hotels in aggregate revenue is believed to exceed 30 percent during the last five years of recession. Most of that market shrinkage is in the banquet and restaurant business, reflecting weakened corporate business sponsors.

Osaka

The Osaka prefecture recently suffered from the largest fiscal deficit at the level of the prefecture government. Many of the area developments have been suspended given the cumulative loss incurred from uncompleted development projects. Kansai New International Airport with only a single runway is so far not generating an expected volume of the inbound arrivals. The bay area developments, including Universal Studio Japan, seem to be among the very few projects to help the Osaka hotel market to correct the current oversupply. In particular, the new luxury entries (e.g., The Imperial, The Westin, Hankyu International and Ritz Carlton) are said to be particularly affected by the slow economy.

1st Tier Hotel Market Trend

Osaka

	1993	1994	1995	1996	1997
No. of Hotels	9	10	10	11	12
No. of Rooms	4,785	5,411	5,411	5,798	6,090
A Year Rooms Supply	1,746,525	1,888,015	1,975,015	2,093,430	2,181,386
A Year Rooms Demand	1,094,612	1,287,157	1,524,876	1,586,068	1,634,953
Occupancy	62.7%	68.2%	77.2%	75.8%	75.0%
Averge Daily Rate (yen)	18,037	16,466	15,703	15,124	15,114

Source: Arthur Andersen Hospitality & Leisure Services, Tokyo

Yokohama

The city is the second largest in Japan in population, and yet is still only one-third the size of Tokyo. The romantic port town atmosphere supported by new area development-including the spectacular bay bridge, international convention centre and the Landmark Tower building-has stimulated new hotel demand. However, as long as the hotels must target the leisure market, which naturally tends to be concentrated to the weekends and holidays, without increasing support in the business segment, Yokohama hoteliers will continue to suffer from reduced demand. The competition among the hotel neighbours lined up along the new bay area called MM21 will remain intense. In addition, new competition also arrived last year with the opening of the Tokyo Bay Sheraton Yokohama in June 1998.

Kyoto

Just 20 minutes away from Osaka by Shinkansen or bullet train, Kyoto is Japan's best known tourist destination for both overseas and domestic tourists. As such, its hotel market tends to be self-sustaining. While the hotel market has not posted a downward trend, it remains weak, however.

1st Tier Hotel Market Trend

Kyoto

	1993	1994	1995	1996	1997
No. of Hotels	10	12	12	12	13
No. of Rooms	3,291	3,836	3,836	3,829	4,008
A Year Rooms Supply	1,201,215	1,198,678	1,400,140	1,401,414	1,417,398
A Year Rooms Demand	796,936	937,177	925,412	976,381	1,008433
Occupancy	66.3%	78.2%	66.1%	69.7%	71.1%
Average Daily Rate (yen)	16,072	15,909	16,223	16,019	15,817

Source: Arthur Andersen Hospitality & Leisure Services, Tokyo

Sapporo

This is the capital city of Hokkaido, the island prefecture situated at Japan's northern territory, which is suffering from a weak regional economy. Hokkaido Takushoku Bank, one of the large commercial

banks headquartered in Sapporo, was the first bank bankruptcy in Japan under "Japanese Financial Big Bang". The city's hotel operators depend on business travel driven from local branch offices of the corporations based in Tokyo and Osaka.

But the primary room demand comes from tourism, which reflects strong seasonal fluctuations. As a result, Sapporo hotels have limited average room turnover due to the seasonal fluctuation and low ADR depressed by the dominant bargaining power of travel agents.

Fukuoka

Fukuoka City serves as the capital of Fukuoka prefecture, as well as the gateway city to Kyushyu Island, located to the southwest of the main island (Honshu). Like Sapporo, Fukuoka

City hosts many branch offices of Tokyo-based corporations. It also maintains close communications and traffic with nearby Asian countries such as Korea, China, Taiwan and Hong Kong, which have become feeder markets of tourists inbound to Kyushu. Reduced travel among Asia nations as a result of recession has had an impact on Fukuoka's hotel market. But a strong mix of tourism resources-the local culture, sea food, tourist points of the sea and mountains, abundant hot springs and large theme parks-also attract leisure tourists from the neighbouring Japanese prefectures of Ohita, Kumamoto, Miyazaki and Kagoshima. Business and conference are also important travel segments. Fukuoka accommodates the most number of medical related conventions in Japan through a year.

Kobe

Like Osaka, Kobe has a large international port with an exotic and romantic ambience, and has long attracted leisure visitors from nearby Yokohama. Kobe, however, continues to recover from the 1995 earthquake, the largest in Japan since 1923. And this recovery has been slower due to the national economy. Kobe tourism, however, has recovered in terms of tourist arrivals.

Nagoya

This city seems to have a better socio-economic outlook compared to the other major "branch-economy" cities in Japan. The city has avoided becoming an economic subsidiary to Tokyo or Osaka, even though main factory lines of Toyota contribute to stabilizing the regional economy. Nagoya will be the host city for the World Exposition expected to be held in year 2005. Also, a new Nagoya international airport is in preliminary survey. Unlike other major cities in Japan, Nagoya avoided the hotel industry recession until recently when rapid increases in the room supply resulted in very tight competition. The competition is expected to become more heated when JR Tokai opens The Nagoya Marriott Associa Hotel in May 2000 with 780 rooms and 17 banquet halls, nine restaurants and wedding facilities.

8

Hospitality Organizing Systems

Introduction

One of the main problems that each enterprise faces is to organize the efforts of the people working on common goals. Most of the solutions to this problem originate from the time before computers became available for practically any company. However, it's a general practice even now, that the developers follow the old management scheme when the company is being computerized, whereas modern computers offer unique opportunities for implementing new, far more effective approaches to management.

We discovered the limitations of existing management schemes while computerizing a small trading company. Our objective was to develop a system able to assist the office workers in all aspects of their routine work. One of our tasks was a conventional one-to support such activities as taking orders, delivering goods, making a phone call, etc. The other one was more ambitious-to register all completed activities and to help plan new activities based on the completed ones.

We realized very soon that our second objective could not be achieved within the functional management scheme adopted in the company. To cope with our task we started to consider the company's activity as a number of processes (such as "processing an order", "closing a deal") without regard to the way these processes were being managed. As a result a new approach to management was developed which we call a process-oriented management. This approach can be described as a project management without project managers, a project manager's functions, e.g., planning, controlling the execution of activities, etc., being distributed among the workers involved in a particular process. The main point with the process-oriented management is that it permits a company to gain full control over all the processes within the frame of the existing, often functionally-oriented, organizational structure. This type of management facilitates also the communication between the workers involved in the same process, and it provides them with actual information on the state of the process, as well as on all activities performed and planned. Below, we present the main ideas of the process-oriented management, and the requirements for a computer system needed to support it.

We tried our best to do that in a very informal way to make it easily understood by all concerned. It should also be mentioned that the author is not a specialist in the field of management, but he worked with experts on management throughout the project. The paper reflects a fresh view of an application developer not spoiled by the experience of the pre-computer management era.

The rest of this paper is organized as follows. In section 2, we outline our view on the management of routine work. In section 3, we present the main principles of the process-oriented management. We look at existing approaches to management of the routine work-the function-oriented management and project-oriented management, and then move on to describing the ways of transforming the project-oriented management into the process-oriented one. We discuss the process-oriented management without regards to computer systems, however, this type of management can't be implemented without computers.

Requirements for a computer system designed to support the process-oriented management are discussed in section 4. In section 5, we discuss the major issues of the development and implementation of such systems. In section 6, we present a short summary of our practical and research work that lead to the development of a process-oriented approach to management.

Management of Routine Work

It's generally recognized that the main objective of management is to ensure a successful achievement of a company's goals at minimal costs. A company has several different types of goals to achieve at any given moment-long-term, short-term, etc. As we are concerned with the management of routine work, it's the "conventional" everyday goals that are of primary interest to us; we call them "operational" goals. A typical operational goal for a trading company is, for example, to "drive" an incoming order through a delivery to receiving payment within certain time limits. A typical operational goal for a hospital is to administer the appropriate treatment to a patient that would lead to his discharging from the hospital. A typical operational goal for a software development company is to build a software system according to the specifications. But for the section of technical support of such company, a typical operational goal is to process a bug report so that the bug is fixed or/and a work-around solution is found.

Though operational goals may be quite unsophisticated, they, nevertheless, constitute the backbone of any business, as they have to be achieved on a day-to-day basis to ensure the proper functioning of the company. The character of operational goals depends on the type of business, but they have a number of common features:

- operational goals pop up more or less regularly;
- there is, usually, a standard procedure for achieving the operational goals of a given kind, which doesn't mean, of course, that a particular goal can't be approached in a different way if needed;
- there is often a set time limit for achieving an operational goal. If the goal is impossible to achieve within the time limit, it is discarded in a standard way.

To achieve an operational goal, a series of activities should be completed. For example, a series of activities aimed at getting payment for an incoming order includes delivery of goods and sending an invoice to the customer. This series may include more items in certain circumstances, for example, if the ordered goods are out of stock, they should be produced or ordered from the suppliers. The activities aimed at achieving an operational goal are not, usually, executed immediately one after another, e.g., if the ordered goods are out of stock, it takes some time to get them from the suppliers. The execution of these activities is a process that continues over some period of time. The main objective for management of operational goals is to ensure that this process results in achieving the goal.

Different activities concerning the same goal can be completed by different workers from different divisions. Another objective of management is, therefore, to coordinate the work of all workers participating in the process of achieving an operational goal.

A Race Towards a Process-Oriented Management

Approaches to management of operational goals may be divided in two types-function-oriented and project-oriented. The function-oriented management (Fn-management) is usually used in the environments where a lot of relatively simple operational goals pop up very frequently. The Fn-management implies that operational goals are handled in a routine manner by the staff where each member has his own function in achieving operational goals. A manager does not coordinate the execution of activities for each goal, workers just react on the incoming documents, phone calls, etc., by completing activities they are assigned, and forwarding the received or newly composed documents further to their colleagues.

The project-oriented management (Pj-management) is usually used with more sophisticated goals such as construction or software projects. The Pj-management implies that a process for a new goal is planned in detail before the work on it starts, and there is someone (e.g., a project manager) who supervises all the work being done.

Fn-management is most cost-effective, but it works poorly when a process of achieving an operational goal deviates from a standard pattern, as it lacks control over individual processes. Pj-management gives full control over an individual process, but it's inefficient when a lot of coexisting processes are involved.

There are working environments where one or the other type of management fits well. But in most environments a combination of these two approaches would be the way to obtain both full control over all processes and efficiency.

Below, we discuss our proposals for integration of the Fn- and Pj-managements. The result is a new type of management which we call the process-oriented management, or Pc-management, for short. This name highlights the main objective of the Pc-management-to control the processes, in contrast to Fn-management that places the emphasis on the execution of activities, and the Pj-management that emphasizes plans. We describe the Pc-management here in the following way. We consider an environment typical for the function-oriented management-a trading company, and try to introduce the project-oriented management in it. The process-oriented management is presented thus as a result of tailoring the project-oriented approach to fit a different kind of environment. We find this way most convenient for discussing our ideas, but it's not, naturally, the only possible one.

The Pc-management is based on the notions of "orgobject", "history" and "dynamic and distributed planning", which we can now turn our attention to.

Orgobjects

The Pj-management involves developing a detailed plan for achieving a project's goal before the work on the project can start. This plan is premised on certain assumptions that may turn out wrong after the project is under way. The plan should then be adapted to the changed conditions. For this purpose, a clear picture of the current state of the project is required to figure out what should be done to complete the project.

A project often involves developing some product that is a physical object, e.g. a software system, a building, etc. This product comes into existence in some form already at the earlier stages of the project, e.g. a half-ready software system or a building under construction. This half-ready product serves as a good representation of the current state of the project. As the half-ready product can be studied without regards to how it has been produced, the plan can be revised without going into details of the project's history.

In cases where the Fn-management is involved, there is no half-ready product to represent the current state of achieving an operational goal. A kind of an abstract object that contains all information on the current state of the process would be helpful here. As it would serve as an organizing device for achieving the goal, we call it an "orgobject".

For example, an orgobject representing a process of "Get payment for an incoming order" may be a record that contains information on: the name and address of the buyer, a description of each kind of goods ordered, the quantity and price per unit of each kind, the quantities of goods already delivered; the amount of money invoiced; the amount of money received. Having this orgobject, the conditions for the successful achievement of the "get payment" goal could be formulated as follows:

- have the numbers representing the quantities of 'goods ordered' and 'goods delivered' equal for each goods kind,
- have 'money invoiced' equal to the sum of 'ordered' multiplied by 'price per unit' for all goods kinds, and
- have 'money received' equal to 'money invoiced'.

As the process develops, the corresponding orgobject should change so that it reflects all the time the current state of the process. As soon as some activity is completed, the orgobject representing the process is to be modified. Thus, in the above example, after the delivery (full or partial), the quantities of the goods delivered are modified; if the customer has changed the order, the types and quantities of the goods ordered are modified, etc. To ensure that the orgobjects are always up-to-date, the routines for every type of activity should list not only the operations required for completing the activity (e.g., packing and shipping for delivery), but also instructions for the appropriate modifications of the relevant orgobjects. Thus, the current state of an orgobject reflects the overall result of all activities completed earlier, and shows what actions should be taken to achieve the goal. To return to our example, if the quantity of the goods ordered is greater than the quantity of the goods delivered, the missing goods are to be delivered. If, on the other hand, the quantity of the goods ordered is less than the quantity of the goods delivered, then the customer should be asked to return some of the goods. Other examples: if the amount of money invoiced exceeds the payment received, then the customer should pay the difference. If the amount of the money received exceeds that of invoiced, then a credit note should be issued.

History

The current state of an orgobject contains only the result of the completed activities, but not a list of them, e.g.: the quantity of the goods delivered, but not the number of separate deliveries; the amount of money invoiced, but not the number of separate invoices, etc. This is OK if all goes as it should. But if something goes wrong, e.g., some goods sent off did not arrive, then the information on all activities performed is vital when figuring out what actions should be taken. This information can be collected through logging all the activities completed in the frame of the given process.

Let's consider the following logging scheme. Every time a worker executes an activity, he/she doesn't physically change the previous state of the relevant orgobject. He/she makes a new record instead which contain the new state of the orgobject and leaves the former one unchanged. For example, after a delivery, a new record is made containing the same information as the previous one except the information on the quantities of the goods delivered. The latter is updated according to the packing list.

The record on the previous state of an orgobject is placed in a special file containing the history of the given orgobject. The worker who completes an activity composes also a report where he/she records: the kind of activity completed, the name of a person who completed it, the date, time, comments, etc. This report is saved together with the previous state of the orgobject in the history file.

Given two consequent states of an orgobject and an activity report, we can reconstruct exactly what happened during the activity execution. For example, in case of delivery, we know exactly by whom and when the goods were delivered, and in what quantities. Thus, our log provides an easy access to the information on both the activity performed, and the state of events before and after it was performed.

Dynamic and Distributed Planning

As it was mentioned above, the Pj-management involves designing a detailed plan for each new process. If we try to apply the same to a Fn-management environment, two problems would arise:

- as Fn-processes are often trivial, their plans would be trivial too, e.g.: 'delivering goods'-'invoicing the buyer'-'getting payment'. It would be meaningless to record such plan for every process (and there are many in this kind of environments),
- unpredictable external events that often occur in Fn-management environments would demand revising the whole plan, e.g.: a customer has changed his order-additional delivery can be required, an invoice is to be sent later than it was initially planned, etc.

Dynamic planning is our answer to these problems. Dynamic planning involves planning only the first few activities at the first stage. As soon as one or several of these are completed, new activities are planned with regard to the emerging state of the relevant orgobject (and standard routines adopted in the company). For example, after a delivery, another delivery is planned if not all ordered goods have been delivered, or invoicing is planned if all goods have been delivered.

The use of dynamic planning is fully beneficial in case of processes that follow a standard pattern. Otherwise, the usual planning is preferable. In case the character of the process (standard/deviating) is difficult to foresee, dynamic planning can be used at first, followed by conventional planning if necessary.

Another poser when trying to introduce the Pj-management in an Fn-environment is how to supervise a process. In cases where the Pj-management is involved, there is usually a project manager who supervises the execution of planned activities, and corrects the plan if needed. In an environment typical for the Fn-management, a project manager supervising each process would result in significant overheads. A solution to this can be described as "distributed planning". Distributed planning implies that the worker who has completed a planned activity himself plans the subsequent activities. Moreover, he/she can assign these new activities not only to himself, but to other people too. For example, a worker who completes a delivery himself plans invoicing to be completed by another worker.

Distributed planning doesn't exclude the possibility of a centralized supervision of a process. In fact, a supervisor may intervene at any time and correct the plan if needed. Moreover, any member of staff can consult the supervisor in case he/she has some problems with his/her work on a particular process. He/she can do it by planning a special activity, e.g., "asking for help", and assigning his/her supervisor to complete it.

Let's have a look at the issue of implementing dynamic and distributed planning. Above, we considered orgobjects and plans as separate entities. Now, we put a plan inside the orgobject representing the corresponding process. As a result an orgobject besides the information on the current state of the process (e.g., on the customer, goods, delivery and payment) will also include a list of planned activities (e.g., delivery, invoicing, etc.), each of them containing information on what should be done, who's to do that and when. Thus, a plan becomes part of an orgobject. Consequently, we can treat correction of the plan as one of the operations of changing the orgobject in the course of completing an activity. In section 3.1, we've already mentioned that instructions for modifying orgobjects should be included in the working procedures for each type of activities. To ensure proper dynamic planning, these instructions should embrace modification of the process's plan. In a simple case, a worker who has completed an activity modifies the relevant orgobject by removing this activity from the list of planned activities. In more complex cases, he/she adds new activities to the list, and/or removes some other activities from it.

Being an integral part of the orgobject representing a process, a plan is subjected to the logging we described above. As a result, all acts of replanning are registered in the same way as other modifications of orgobjects. Thus, for example, the name of a person who modified the plan is recorded, which may prove to be useful in case of conflicts.

Advantages of the Process-Oriented Management

The main advantage of the Pc-management is its flexibility. The Pc-management permits to choose the optimum approach to coping with each process, and within the same management scheme. Thus, simple processes that follow a standard pattern are dealt with in a completely decentralized manner, whereas some more sophisticated case will be dealt with by centralized individual planning and supervising. Moreover, the same process may be treated differently at different stages. For example, it may be started as a standard one, but later it can be planned and supervised individually. As a result, full control over all kinds of processes is gained and efficiency is not sacrificed.

Another important thing is that the Pc-management is not bound to any particular type of organizational structure. It can be used both in case the same member of staff completes all the activities required for achieving an operational goal, and in case each activity type is assigned to a particular worker. This permits to preserve the same management scheme when the organizational structure is changed, e.g., in case of a company's expansion.

Some other advantages are as follows:

1. Orgobjects provide a perfect insight into the company's state of affairs. The information stored in the orgobjects is of great help to the management staff as it permit to quickly evaluate the state of a process (without going into its history). It also helps to give prompt answers to customers' questions. This kind of information is not easily obtainable when traditional managements schemes are used. Thus, when the Fn-management is used, only the information on the executed activities of a given type is easily accessible, and when the Pj-

management is used, only the information on the state of the plans execution is easily accessible.

2. Histories of orgobjects permit to easily trace all the activities completed on a given process, which helps to devise plans for complicated cases. They are also a very important source of data for all kinds of statistical analysis, and other types of information processing required for decision-making.
3. The company's staff becomes goal-and process-conscious, as it is easy for any person to overview all the activities (one's own and those of others) completed in a process he/she is involved in. The history of old orgobjects is useful for "learning by example", which may help a worker to find solutions in difficult cases. The goal-and process-consciousness isn't easy to acquire with a traditional management scheme. Under the Fn-management, a worker doesn't see how a process he/she's in is accomplished. His/her personal goal becomes to complete as efficient as possible the activities he/she is responsible for. That may result in, e.g., a seller concentrating on making telephone calls most of which don't get him to closing a deal.
4. The Pj-management emphasizes following the schedule, which becomes the main goal of the workers engaged in a project. There is a danger that the workers do not keep their eyes open for changes in the surrounding world, which is, e.g., the main reason why large software projects often produce out-of-day systems.
5. As all the information on the past is being stored, the management staff is in a better position concerning various kinds of conflicts, internal conflicts among workers engaged in the same process, and external ones, e.g., with customers or suppliers.
6. Distributed planning is a very powerful tool for coordinating the work which makes unnecessary the intensive communication (exchanges of documents, phone calls, etc.) among the workers engaged in the

same processes. They get the required information from the current states of orgobjects and their histories.

An Orgsystem Wanted

Let's imagine you are fascinated by the Pc-management and decide to implement it in your company. A lot of orgobjects start circulating around, each accompanied by a huge history file. You don't find the one you need, you never know which of the orgobjects contains the planned activities assigned to you, and when these activities should be completed. You strove for a better order and got yourself into a mess.

And, as if that were not enough, you have a lot of extra work to do. You should construct a new state of an orgobject for each completed activity, and remember to put the new activities on the list and assign them to yourself and others. You wanted to improve the efficiency, but it sinks instead. There is no need to worry, there is a means to restore the order and efficiency, and that's, naturally a computer system. It's primary aim is to make you happy with the Pc-management doing away with the chaos, that's why we call it an "organizing system", or orgsystem for short.

Let's have another look at the Pc-management, this time supported by an orgsystem. Orgobjects do not circulate between various members of the staff who are to work with them, they stay in the same place together with their history and plans, and are easily accessible to all workers involved. All planned activities assigned to a given individual appear immediately in his/her personal calendar, so that each worker knows exactly what activities he/she has to complete and when.

An orgsystem provides the means to increase the efficiency by:

- assisting workers in executing each activity,
- providing an extremely user-friendly interface.

These two features are a key to successful implementation of an orgsystem. Without them people would not be motivated to use the system, consequently the Pc-management wouldn't work. Let's look at these features in more detail.

Level of Help

All operations needed for executing an activity under the Pc-management belong to one of the two groups:

- external operations-operations that affect the "external world", and
- maintaining operations-operations aimed at maintaining orgobjects.

The character of external operation depends on the type of activity, e.g., packing and shipping for delivery, programming and testing for developing a software module, etc. Maintaining operations are the same for all activities. They include:

- updating the information contained in the relevant orgobject,
- correcting the plan,
- logging the preceding state of the orgobject.

An orgsystem assists a worker to complete both the external operations and the maintaining ones.

1. *External Operations:* Level of help which is possible to offer for completing the external operations depends on the type of activity. For example, programming and testing of a software module are usually performed inside the computer, and they are already fully computerized. Here, an orgsystem should just integrate the existing tools for software development, e.g. editors, debuggers, etc., so that a proper tool is invoked when a user chooses to execute these operations. Packing and shipping are not that easily computerized, not now anyway. But even there, an orgsystem can be helpful to some extent by, e.g., making up a packing list. It's important to give a hand in completing the external operations for each kind of activities. There's a risk otherwise. If some activity is left without the orgsystem's assistance, a worker who completes it can easily forget to make the appropriate changes in the orgobject concerned. In that case, the completed activity will still remain on the list of planned activities and the orgsystem will keep reminding the

worker to complete it. There is also a danger that the same activity will be completed several times.

2. *Updating:* Modification of an orgobject can often be done on the basis of the information collected in the process of executing the external operations. For example, an "order" orgobject contains the information on the quantities of the goods already delivered. This information should be updated after each separate delivery. The new quantities can be easily calculated based on the packing list that was made at the previous step, which permits an orgsystem to update the orgobject without assistance from the users.
3. When correcting a plan, a worker is prompted by the system on the appropriate activities to plan next; in simple cases the plan is corrected by the system itself. This is possible, as an orgsystem possesses two type of knowledge:
   - on the working procedures used in the company, which helps to plan new activities, and
   - on division of responsibilities between different divisions, sections, and workers, which permits to correctly assign new activities.
4. Logging includes two operations:
   - saving the old state of the orgobject, and
   - making a report on the activity completed.

Saving the old state of an orgobject is done by an orgsystem without any user assistance, but an activity report needs a human participation. Even there, an orgsystem helps by automatically supplying the information on what activity has been executed, by whom and when. The rest of the report, e.g., comments, is of course the responsibility of the worker.

User-interface

Conventional computer systems are designed as a set of functions operating on a common database, the main facility of the user-interface being multilevel menus. This type of the user-interface provides the user with a quick access to a function he/ she wants to complete. It reflects the objective of a conventional computer system which is to help workers to cope with single activities like updating information, printing a report, etc. An orgsystem objectives are much wider, which brings about the need for a completely different kind of user-interface.

An orgsystem's user-interface permits end-users to freely choose between the object-oriented and activity-oriented way of working with orgobjects, as well as easily switch from one to the other. The object-oriented approach is applied when a user wants to work with a particular orgobject for a longer time. In this case, he/she may need to look at the object's current state and its history, as well as to plan and execute various activities involving the orgobject. The activity-oriented approach is applied when a user wants to complete the same activity for a number of orgobjects. In this case, the dialogue designed for a given activity is repeated for all relevant orgobjects.

The object-oriented way is particularly useful when one worker is responsible for many activities involving an orgobject. It is also the way that management staff can use when there is a need to evaluate the state of a particular process and to devise a plan for a difficult case. The activity-oriented approach is preferable if a worker is responsible for only one type of activities. It's also the right approach to completing simple activities that do not require much human assistance, e.g., printing an invoice, etc.

Another distinguishing feature of an orgsystem's user-interface is that it maintains personal calendars. A personal calendar is a list of activities assigned to a particular worker. The point is that these activities are included in different orgobjects and the calendar permits a perfect overview of a persons' many tasks. The orgsystem offers a variety of ways to use the calendar. A user can browse through his/her calendar, or some parts of it, e.g., to see all activities planned for a particular day, all activities of a certain type, etc. When browsing, he/she can start the execution of his/her activities (activity-oriented approach), or move to the orgobject where a particular activity belongs and start working with this orgobject in the object-oriented manner. To maintain its user-friendly character, an orgsystem's user-interface should satisfy a number of general requirements. Most important are the following two:

- easy access to all information required for working with orgobjects. For example, when working with an orgobject representing an order, a user should have access to all information related to the customer who ordered goods: his address, previous contacts with him, etc.;
- consistency. There should be standard procedures for navigating to an orgobject, for getting information (e.g., a company's address), for planning, for starting the execution of activities, etc. These standard procedures should be the same for all types of orgobjects and activities.

Joys and Hardships of an Orgsystems Developer

There are, naturally, technical problems to solve in the development of an orgsystem. The system requirements discussed in the previous section must be met. However, an orgsystem designer's greatest problem is that he starts the development in an environment initially not based on the Pc-management, which makes both design and implementation of an orgsystem far from trivial tasks.

Orgsystems Design

An orgsystem designer should begin with:

- identifying the company's operational goals,
- figuring out what processes are used to achieve them, and
- designing orgobjects to represent these processes.

His/her next task is to review all the working procedures and tailor them to fit the Pc-management scheme (by adding maintaining operations to each activity). This is often a tough job, as there are seldom some written descriptions of the working procedures, and if they exist, they are far from complete. The only way to cope with the job is to try and get the missing information from the company's workers.

The workers would, naturally, know nothing about orgobjects, but they know their job. The conditions in which an orgsystem designer works are similar to those of a linguist who studies a language that exists only in the spoken form. Linguists have special methods permitting them to get the necessary information from the native speakers without teaching them any linguistic notions. Moreover, it's considered a wrong practice to teach informants linguistics, as it may only spoil them. An orgsystems designer needs similar methods that would permit him to redesign the company's working procedures without introducing the workers into the world of orgobjects, distributed planning, etc. We believe that rapid prototyping is the right method. As soon as a designer has identified the company's operational goals and processes, and designed the orgobjects to represent them, he/she should make a prototype of the system and let the future users test it. To be able to use prototyping, an orgsystem designer needs appropriate application development tools. These tools should allow him to quickly produce a sketch of the system that has "look-and-feel" of a real system, but lacks processing routines and database access. It's this sketch that we call the prototype of the system. Working with it, a user can navigate among orgobjects in the same way as he would do that when the orgsystem is ready. He can modify existing orgobjects, create new ones, and see how to start different activities. But he can't save the information or see the results of the completed activities.

After the future users have accepted the prototype, the designer can stepwise add database access and processing routines, which would be also done with the help of the above mentioned application development tools.

Orgsystems Implementation

Implementing an orgsystem means introducing the Pc-management in a non-Pc-management environment. This may be achieved in one of two ways:

- by substituting all the old working procedures in the company at once, or
- by gradual introduction of the new working procedures.

The first approach may suit small companies whose workers often switch from one activity type to another. An orgsystem would help to do these switches very quickly, and it would help the workers, who usually have a lot of different things to do, to preserve the order in their affairs. The staff of a small company would easily understand the advantages of using all facilities provided by an orgsystem: object-and activity-oriented ways of working, personal calendars, easy access to the history, etc.

However, in case of large companies, the second approach may be the best choice. Large companies usually, have a lot of workers who are involved only in one or several activities for each process. These workers may believe that an orgsystem is too complex for their simple tasks. It would be difficult for them to see the advantages of the object-oriented user-interface, and their earlier experience of traditional computer systems can only make the things worse.

Luckily, an orgsystem provides a means for working in the activity-oriented manner, which would put the workers competing simple activities at ease. There would be no problem to teach them to use the orgsystem in the activity-oriented way, because it resembles their old manner of doing things. Later, the workers could be taught the object-oriented way as well, which would give them better possibilities to take the initiative and find solutions for difficult cases. But even if most of the office workers continue to use the activity-oriented approach, there would always be some key people who benefit from the object-oriented approach, e.g., management staff.

Bibliography

Apostolopous, Y and Leivadi, S: *Sociology of Tourism, The: Theoretical And Empirical Investigations*, London, Retailed, 1996.

Ashworth, Greg and Larkham, P J: *Building a New Heritage: Tourism, Culture & Identity in the New Europe*, London, Routledge,1994.

Beeho, A & Prentice, R: *Conceptualising The Experiences of Heritage Tourists*, 1997.

Boniface, Priscilla and Fowler, Peter: *Heritage and Tourism: In the Global Village*, London, Retailed, 1993.

Brunt, Paul: *Market Research in Travel and Tourism*, Oxford, Butterworth Heinemann, 1997.

Clark, Mona: *Interpersonal Skills for Hospitality Managers*, London, Chapman Hill, 1995.

Coccosis, Harry and Nijkamp, Peter: *Sustainable Tourism Development*, Aldershot, Avebury, 1995.

Cournoyer, Norman G.: *Hotel, Restaurant, and Travel Law: A Preventive Approach*, Albany, Delmar Publishers, 1993.

Davidoff, Donald M.: *Customer Service in the Hospitality and Tourism Industry*, Englewood Cliffs, Prentice Hall, 1994.

Donald E. : *Public Personnel Management: Contexts and Strategies*, Upper Saddle River, NJ: Prentice Hall, 1998.

Eberts, Marjorie: *Careers in Travel, Tourism, and Hospitality*, Lincolnwood, VGM Career Horizons, 1997.

Edgell, David L: *International Tourism Policy, New York,* Van Nostrand and Reinhold, 1990.

Frechtling, Douglas C: *Practical Tourism Forecasting,* Oxford, Butterworth Heinemann, 1996.

Gunn, Clare and Var, Turgut: *Tourism Planning,* London, Retailed, 2002.

Harron, S and Weiler, B: *Ethnic Tourism,* Belhaven/Wiley, 1992.

Hays, Judi Radice: *Restaurant & Food Graphics,* Glen Cove, PBC International, 1994.

Hinkin, Timothy R.: *Cases in Hospitality Management: A Critical Incident Approach,* New York, Wiley, 1995.

Horner, S. and Swarbrooke, J.: *Marketing Tourism, Hospitality and Leisure in Europe,* London, International Thomson Business Press, 1996.

Judd, D R: *Promoting Tourism* in US Cities, 1995.

Kharbanda, O. and E. Stallworthy: *Waste Management Towards a Sustainable Society,* Auburn House, New York, 1990.

Lucas, Rosemary E.: *Managing Employee Relations in the Hotel and Catering Industry,* London, Cassell, 1995.

MacCannell, Dean: *Tourist, The: A New Theory of the Leisure Class,* London, Macmillan, 1976.

Peters, M: *International Tourism,* London, Hutchinson, 1969.

Rogers, H Anthea and Slinn, Judy A: *Tourism: Management of Facilities,* London, Pitman: M & E, 1993.

Tribe, John *Corporate Strategy for Tourism, London,* International Thomson Business Press, 1997.

Wahab, S A: *Tourism Management,* Tourism International Press, 1975.

Yale, Pat: *From Tourist Attractions to Heritage Tourism,* Huntingdon, Elm, 1991.

Index